EVOKING TRANSFORMATION
Visual Redress at Stellenbosch University

Edited by Aslam Fataar and Elmarie Costandius

Evoking Transformation: Visual Redress at Stellenbosch University.

Published by African Sun Media under the SUN PReSS imprint

All rights reserved

Copyright © 2021 African Sun Media and the Aslam Fataar and Elmarie Costandius

This publication was subjected to an independent double-blind peer evaluation by the publisher.

The editor(s) and the publisher have made every effort to obtain permission for and acknowledge the use of copyrighted material. Refer all enquiries to the publisher.

No part of this book may be reproduced or transmitted in any form or by any electronic, photographic or mechanical means, including photocopying and recording on record, tape or laser disk, on microfilm, via the Internet, by e-mail, or by any other information storage and retrieval system, without prior written permission by the publisher.

Views reflected in this publication are not necessarily those of the publisher.

First edition 2021

ISBN 978-1-991201-08-9
ISBN 978-1-991201-09-6 (e-book)
https://doi.org/10.18820/9781991201096

Set in Adobe Garamond Pro 12/18

Cover design, typesetting and production by African Sun Media

SUN PReSS is an imprint of African Sun Media. Scholarly, professional and reference works are published under this imprint in print and electronic formats.

This publication can be ordered from:
orders@africansunmedia.co.za
Takealot: bit.ly/2monsfl
Google Books: bit.ly/2k1Uilm
africansunmedia.store.it.si *(e-books)*
Amazon Kindle: amzn.to/2ktL.pkL

Visit africansunmedia.co.za for more information.

Contents

1. Introducing a reflective perspective on 'visual redress as transformation' at Stellenbosch University 5
   Aslam Fataar and Elmarie Costandius

Section A: Visual redress trajectories at Stellenbosch University

2. 'Discourse speaks us': Visual redress at Stellenbosch University, 2000–2021 21
   Aslam Fataar

3. Transforming the Stellenbosch University landscape(s): The journey of visual redress at Stellenbosch University 51
   Leslie van Rooi

4. Visual redress at Stellenbosch University: A reflection on practice from 2010 to 2021 73
   Elmarie Costandius

Section B: Site-based visual redress initiatives at the university

5. Preserving knowledge: The Stellenbosch University Library visual redress journey 119
   Ellen Tise, Stephané Conradie and Mimi Seyffert-Wirth

6. Reflections on visual transformation in a science context and future implications... 145
   Faadiel Essop - Centre for Cardio-metabolic Research in Africa (CARMA), Department of Physiological Sciences, Faculty of Science, Stellenbosch University

7. Committed to Transformation: The journey of the Faculty of Medicine and Health Sciences' Charter... 173
   Khairoonisa Foflonker

8. Law and visual redress: The space between insider and outsider 199
   Bradley Slade

9. Visual redress: Decolonising the Faculty of Theology at Stellenbosch University?. 223
   Reggie Nel

Section C: Voice and agency enunciations amid visual redress experiences at Stellenbosch University

10. Visual redress as restitution: Conversation... 245
    Renee Hector-Kannemeyer and Otto van Noie

11. Work IN Conversation: Discussing one artist's creative interventions on Stellenbosch University campus 273
    Gera de Villiers and Charles Palm

12. Indexing visual redress at Stellenbosch University: Ways of viewing and reading while walking through the Arts and Social Sciences Building............................... 297
    Faaiz Gierdien

Section D: Reflexive considerations on the transformative potential of visual redress

13. Functions and uses of visual redress initiatives... 313
    Nico Koopman

14. Bibliography on visual representational culture at Stellenbosch University 329
    Mimi Seyffert-Wirth

Notes on contributors 339

Chapter 1

Introducing a reflective perspective on 'visual redress as transformation' at Stellenbosch University

Aslam Fataar and Elmarie Costandius

This book presents a reflective account of a pertinent aspect of institutional transformation at one South African university. It contains chapters written by institutional actors from across Stellenbosch University (SU) who have been doing generative work in the area of visual redress. In this book, 'visual redress' refers to processes involving changes in the university's visual environment and culture that promote restitution, inclusivity and institutional cohesion. Visual culture can be described as visible and tangible expressions of people that reveal who they are and reflect the vision they have for the institution's future. This book's visual culture relates to activities undertaken to change the University's symbols, names, statues and institutional spaces. It also refers to developing new visual symbols and icons that represent the zeitgeist of democratic change on the University's campuses.

Transformation-related activity in the visual culture domain of the University is located within an institutional history of more than 150 years since its founding in the 1870s and official university status acquired in 1918. The visual culture of the University depicted an Afrikaner identity founded on a history of colonial segregation and apartheid. Freschi, Schmahmann and Van Robbroeck (2020:7) point out that "art and visual culture helped to secure the hegemonic claims to the [white] nation-state via the construction of a unified Afrikaner imaginary". Visual culture aligned with the exclusionary and race-based institutional culture and functioning of the University until the onset of the country's democracy in 1994. This apartheid-based visual culture continues to be visible, and its exclusionary effects are still experienced in the present period.

The visual culture of the University has historically offered an 'aesthetic gloss' that was experienced by its mainly white Afrikaner students and staff, which accompanied its welcoming practices, an institutional curriculum that promoted racial stratification and a version of science that justified racial and ethnic separateness (see Jansen & Walters, 2020). As a mode of representation, the University's visual culture signalled the triumph of the ideology of Afrikaner nationalism at the "university of apartheid", a term coined by Lalu (2007) to describe the operations of apartheid knowledge formation and categorisation at South African universities in general. SU was the country's premier university of apartheid. The University's visual depictions portrayed to the world that it was the site of the production of knowledge for separateness. This was founded on arbitrary constructions of humans based on racial superiority and inferiority. Its raison d'être was the nonsense of racial separateness.

Schmahmann (2020:148) observes that SU "was slow to take cognisance of visual culture on campus and to engage actively with it". While she is correct to describe the pace as slow, the various chapters in the book discuss the considerable number of visual culture changes at the University since 2000, including visual redress activities since 2015. These visual redress activities represent an attempt to change the institutional terms on which the University functions. The shift is from a discourse of racial exclusion towards a discourse that signifies the University's symbolic commitment to redress, restitution and inclusion. Such a change is enunciated in the University's current draft Visual Redress Policy, which is discussed in various chapters of the book. The ongoing visual redress activities on campus are galvanising University staff members to become involved in institutional processes that are defining its broader transformation commitments.

The draft Visual Redress Policy encourages a deliberate participative approach to activities, which combines a focus on normative commitments with the policy's framing values and dialogue among participants. Dialogue is intended to persuade about, and build trust in, visual culture choices. What has been emerging is a visual redress praxis that emphasises inclusive, participative dialogue as key to producing the visual redress activities and outcomes. Creating artefacts is as important as the processes from which they emerge. The draft policy also anticipates that visual redress processes and activities become mainstreamed in the faculties' and departments' curriculum offerings. Importantly, it is hoped that visual redress processes can provide an impetus for broader institutional transformation work in other sectors of the University. These would include developing an 'at home' culture that accommodates the growing diversity among staff and students, and the transformation of the University's teaching, learning and support environments.

The opening to visual culture as redress occurred in light of a decisive shift in the institutional discourse at the University. Aslam Fataar and Leslie van Rooi's chapters discuss the dynamics that made up the discursive shift that was precipitated by the student protests of 2015 and 2016. In concert with students at universities across South Africa, SU students delivered a vehement and compelling critique against the University's ongoing exclusionary culture and lack of transformation. The University's response during the ensuing years amounted to a significant institutional commitment to change by adopting policies, structures and processes to facilitate a systemic approach to transformation on campus. Visual culture based on redress and transformation increased markedly after 2015. As various chapters in the book describe, the Rooiplein, the SU Library, the Arts and Social Sciences Building and the Lückhoff precinct became the focus of numerous visual redress activities that emphasise symbolic restitution. Site-based activities occurred via committee processes in the faculties of Science, Medicine and Health Sciences and Law and Theology. Elmarie Costandius, an academic member of the Department of Visual Arts, played a key consulting role in the visual redress activities, which she discusses in Chapter 4. A visual redress committee to oversee activities was established in 2017. A Visual Redress Policy, in addition to a policy on the naming and renaming of buildings, is being finalised through a University-wide consultation process.

While the greater institutional commitment to transformation provided an opening, it was the commitment of individual persons in a range of University spaces that made visual redress practices possible. The chapter contributors are institutional actors who led practices in specific University spaces, such as in committee structures and site-specific processes. This book was written via a set of reflection and conversational processes that involved all the chapter contributors. They were involved in tireless voluntary visual culture work. Carrying deep ethical commitments to transformation and a politics of reparation and care, their work in the visual redress domain goes beyond their required professional obligations.

They are involved in this work to give expression to active participation and leadership in often difficult circumstances where they met recalcitrance, objection and challenge. They approximate the organic intellectuals whom Said (1996:x) describes as those who make an "effort to break down the stereotypes and reductive categories that are so limiting to human thought and communication". They refuse to adopt a "careful silence, patriotic bluster, and retrospective and self-dramatizing apostasy" (Said, 1996:xv). Their core institutional identity is that of agents who, in speaking truth to power, are imagining and authoring a new set of visual culture experiences. Their work has invited the University community to build an ethical pathway towards restitution and full human inclusion.

The contributors to this book are public institutional intellectuals from various faculties who normally publish within their own specialised fields, but in this book many authors were challenged to write outside of their field and address transformation related to socio-political issues that are often not engaged with. The lecturers were called upon to think strategically in response to the micro-political exigencies of their institutional contexts. They are charged with ethical intent, yet they actively read and engage the realpolitik of their environment. They work hard to understand what the possibilities for change in their settings are and go about, strategically, to lodge processes, norms and practices in open-ended dialogue. It is in exercising strategic wisdom that they get things done. They apply insight in managing the problematic emotions that accompany work relationships, especially where they receive pushback, negative comment and even open resistance and insult. These public institutional intellectuals learn how to manage their own and their co-creators' emotional responses for the good of change in the institution. They engage in "strategically mobilizing both emotions and meanings as resources" (Moisander, Hirsto and Fahy (2016:981) to gain support for their transformation work. The chapters in the book illuminate their investments in the emotional work that make up their visual redress activities as a necessary means of securing optimal outcomes. Such visual redress activism is aptly captured by Moisander et al. (2016:981):

> In the politics of institutional work, the control of discursive spaces is therefore important, especially for actors who seek to gain acceptance for particular issue interpretations and institutional projects. ... [E]motions may be mobilized and used as resources for the exercise of episodic power and over particular discursive spaces. ... [Their] emotional work is implicated in the discursive practices

through which power/knowledge is exercised in institutional processes … [which] institutional actors may enact in relation to institutional creation, maintenance, and disruption.

Visual redress activity has lodged a range of norms in various University sites. It has centred restitution, decoloniality, inclusion and human rights as ideals to inform the institution's aspirational vision. Visual redress actors on campus sites succeeded in developing consensus-seeking dialogue and participation that decided on the normative intent of their representational activity. In Chapter 7, for example, Khairoonisa Foflonker discusses the process that produced the Faculty of Medicine and Health Science's Charter. The 18-month process involved a wide range of Faculty actors who shared perspectives, engaged in challenging dialogue and built the necessary trust that produced the Charter.

Other site-based initiatives experienced contestation about the chosen visual activity, which led to adjustments. One key example is the Faculty of Law's project to install the Preamble of the country's Constitution on boards outside its building, the historic Ou Hoofgebou (Old Main Building). Bradley Slade discusses in Chapter 8 how the installation was delayed by more than two years as a result of the objections of an interest group based in the town to the technical and design dimensions of the installation. In Chapter 6, Faadiel Essop provides an account of the objections to the collage produced by a visual redress process in the Faculty of Science. These objections raised the need to use more than one language on the collage, which was incorporated in the collage. It also pointed to the hindering impact on visual redress activities by a discourse of scientific elitism coming from some quarters of the Faculty. It was the ability of those persons who participated in the visual redress activities to mediate tensions and objections that led to the successful production of transformative visual spaces and artworks that represented the ideals of transformation and redress.

The visual redress activities on campus are tied to decoloniality, restitution and human rights. Instead of division and exclusion, the activities illustrate the University's willingness to enter into a space of experimentation and participative dialogue capable of producing shared institutional norms and practices. The visual redress activities are hacking away at the older norms of exclusion while instantiating an 'all-included' understanding of the University's aspirational functioning. Visual culture changes signal what the University can become. It gestures, persuades and invites an embracing of the need for broader transformation on campus. Mbembe (2015:5) explains that the "*decolonization of buildings and public spaces* is therefore not a frivolous issue. … [It] is inseparable from the *democratization of access*" (original emphasis). Visual redress, therefore, signposts the University's commitment to its broader public purposes.

The chapters in the book

The chapters in the book are divided into four sections. The first section features a set of chapters that concentrate on the overall development of visual redress trajectories on campus from roughly 2000 onwards. Aslam Fataar's chapter is a reading of visual redress in light of the broader constitutive discourses in the University. A member of the Visual Redress Committee, he adopts a historicising approach to argue that the racially based visual culture established during the decades that preceded 1994 continues to impact the terms of visual culture activities and meanings on the campus. His chapter offers an analysis of how the changing national and institutional political discourses influenced transformation at SU. He argues that the nature and types of visual culture changes after 2000 were determined in interaction with the discursive shifts at the University. Together with other authors in the book, Fataar suggests that the student protests of 2015/6 introduced a decisive change in the University's discursive terrain, with implications for its commitment to transformation. This discursive shift led to the 'institutionalisation' of transformation at the University, which presented a productive opening to enact transformative visual culture activities. The emerging visual culture activities on campus after 2015 articulated a vision of redress, restitution and inclusion that portend commitment to systemic transformation across all sectors of the University.

Leslie van Rooi's chapter focuses on the institutional journey of visual redress at SU over the years past. In particular, focus is given to the post-FeesMustFall era, the removal of the Verwoerd plaque and its effect, the formalisation of visual redress (among others through standing committees) and the link between visual redress and name changes at SU. Currently holding the position of SU's Senior Director: Social Impact and Transformation, Van Rooi's chapter includes a discussion of current and ongoing visual redress projects at SU. The chapter ends with a reflection on how visual redress plays out at other universities in South Africa. Some suggestions are then made on a possible way forward.

Elmarie Costandius's chapter concentrates on various visual redress art-based projects that she facilitated since 2010 as part of her own teaching practice, but also on how the projects were extended to work interdisciplinary with other faculties and communities outside SU. Costandius is currently an associate professor in the Department of Visual Arts and a significant contributor to the University's work on visual redress. Her visual culture work is founded on a new materialism framework, which emphasises the importance of embodied learning and the affective reaction of the body in relation to cognitive experiences of learning. The outcome of visual redress is to create social cohesion, and social cohesion is learned not only cognitively, but very importantly also in a bodily way. In this chapter, art-based processes as a potential transformative method are put forward as a valid alternative mode of enquiry to traditional learning and research.

The second section focuses on site-based visual redress initiatives on the University's campuses. All the chapter authors in this section are professionally located in the sites discussed by them. They are either academics in these specific sites or senior academic support staff. Most of them initiated and/or led the visual redress processes that produced the specific visual culture outcomes for their sites. A significant aspect of these processes was their ability to develop inclusive and dialogical processes on which choices over visual representations were made. Collectively, these visual redress processes and outcomes made a considerable contribution to authoring transformation-informed activities in the sites, which are helping to forge a productive and inclusive institutional path for the University.

Ellen Tise, Stephané Conradie and Mimi Seyffert-Wirth's chapter discusses the SU Library's visual redress journey within the context of the Library's mandate of preserving knowledge past and present. The chapter covers the SU Library's visual redress activities within this context and the broader SU visual redress projects. The chapter provides a brief historical overview of the Library as well as a historical overview and current depiction of the Library's Special Collections division. This is followed by a discussion of significant visual redress initiatives, such as the name change of the SU Library and a Visual Arts student project in Special Collections. Other visual redress processes and outcomes in the Library, such as signage, replacement of historical artefacts and maps, refurbishment of spaces to make the Library more inclusive and the 2018 centenary exhibition are also discussed, which also include personal reflections.

Faadiel Essop's chapter focuses on equity and redress with respect to the institutional culture in the Faculty of Science at SU. The chapter specifically explores the process and implications of a visual redress initiative conducted in the Faculty of Science. Here, it emerged that the process adopted allowed for difficult issues regarding identity, redress and transformation to be dealt with in a sensitive and harmonious way. Based on Essop's reflections on the process, the chapter discusses the impact of the power plays of institutional bureaucrats on the process. He suggests that the notion of 'scientific elitism', which he views as a stumbling block for transformation in science-related fields, should be tackled through making scientists aware of the broader and multifaceted socio-political and historical contexts. Essop concludes that a more diverse student and staff cohort together with a robust inclusive ethos should in turn be a strong catalyst to further propel scientific research endeavours, innovation and excellence.

Khairoonisa Foflonker's chapter explores the development of the Charter of the Faculty of Medicine and Health Sciences at SU and demonstrates how both the development of the Charter and the accompanying visual redress process have made a significant contribution to transformation and decolonisation. The Faculty Charter is a pledge to create inclusive, fair and friendly environments in every aspect of daily interactions. Moreover, the Charter recognises the pain and injustices of the past, while simultaneously offering an aspirational guideline for the future. Visual representations of the Faculty Charter include Perspex panels, brochures, slogans and symbolic stickers as reminders of the individual and collective commitment to the processes of transformation and decolonisation. Foflonker's chapter offers a detailed discussion of the complex dynamics involved in a faculty-based visual redress process that occurred over 18 months. Her account discusses the work that went into building trust and shared perspectives among those who participated in the process that made the Charter as a visual culture outcome possible.

The chapter "Law and visual redress: The space between insider and outsider" by Bradley Slade considers the role of law during the colonial and apartheid eras in establishing the prevailing visuals on SU's campus. Slade argues that the combined effect of these visuals contributed towards an institutional culture that alienates and still largely excludes representation of black bodies. The chapter presents two visual redress processes in the Faculty of Law with the aim of unpacking the transformative effect that visual redress processes had and can have at institutions of higher learning. The chapter also offers the implementation of the Preamble to the Constitution of the Republic of South Africa, 1996, in front of the Faculty of Law as a guide in undertaking visual redress processes.

Reggie Nel, in his chapter titled "Visual redress: Decolonising the Faculty of Theology at Stellenbosch University?", argues that the Faculty of Theology is currently housed at what is often considered one of the most historic parts of Stellenbosch, and its specific location and visual representation of the building are therefore still essential to its identity. This history of the Faculty is closely tied to the history of the town, but it is also a reminder of the traumatic events of displacement and misrecognition of its inhabitants. The chapter tells the story of addressing this legacy through a journey of systemic visual redress processes. Three streams that gave impetus to this process are described in the chapter and as a conclusion, Nel, who is the current dean of the Faculty of Theology, suggests a systemic process of transformation, or what is also described as the process of decolonisation.

The third section of the book features chapters by critical visual redress voices at the University. The authors offer chapters organised around the centrality of their own voices and experiences of their visual redress participation and activities. While the voices of the authors of the preceding chapters are also present in their account, the chapters in this section turn primarily to the authors' personal encounters with respect to the visual redress activities. These perspectives present the authors as multidimensional interlocutors with deep subjective and ethical investments in processes of transformation. The chapter by Renee Hector-Kannemeyer and Otto van Noie explores a 'restitution-seeking' journey by the local Stellenbosch community and SU. The chapter is based on a dialogue between two voices with strong ties to the community. The chapter is aimed at advancing a process of redress that will be respected by all parties, heal broken social relationships and lay a foundation of restorative justice. The authors propose a methodology of critical participatory action research, based on co-equal University and community ownership and participation. This action research process should be located at the Lückhoff precinct, which is a key site identified with the trauma of forced removal and some of the University's attempts at restitution. The authors make a case for locating the community's experiences of loss, recurring trauma and humiliation at the centre of restitution processes, which in turn would be put to critical use in empowering and capacitating the community to construct viable livelihoods and critical citizenship decades after their forced removal from the centre of Stellenbosch. Ongoing visual redress processes would be central to these University–community restitution processes.

Next is an interview-style chapter based on a discussion with Charles Palm, a visual artist and SU student, about his visual culture work on campus since 2018. The chapter was produced from an interview between Palm and Gera de Villiers, a postdoctoral fellow for the visual redress project at the University. During 2018 and 2019, Charles Palm enacted three works on the Rooiplein – *Obscure Stellenbosch*, *Work IN Progress* and *Die Voo'kamer* – that sought to provide spaces for previously marginalised histories to be considered and contemplated. The Rooiplein is a highly trafficked pedestrian throughway and communal gathering area at the heart of SU's main campus. It is a semiotically charged space, where multitudes of people from different social and cultural backgrounds converge, and is therefore an ideal space to enact engagement.

Faaiz Gierdien, in his chapter titled "Indexing visual redress at Stellenbosch University: ways of viewing and reading while walking through the Arts and Social

Sciences Building," uses notions of indexicality and visuality to read visuals inside this building depicting the erasure of the Die Vlakte residents. Gierdien's chapter is based on reflections of his encounter with the building while walking through it on his way to offer his lectures in mathematics education. Gierdien became aware of the haunting presence of the Die Vlakte incidents and ways in which SU is also implicated in the banishment of residents from the current Arts and Social Sciences Building site. He suggests that the visual redress representations in the building meet him halfway by pointing him into specific directions, informing his meaning making, which presents him with the challenge of filling in the gaps and making his own sense, mapped onto his subjectivity of a walker. His chapter is a call for a type of historicised walking that adds new angles and meanings. His chapter is an example of how the intentions and depictions of visual redress as a new form of representation impel active readings and interpretations, lest one is presented with a visual gloss that covers up the past instead of opening critical conversations about people's place in the world.

The last section consists of the chapter "Functions and uses of visual redress initiatives" by Nico Koopman, who is the University's current Vice-Rector: Social Impact, Transformation and Personnel. This chapter draws upon insights from discourses on the public roles and functions of religion in order to enrich discussions on the role and functions of visual redress initiatives on university campuses and at other institutions of democratic societies. These functions might assist our quest to develop visual redress policies and practices and to launch visual redress initiatives that serve dignity, healing, justice, freedom and equality for all. Five of these functions are the envisioning and imagining of a new reality; the criticising and rejecting of an old and still prevailing reality of dehumanisation, injury, injustice, oppression and inequality; the telling of stories of both hurt and healing; the practising of scientific and technical analysis; and the developing of policies and practices in service of dignity, healing, justice, freedom and equality for all.

The book ends with a bibliography on visual representational culture at SU by Mimi Seyffert-Wirth.

Conclusion

In conclusion, this book represents an attempt by its authors to offer an account of working in the domain of transformation at SU. 'Evoking transformation' signals the modest intent of presenting a set of insights into the work of transformation institutional agents in various spaces at the University that is redolent of contingency and human and cultural complexity. Evoking transformation refers to calling forth, bringing to mind, recollecting and evoking memories, and inciting and conjuring new meanings. In this sense, 'visual redress activities on campus involve' a type of relentless practical commitment to change at the University, chipping away at old edifices, whether physical, psychic or affective. The work of these agents also points the way to what is achievable in specific discursive and contingent circumstances. Eschewing an all-or-nothing approach to transformation, the book highlights the uneven pace, messiness and contestation of transformation work. An understanding of transformation is therefore emerging in this book worthy of further exploration: Such an understanding, or working theory, must account for the interaction between the impact of a university's historical situatedness, discursive contestation, policy and micro-political processes, and the institution's willingness and ability to engage in inclusive institutional change across its various operational arenas. As this book illustrates, what is central to an account of transformation is the intellectual, organisational and affective terms on which institutional transformational agents encounter and engage change processes inside the contingencies of particular University sites. It is the active ethical agency of actors within specific University sites that advances transformation at the University.

References

Freschi, F., Schmahmann, B. & Van Robbroeck, L. 2020. Troubling images: An introduction. In: F. Freschi, B. Schmahmann & L. van Robbroeck (eds.). Troubling images: *Visual culture and the politics of Afrikaner nationalism. Johannesburg*: Wits University Press, 1-22. https://doi.org/10.18772/22020024716.5

Jansen, J. & Walters, C. 2020. *Fault Lines: A primer on race, science and society.* Stellenbosch: African Sun Media. https://doi.org/10.18820/9781928480495

Lalu, P. 2007. Apartheid's university: Notes on the renewal of the enlightenment. *Journal of Higher Education in Africa*, 5(1):45-60.

Mbembe, A. 2015. *Decolonizing knowledge and the question of the archive.* Retrieved from https://wiser.wits.ac.za/system/files/Achille%20Mbembe%20-%20Decolonizing%20Knowledge%20and%20the%20Question%20of%20the%20Archive.pdf [Accessed 27 November 2020].

Moisander, J., Hirsto, H. & Fahy, K. 2016. Emotions in institutional work: A discursive perspective. *Organizational Studies*, 37(7):963-990. https://doi.org/10.1177/0170840615613377

Said, E. 1996. *Representations of an intellectual.* New York, NY: Vintage Books.

Schmahmann, B. 2020. Knocking Jannie off his pedestal: Two creative interventions to the sculpture of JH Marais at Stellenbosch University. In: F. Freschi, B. Schmahmann & L. van Robbroeck (eds.). *Troubling images: Visual culture and the politics of Afrikaner nationalism.* Johannesburg: Wits University Press, 140-166. https://doi.org/10.18772/22020024716.11

Section A

Visual redress trajectories at Stellenbosch University

Chapter 2

'Discourse speaks us': Visual redress at Stellenbosch University, 2000–2021

Aslam Fataar

Introduction

The chapter discusses visual redress at Stellenbosch University (SU) from 2000.[1] It is based on institutional documents and interviews with key institutional actors. Consonant with the other chapters in this book, I argue that the period after 2015 represents a qualitative shift in visual redress activities, emanating from what I call the University's institutionalisation of transformation during the period. In contrast to the period before 2015, a concerted institutional commitment to changing core aspects of its visual culture emerged after this period. This gave rise to an increase in visual redress initiatives across the University. Undertaken via differing dynamics and processes across the University, a range of meanings associated with the emerging visual culture has taken root. Visual cultural representation at SU has taken on heterogeneous expressions and forms.

The chapter presents the specific institutional discourse and dynamics since 2000 as the background text for visual redress processes. The focus is on the interaction between visual redress discourse on the one hand and the type of visual redress initiatives that have taken place across SU's campuses on the other. It is the dynamic relationship between these two aspects – visual redress discourse and visual redress initiatives – that determined the specific trajectory of visual redress at the University.

Discourse refers to those social and knowledge practices that define what is allowable or do-able in everyday life, institutions and social practices. Discourse governs how we talk, our conduct and what we can do in specific circumstances. Hall (1992:291–292) explains that discourse imposes the authoring bases for the texts or activities that are produced by individuals or institutions. People or institutions do not behave outside of discourse. They are subject to the rules and conventions of discourse. The power of discourse lies in its ability to determine how knowledge in the world is categorised and what type of action is possible in specific

---

1 The term 'visual redress' emerged in SU's policy documents from around 2013 in the context of the institution's grappling with establishing a welcoming culture. The term refers to processes involving changes in the visual culture of the University to promote restitution and inclusion. It became parlance in the SU's discourses and structures after 2015.

contexts. Institutions such as universities operate inside discourse. Ball (2006:48) explains that "discourses are about what can be said, and thought, but also about who can speak, when, where and with what authority. … Thus, certain possibilities for thought [and action] are constructed".

Institutional behaviour is subject to certain dominant discourses in specific periods, which gather authority and have an impact on the institution's decisions and policy directions. Here the focus is on how discourse shapes meaning systems that gain the status of 'truth' and come to dominate institutional behaviour while marginalising other forms of behaviour (Pinkus, 1996). A discourse analysis throws the spotlight on how these processes constitute, for example, the career of institutional change and adaptation at universities.

However, the focus is not only on domination. Dominant discourses are not static or closed systems (Hall, 1992:87). They shift over time, depending on changes in the broader cultural, political and economic environment in which institutions are located. For example, the democratic changeover from the apartheid to the post-apartheid period represents a clear shift in the political discourse that affected the way universities functioned. Discourse theorists (see Foucault, 1982; Hall, 1992) emphasise that we are entangled in a variety of contradictory discourses, and that subjugated, or non-dominant knowledges and behaviour, may emerge from time to time, which challenge the dominant discourses and make certain resistant practices possible. The 2015/2016 #FeesMustFall struggles led by students introduced a decisive shift that changed the discursive environment of universities. The students lodged the quest for radical institutional change and the decolonising of education as critical tropes in the country's universities. As discussed below, this shift in discourse changed the institutional terms upon which visual redress as transformational practice proceeded at SU. The key argument presented here is that the visual redress initiatives that emerged at SU since 2000 are the outcome of the shifting institutional discourses that made certain types of visual redress activities possible.

Historicising visual redress at the University

This section offers a brief discussion of some dimensions of SU's visual culture during its more than 100 years of existence. Historical antecedence has an impact on current-day visual redress activities. In its centenary commemoration in 2018, the University released a statement that explained that it "celebrates its successes and achievements" and "acknowledge[s], with deep regret, [its] role in the injustices of the country's past" (SU, 2018:n.p.).[2] The statement was presented in the three regionally dominant languages of the Western Cape, namely isiXhosa, Afrikaans and English. This multilingual approach is a break from the dominance by the Afrikaans language at SU. The centenary statement was prominently displayed on the University's promotional literature and at the entrance of the newly named Stellenbosch University Library.[3] Following on SU's acceptance of its Transformation Plan (SU, 2017b), the centenary statement positioned the University community to engage in practices of restitution in respect of SU's complicity in the inequalities and iniquities associated with the country's colonial and apartheid past. Redressing visual culture is accorded a prominent role in this regard.

Historicising the University's visual culture reveals its impact on recent experiences of the campus. The symbols, statues and names, chosen in an earlier period, have implications for the way people relate politically and emotionally to an institution. Choices over symbols and memorialisation inform these developments. They represent a specific depiction of an institution's memory, which mobilises a specific version of history that reflects its temperament in the light of the dominant politics of the moment. Changing names and symbols are made at different political moments in the University's life. The political rupture caused by the break from apartheid and democracy placed SU on a changed discursive path. The University struggled to adapt to such a path during the 1990s and early 2000s. Moving to

---

2   See Chapter 4 by Elmarie Costandius in this book for the full statement. SU was founded as a fully-fledged university in 1918 by an Act of Parliament. Two other universities, Cape Town and Fort Hare, were similarly accorded university status.

3   The Library's name was changed from the JS Gericke Library to the Stellenbosch University Library in 2017 as part of the Library's commitment to visual redress transformation. See Chapter 5 by Ellen Tise, Stephané Conradie and Mimi Seyffert-Wirth in this book for a discussion of visual redress activities in the Library.

inclusiveness and adaptation to the democratic dispensation proved contestable and challenging. The pace of incorporating students and staff from broader demographic categories and shifting its institutional culture towards greater inclusion was slow.

The changes in the visual culture of the University soon after 2000 were made via bureaucratic processes to mollify the political temperature of the early democratic transition in a context where the University remained mostly untransformed. Changes to the visual culture during this period illustrate the contested meanings and impact of these changes. The example of changing the name of the BJ Vorster Building to the Arts Building in 2002 illustrates how these changes contributed to the further marginalisation of black people and communities. It was built during the early 1970s and named after a sitting prime minister. Vorster was also the University's chancellor at that time. The 1960s and early 1970s were the heydays of the apartheid era. The link between the hegemonic Afrikaner nationalist politics and the University was strong. The building's modernist architecture reflects the triumphalism and nascent worldliness of Afrikaner nationalism that emerged during the period. The building's architecture was similar to other projects that provided for Afrikaner educational advancement during the period. These included the modern, yet laager-like, Rand Afrikaans University (Schmahmann, 2013:6), now the University of Johannesburg, and the University of South Africa's imposing campus in the capital city of Pretoria, now Tshwane. This was a time of Afrikaner confidence based on the nationalist vision of grand apartheid: homelands, forced removals, rigid racial segregation and apartheid education.

The BJ Vorster Building was however built on a terrain called Die Vlakte, where a large section of Stellenbosch's coloured community resided. The building rose out of the ashes of the forced removal of people from Die Vlakte in the 1960s. SU took over parts of the terrain and also took ownership of Lückhoff School, which, in the eyes of the Die Vlakte residents, represents the high watermark of the University's complicity with the removals for which community members have been seeking proper recompense. A prominent community member described the University's takeover of Lückhoff School as its 'original sin', whose restitution remains a challenge, aspects of which are discussed below and treated in greater depth in Chapter 10. The people of Die Vlakte have a difficult, some say distrusting, relationship with the University and the town (Biscombe, 2006). Die Vlakte was situated in the centre of this University town. Its people stayed among white Afrikaner people in the town, yet attending the University was disallowed because of its racial exclusivity.

While renaming the building to the neutral 'Arts Building'[4] served the purpose of distancing the University from National Party politics, it deepened the misrecognition of the impact of the Die Vlakte forced removals. In an attempt to mollify expectations for the University to align itself with the new political democracy, the name change of the building and other similar name changes on campus revealed a propensity for tactical measures. These measures, however, failed to signal an intention by the University to undergo serious restitution processes. The name change further alienated the Die Vlakte community, which became the focus for restitution-type visual redress activities in later, changed circumstances.

The discursive environment at the University needed to shift towards a more concerted focus on transformation for in-depth restitution efforts to become possible. The visual culture event that signposted such a shift was the installation of the so-called Pink Piet statue at the University's Faculty of Theology in 2006. The statue was commissioned by the supporters of Prof. Johannes du Plessis and placed in the town in 1946. Prof. Du Plessis was a lecturer at the University's Theology Seminary from the early 1920s (Schmahmann, 2013:40). He was dismissed from his post in 1930 after he was found guilty of heresy because he supported an open-ended reading of theology. He questioned, among other things, the Bible in the light of science and as the literal word of God, and Jesus' capability for error (Lategan, 2001:63–64). He also held liberal views of justice and racial equality. While he successfully challenged his dismissal in the Cape Town Supreme Court and was technically reinstated by the University, he was never allowed to teach at the University again. Prof. Du Plessis challenged the nature of theological studies at SU. His example of pursuing dissident scholarship was later emulated by a small but growing number of dissident scholars whose academic work challenged the dominant scholarly orientation of SU.

---

4   The building was renamed the Arts and Social Sciences Building in 2007.

The Pienk Piet statue was installed in the garden of the Faculty of Theology building in 2006, where it joined other statues of past Theology professors. The installation was part of the Faculty's 150th anniversary commemoration. This early visual redress initiative gestured towards the need for the critical academic study of theology based on plural and inclusive scholarly approaches that are disconnected from support for party politics and separatist ideologies. Representing a 'family fight' in Afrikaner academic circles about the type of academic orientations allowed at the University, installing Prof. Du Plessis's statue signalled the Faculty of Theology's willingness to adopt scholarly approaches founded on integrity and academic openness to requirements of a democratic dispensation. More broadly, such a perspective has dislodged the University's academic ties to its erstwhile narrow racially based sectarian politics.

Compared to the productive use of symbolism associated with the centring of the Pink Piet statue, the University's response to the imposing statue of Jan Marias, the University's primary benefactor at its origin in 1918, has no easy resolution.[5] Two artistic performances by students of the University's Department of Visual Arts in the post-2015 period engaged in what decolonial scholar Boaventura De Sousa Santos (2018:202) calls artistic insurgence, which took place on the centrally located Rooiplein public square of the University. Their art performances challenged what is experienced by many students as the grotesque presence of the Marais statue on the square. The two performances centred powerful, yet short-lived, conversations about the statue's ongoing circulation of racially paternalistic meanings decades after its erection. The statue was installed in 1950 as a tribute to Marais's financial contribution to the development of the University. However, in the post-2015 period, many students objected to his presence on the basis that he benefitted only Afrikaner students.[6]

---

5   See Schmahmann (2020:140–165) for a comprehensive discussion of the JH Marais statue at the University, which was produced by sculptor Coenie Steynberg and unveiled in 1950.

6   Some students also expressed their support for the statue to remain on the Rooiplein. See Chapter 3 by Leslie van Rooi in this book for an explanation of the expressions of support and opposition to the statue during the #RhodesMustFall and #FeesMustFall student protests.

A Visual Arts student designed a wooden staircase that went up the Marais statue. Naming her intervention *Flight* in order to signify the statue's role in absolving the University from accounting for all its students, she mounted the stairs and defiantly looked Jannie Marais in the eye. She meant her protest as a challenge for him to step down, in other words, for the statue to be removed. As Schmahmann (2020:153) suggested, it was …

> … a call for the university to cease conceiving of itself as, in essence, home for white Afrikaners, and instead to explore ways of embracing cultural diversity. In other words, rather than the actual statue, it is what Jannie Marais himself seems to symbolise that is being called to 'step down'.

The University's security teams removed the stairs after an hour of the performance. The stairs were dumped in front of the Department of Visual Arts building, which is itself an indication of the difficulty of sustaining a conversation about the visual culture of the University that is made up of artefacts that have taken on a life of their own due to their long presence on campus. Many students and staff are unaware of their political meanings. There is also the difficulty of developing alternative-use ideas for statues of such enormous size.[7]

In a separate performance, another student from the Department of Visual Arts presented a challenging performance that interacted with the Marais statue, which entailed the positioning of two benches within metres from the statue, one occupied by the student staring at the statue. The performance engaged the statue as a form of traumascape (see Breyne, 2018), which has the potential of evoking discussion about the trauma and hurt suffered by those affected by injustice and exclusion. The benches invoked the episode where learners from Lückhoff School in 1969 were required to carry their benches from the school in Die Vlakte to their replacement school in the nearby coloured township of Idas Valley. The three-hour performance called attention to the role of the University in this process. It presented the "campus of SU and the monument of Jan Marais as a traumascape in the sense that they

---

7   The size of the Marais statue is, for example, rivaled by the Steyn statue that was erected on the campus of the University of the Free State in 1929 (Jansen 2020). A proposal to erect a statue of local King Moshoeshoe elicited strenuous rejection in the media from Afrikaners who were appalled by the equivalence that such an addition would draw between the two men.

are part of the geographic epicenter of a suppressive historical political system of apartheid that was extremely violent and traumatizing" (Breyne, 2018:43).

Both performances raised questions about continuing violations associated with practices of exclusion and symbolic violence in on- and off-campus interactions. Visual cultural expressions have a traumatic afterlife, especially in terms of the impact they have on those excluded from the symbolism associated with racial domination. Ghostlike in its impact, it serves to disorientate and alienate people who reject these racial tropes. The two engagements with the Marais statue referred to above illustrate the power and limits of insurgent questioning dialogue with visual images. As dialogues of challenge and discomfort, they open reckoning with the exclusionary nature of symbols and the politics that they represent. The fleeting nature of their performances has yet to translate into more substantive visual cultural restitution. Their example illustrates the troubling consequences that the untransformed visual culture has for experiences of the broader institutional culture of the institution. It signals the need for more fundamental changes to the way students and staff experience an institution that struggles to establish the type of changed inclusion practices that are worthy of their presence.

This section discussed the challenges associated with shifts in the visual culture of the University. It showed how the changing of visual symbols and statues and the naming of buildings are the outcome of the institutional culture and politics of specific periods. These adaptations create the semiotic and conceptual grounds for further adaptation when the institution's visual representations come under pressure from the imperative to transform the University's institutional culture. The chapter now turns to a discussion of how SU has adapted its visual cultural representation to align with its transformation agenda in the post-2000 period.

Visual redress between 2000 and 2015 in light of an emergent transformation discourse

Visual cultural change at SU unfolded at a slow pace during the period 2000–2015. Its ties to institutional transformation emerged unevenly during the period.

The visual cultural changes wrestled with the requirements for restitutive dialogue and institutional inclusivity. This section discusses the interaction between transformation as discourse and the type of visual cultural changes that took place until 2015.

Like all other South African universities, SU was confronted by the new political dispensation's requirement to align with the democratisation of society. A range of government regulatory and policy instruments emerged to facilitate change at universities (see DoE, 1997; NCHE, 1996). Government's institutional change agenda for universities was far-reaching and ambitious. Transformational change requires a range of structural change processes in the various institutional environments of universities that would facilitate access to previously excluded groups. The universities' responses to the transformation agenda were uneven, determined as they were by their institutional histories, leadership orientations and financial positions, and the particular choices they made to survive and adapt to the emerging higher education regulatory environment.

SU's adaptations during the 1990s are described as a 'wait-and-see' and 'business-as-usual' attitude (Baumert, 2014:187–241), which refer to the University remaining relatively inert to the pressures to, for example, change its Afrikaans-dominant institutional culture and language policy to enable greater access by black students and staff. The University mostly abjured such change during the mid- to late 1990s. This was, however, not a case of simple refusal and sitting back to wait for external intervention. The University used the period to assert its institutional autonomy from government interference to retain control over its change processes.[8] The search for financial viability caused the University during the 1990s to increasingly turn to international partnerships and third-stream income to augment its funding base.

---

8   The ruling African National Congress's commitment to reconciliatory governance resulted in a position of government adopting a hands-off approach to the University, in other words, a situation where SU would not be unduly pressured to change. Presidents Mandela and Mbeki, on separate occasions, assured the University of the continued viability of Afrikaans as a key language of instruction. Such a situation was however not meant to result in the continuation of racial exclusivity or the dominance of one language. Expressing frustration with the lack of change at SU, the minister of Education, Prof. Bhengu, questioned its lack of meaningful change to secure greater inclusiveness.

The University adopted a range of management and performance instruments to secure greater efficiencies. It paid attention to shoring up its research platform and undertook programme realignments across its campuses.

Once it had a firmer institutional platform to mitigate the pressures for change, the University opened the door to a conversation about transformation. Such a conversation was led by a small group of reform-minded academics who had a history of supporting greater responsiveness to the transformation agenda. The University produced its first authoritative document that emphasised its perspective on transformation in 2000. Titled *A strategic framework for the turn of the century and beyond* (SU, 2000), the document remained the key reference text that guided transformation work for the ensuing decade. The document emphasised the importance of maintaining quality in its programme renewal, internationalisation, efficient management and financial diversification. These dimensions became key framers of institutional dynamics during the period and beyond. Afrikaans as the dominant language of the institution was emphasised. The struggle over its retention provided the critical discursive marker for debates on institutional change during the period. The document included statements on the need for redress, inclusion and adapting its institutional culture in support of greater diversification. Recruiting students and staff in support of greater diversity was mentioned, although the dominance of Afrikaans would impede the attainment of this objective considerably. The University had, for example, only decreased the percentage of white students from 72% in 2006 to 67% in 2012 (SU, 2013b:13).

What was significant about this document, and an accompanying implementation document, was that for the first time, SU had committed itself in clear policy terms to transformation objectives that included redress, equity, diversification and inclusion. In other words, the document provided an essential opening for addressing the transformation imperative on campus. The new rector, Prof. Chris Brink (2002–2006), was recruited to implement the content of the document. Billed as a 'transformer' (*omvormer*) rector, Brink used the 2000 strategic document to develop a five-point vision statement that would guide a streamlined and targeted approach to transformation.

This vision statement also informed the leadership approach of the next rector, Prof. Russel Botman (2007–2014), who hitched Prof. Brink's vision statement onto the sustainable development goals and his signature HOPE Project campaign as a means of providing greater impetus to transformation. Prof. Brink continued the University's emphasis on internationalisation, managerial efficiency and curricula responsive to transdisciplinary knowledge. Continuing along this part, Prof. Botman emphasised the University's local and national relevance as well as its commitment to African content.

Turning to the visual cultural adaptation at the University, SU's activities revealed three different types that ran parallel to each other during the period. They each reveal specific institutional dynamics that informed its operations. The first type that emerged was the removal of symbolic depictions that tied the University to Afrikaner National Party politics. In addition to changing the name of the BJ Vorster Building to the Arts Building in 2002, the names of other prime ministers, such as JC Smuts, DF Malan and HF Verwoerd, were removed from campus buildings in 2004.[9]

Activity in the University's library from 2005 onward also followed the model of removing potentially offensive symbols. Artwork, pencil drawings and staff photos were removed from places such as the library foyer and staffroom. The bust of JS Gericke, a former rector after whom the library was named, was removed and placed in the library's Africana section. This was about the time that conversations started emerging about changing the library's name, which eventually occurred in 2017. This model of removing offensive symbols continued for some visual culture adaptation activities at the University throughout the 2000–2015 period.

The second type of visual adaptation is represented by name changes that mostly involved politically uncontentious choices. This involved the type of naming that described the core activities of the buildings or lecture theatres. Others were named after donors or named for ethically aspirational concepts such as metanoia

---

9 The JC Smuts Building was renamed the Biological Sciences Building, the DF Malan Building was changed to the Mike de Vries Building, named after a former rector, and the HF Verwoerd Building was renamed the Accounting and Statistics Building.

and *ubuntu*. The acceptance of a naming policy in 2010 facilitated such neutral types of name changes.[10] The policy guided the decision-making regarding the granting of naming rights. It emphasised community participation where names after persons are considered.

The renaming activity that took place after the acceptance of the naming policy mostly followed the model of uncontentious choices of about 14 renaming activities across the University. The restitutive imperative did not surface as a vital feature of visual cultural activities on campus between 2010 and 2015. This is an aspect addressed by the visual redress policy developed from 2018 by incorporating a more decisive visual redress impetus to visual cultural adaptation and naming processes[11].

The third visual cultural adaptation response by the University happened in the context of its attempt to engage in restitution-orientated visual transformation activities concerning the Die Vlakte community. A set of activities from 2002 represents the University's first attempt at visual culture tied to transformation. A particular understanding of visual culture as restitution crystallised around activity at Lückhoff School. Redress activity connected to the Die Vlakte community was spurred by a book-writing project that memorialises the lives of people who lived in Die Vlakte. The book project emerged out of a meeting between senior members of the SU management team and persons attached to the Die Vlakte community a few months before the start of Prof. Brink's rectorship in 2002. The meeting took place in the Volkskerk, which was a prominent independent church built by, and serving, the people of Die Vlakte. The meeting discussed SU's intention to establish a relationship with the Die Vlakte community. SU offered its support for the writing of the book. The Department of History was involved in the logistical and academic planning of the research for the book. The research was preceded by planning conversations between Department members and the project team, the latter made up of community members of, or related to, the Die Vlakte community. The Department of History offered workshop training sessions to members of the

---

10   The naming policy is contained in a policy document titled *Policy on the naming of buildings, venues and other facilities/premises* (SU, 2010).

11   It is anticipated that the visual redress policy, currently in a process of drafting, will be finalised and become university policy during 2021.

research team on oral story collection methods. The project team members travelled widely to collect stories from people who lived in Die Vlakte. The team met for frequent planning meetings in the Lückhoff School building, which housed the University's Division of Community Interaction.

The book titled *In ons bloed* (In our blood) was published in 2006. It was researched by a group of community members and compiled by former Die Vlakte resident Hilton Biscombe. It consisted of stories, descriptions and photos arranged thematically on various aspects of life in the area, such as religion, sport, culture, politics, Lückhoff School and Die Vlakte's relationship to the University. The book was launched at a ceremony in the University's HB Thom Theatre.[12] Prof. Brink commented in his foreword that the book is a cathartic moment for the University. He explained that it is about a time when the people of Die Vlakte were consciously and brutally driven out in order to fit into the separate compartments that were then regarded by apartheid as a solution to the 'race problem'. Committing the University to establishing a restorative relationship with the community, he explained that the University has to understand the past, and remember and learn from it (Biscombe, 2006:ix).

Prof. Julian Smith, Vice-Rector: Operations, who had executive responsibility for the Division of Community Interaction,[13] referred to the book as articulating a dimension that was hidden and silenced and said it allowed the University to give a sharper definition to its community role (Biscombe, 2006:vii). In this respect, the book presented the University with an opportunity to launch its first visual redress activity with respect to the removed Lückhoff School where, in its place, the Division of Community Interaction was based. Capitalising on the relationship that University members established with the Die Vlakte community members, the Division, under the leadership of Dr Jerome Slamat,[14] shepherded several processes that opened a conversation about restitution. The Division facilitated the renaming of the building

---

12 The HB Thom Theatre was renamed the Adam Small Theatre in 2018 after a renowned academic, poet and author.

13 This division has been renamed the Division for Social Impact.

14 Dr Slamat was the Senior Director: Community Interaction at the University at the time. I wish to thank him for his considerable input in the narrative told here about Lückhoff School.

from the US Gemeenskapsdienssentrum to Lückhoff School in consultation with community members. The naming intended to signal the University's regret over its complicity in the Die Vlakte forced removals and the takeover of the building, and its seriousness in helping to restore the building to the community. Such a gesture was intended as a necessary first step to restore co-ownership to the community, the exact form of which is the subject of ensuing processes. The Division facilitated the renaming process. The launch of the renaming of the building was presented as the reinstatement of the original name of the school that was closed in the 1960s as part of the area's forced removals. Hosted by Prof. Botman on 15 October 2007 at Lückhoff School, the invitation billed the event as the "Rededication of the Lückhoff School in Banhoek Road" under the theme "Future, Hope and Healing". A photo exhibition was opened at the event. Local community leaders, politicians, the rector and the premier of the Western Cape gave addresses.

The University continued its efforts to pay tribute to those affected by the forced removals. At the beginning of 2008, a collaborative effort was made by members of the broader Stellenbosch community and the Division of Community Interaction to memorialise the school. Financially supported by the Het Jan Marais Nationale Fonds, a permanent visual representation of the school's history was produced by using photos and other memorabilia obtained from ex-learners, an exhibition of which was launched in October 2008 at the school. Curated by a committee consisting of Division and community members, the exhibition consisted of a collection of stories and photos that were collected via an advertisement in the local newspaper that asked people to submit school-related photos, which received a good response. The photos were digitised and returned to their owners. A former staff member of the Department of Visual Arts, Mr Victor Honey, did the layout of the photos for the exhibition. The late ex-principal of the school, Dr Fred Backman, gave an address at the launch. The event also celebrated 'uitstygers' (achievers) among learners who attended Lückhoff School. The event happened under the theme "Let Me Tell You about Lückhoff".

The visual culture activities at Lückhoff School represent the University's foray into a restorative approach. It laid the basis for the more concerted visual redress approaches after 2015. Based on a University and community partnership, the Lückhoff School activities represent what Santos (2018:200) calls the workings of a palimpsest archive in reference to visual work that "identif[ies] the marks, traces, shadows, and silences of what was destroyed or produced as absent, invisible, and irrelevant in building the achievable world". Such an approach is based on what he calls a "sociology of absences" (Santos, 2018:200), which confronts the erasures and silences that were associated with the forced removals. Such an approach provides the basis for engaging in healing, restoring memory and empowering those communities whose development have been ravaged by apartheid. Prof. Botman[15] enunciated a commitment to such a restorative approach to visual redress by proposing a co-ownership model for Lückhoff School. This model would involve the University and the community running the building as a creative hub for a range of empowerment initiatives, including community and literacy education, youth employment training and community-building activities. The community received the idea with enthusiasm, but it stalled in light of Prof. Botman's untimely death on 27 June 2014. The University is currently pursuing the co-ownership idea in a community partnership, which is the subject of discussion in Chapter 10 of this book.

By 2014, transformation had stalled at the University. Dissatisfaction with the pace of transformation was expressed in a contentious university document.[16] This document explained that "the time has come for robust dialogue about transformation. … the slow pace of fundamental institutional change thus far calls for acceleration, with a refocusing drive for transformation" (SU, 2013b:1–2). While the document refers to the broader trajectory of the University's experiences with the directions of institutional change, the related visual cultural activities have by the same time been experienced as halting and uneven across the University's campuses. The types of visual adaptation activities that emerged struggled to connect with the imperatives for restitution-type visual redress activities associated with transformation. This was also

---

15   Prof. Botman's HOPE Project yielded a productive set of renovations in the University's main library, which introduced new African artwork, and the research and learning commons, which was a flagship initiative of the HOPE Project. It opened its doors in 2010, followed by the state-of-the-art Carnegie Research Commons, which opened a year later in 2011. See Chapter 5 for a discussion of these additions.

16   The document was titled *Transformation at Stellenbosch: Future strategies* (SU, 2013b).

a reflection of the lack of a broader welcoming institutional culture at SU.[17] Despite the three types of visual adaptation during this period, visual cultural transformation had taken a back seat by 2014. It lacked impetus and momentum similar to the stalled transformation trajectory of which it was a part. This situation was upended in 2015 when the student protests changed the discursive environment in which universities functioned, which had implications for the transformation imperative at SU and its visual cultural adaptation activities.

Visual redress as transformation in the post-2015 period

This period witnessed the institutionalisation of a visual redress impetus at the University and an increase in visual redress activities on the University's campuses. This section discusses the nature of the discursive shift that emanated from the student struggles on campuses all over South Africa and at SU. This discursive shift had a decisive impact on institutional discourses. It led to several processes, policy developments and initiatives that determined the direction of visual redress at the University. While related to visual cultural adaptation in the previous period, the particular expression of visual redress took on a qualitatively different form in the direction of a more concerted transformative approach. Two key conceptual points are developed in this section. The first is that an institutional policy to regulate visual redress activities emerged alongside and after the implementation of a range of visual redress activities during the period. It could be said that those who wrote the policy learnt from the implementation of these activities. The second related point is that the period gave birth to a conception of visual redress as 'transformation praxis', which holds lessons for future visual redress activities at SU and other universities.

The student struggles from 2015 onwards emanated from experiences of marginalisation that confronted students in the country's universities. Black and poor, the students bore the brunt of debt, financial exclusion, failure and high attrition rates. They complained of being exposed to untransformed curricula and

---

17 Prof. Botman instituted a welcoming culture task team to produce a report and a set of recommendations to improve the University's welcoming culture. A report was produced that mentioned visual renewal as one key dimension of such a welcoming culture. The report was titled, "Task Team on a Welcoming Culture at Stellenbosch University" (SU, 2013a).

racist university practices. Visceral expressions of pain and alienation marked the student protests. Framed by them as a generational chasm between their parents' generation, who accepted the empty promises of democratic change, the students rejected transformation discourses that failed to address unequal power arrangements at universities. I argued as follows in a 2018 article (Fataar, 2018:599):

> The students railed against a politics of patience. Their strategy of occupying university spaces and buildings was an attempt to call attention to the university's suffocating and racist institutional culture, exclusionary governance processes, and the prevalence of a colonial curriculum.

The Open Stellenbosch student movement crystallised the vision of the broader student protests within the specific context of SU. It engaged in several campaigns and protests on campus that highlighted students' negative experiences at the University. Open Stellenbosch served as a hailer for students' alienating experiences in their lecture theatres and residences and their experiences of discrimination on the broader campus. They engaged with the exclusionary depictions of the University's architecture, building names and statues. The Rooiplein became a stage for their resistance and questioning performances. The space witnessed numerous spontaneous student performances that, among others, questioned the University's visual depictions. The period also saw some Visual Arts student projects on the Rooiplein that challenged the semiotics of the campus.[18]

A crucial moment in the University's response to the student protests was the emergence of the 'Luister' video. The video is a visceral portrayal of the negative experiences of black students at an agricultural training institute associated with SU.[19] The video portrayed their experiences as a result of the racist practices at their institution where the domination of Afrikaans as the primary institutional language generated disaffection and anger. The video created a national uproar. It was discussed in the country's parliament, which called on the University to explain its content.

---

18 See Chapter 4 by Elmarie Costandius and Chapter 11 by Gera de Villiers and Charles Palm in this book for a discussion of student-led visual redress performances and artwork on the Rooiplein from 2015 that were inspired by the Open Stellenbosch-led student protests.

19 The Luister video was shot at the Elsenberg Agricultural Training Institute. The Institute offers an undergraduate degree in agriculture in association with SU (see Nicolson, 2015).

The University had to defend its commitment to transformation at a parliamentary hearing. The association made on social and mainstream media between the video and SU placed the University on the back foot and arguably played an important role in shaping its response to the student protests.

Under the tenure of the new rector, Prof. Wim de Villiers, who started his rectorship in April 2015 shortly after the protests erupted in March 2015, the University embarked on an institutional path that was responsive to the demands for change. The removal of a plaque depicting National Party prime minister Verwoerd was removed from the Accounting and Statistics Building. The plaque, which commemorated Verwoerd as the 'architect of apartheid', was placed in the University's archives and the hole in the wall where it stood was covered with the country's national flag as a symbol of reconciliation. This followed on a short committee process in which the decision for the removal was taken. The official removal took place on 27 May 2015. Verwoerd's grandson, Willem Verwoerd, spoke at this occasion. He expressed the hope that the act of removal would convey a sense of healing. Prof. De Villiers explained at the event that the removal expressed the University's commitment to redress and the creation of a welcoming culture (News24, 2015).[20] Strikingly, members of Open Stellenbosch staged a silent protest by sitting through the ceremony with their lips taped. Explaining their response, the organisation stated on its Facebook page that "it supports the removal of the Verwoerd plaque. It has been long overdue. … Open Stellenbosch is committed to engaging with the institution in every way to ensure that transformation takes place" (Open Stellenbosch, 2015:n.p.).

The decisive intervention by the University that signalled its commitment to transformation was the acceptance of a language policy that stressed multilingualism. Language is a contentious matter at the University, and as alluded to earlier, it is a

---

[20] The event programme gave the following raison d'être for the removal:
The removal of the Verwoerd commemorative plaque from the Accounting and Statistics Building (formerly the HF Verwoerd Building [name changed in 2004]) illustrates the commitment of Stellenbosch University to create a welcoming culture for all and to remove obstacles in the path to unity and progress on campus. This event serves as an affirmation of the University's acknowledgement of its contribution to the injustices of the past, and its commitment to appropriate redress and development initiatives in its Strategic Framework (2000). We, the witness of today's event undertake to remind our campus and town community of where we come from and where we are heading with our democracy (SU, 2015).

placeholder for broader struggles over the future of the University. The University was under considerable pressure by alumni and others associated with the University's Afrikaner identity to keep Afrikaans the primary language of instruction. On the other hand, as the pressure for greater inclusiveness increased, the University had to confront the language matter as one of the primary obstacles that prevented it from welcoming greater numbers of black students and staff. Under Prof. De Villiers's leadership, the University embarked on a language revision process that started in late 2015. Despite legal and political contestation and media pressure from Afrikaans newspapers against dropping Afrikaans, the process culminated in a new multilingual language policy that was accepted by the University's Council in June 2016. The policy aimed to …

> … increase equitable access for all students and staff and to facilitate pedagogically sound teaching and learning. Since our campuses are situated in the Western Cape, we commit ourselves to multilingualism by using the province's three official languages, namely Afrikaans, English and isiXhosa (SU, 2016:1).

The acceptance of the new language policy reflected the impact of the shifting institutional discourse at the University. Transformation as a University imperative became a firm part of SU's agenda. One of the vice-rector positions was redesignated to the title Vice-Rector: Social Impact, Transformation and Personnel. Prof. Nico Koopman was appointed to this position in 2016.[21] Another critical position in this line function was that of Senior Director: Social Impact and Transformation, a position held by Dr Leslie van Rooi. The University's Transformation Office was set up to implement its transformation agenda across campus. A Transformation Plan was accepted in 2017 to guide transformation-oriented work on SU's campuses. The Plan enunciated an ambitious agenda of institutional change by stating as follows:

> Transformation at SU is viewed as **systemic transformation**. This implies that all dimensions of university life are involved in the transformation and renewal process. Systemic transformation also implies that all dimensions of university life contribute to the transformation of society. Transformation is therefore described as

---

21 Prof. Koopman acted in the position of Vice-Rector for Community Interaction and Personnel which was the previous designation of his current position.

transformation of the University and transformation through the University (SU, 2017a:10, emphasis in the original).

As instructed by the Plan, the Institutional Transformation Committee was set up to provide guidance and advice to the Transformation Office and the Rector's Management Team on the direction of transformation at the University. Transformation was given further impetus by the hosting of annual indabas that involved staff across the University in discussion about institutional processes and objectives, and an annual report on transformation targets and accomplishments. A criticism of transformation at SU is that it is not sufficiently mainstreamed into the teaching, learning and research processes in the University and that faculties are struggling to develop coherent implementation strategies across their operations to advance transformation objectives.

What is clear is that the institutionalisation of transformation at the University since 2015 has galvanised a concerted University institutional focus, which has given impetus to wide-ranging activities at SU. The Plan's targeting of changes in the institutional culture has culminated in a strengthening of its visual redress campaigns. The Plan explains: "**Institutional culture** refer[s] to the subtle and subconscious pictures, expectations, perceptions, perspectives, prejudices, attitudes and intellectual frameworks with which people live and which determine the visions, values, ideals, communal identity and collective character of an institution" (SU, 2017b:10, emphasis in the original).

The Plan's strong focus on visual cultural alignment to the vision and values of transformation has resulted in a range of visual redress activities at the University from 2015. These activities have been directed and informed by a Visual Redress Committee that was set up in 2018.[22] This is an advisory committee that deliberates on the merits of initiating specific visual redress activities in addition to dealing with disputes and challenges that emerge concerning these activities. It also advises the Rector's Management Team on visual redress matters.

---

22 I have been serving on the Visual Redress Committee since its inception.

Some initiatives that emerged in the light of a more significant institutional commitment to visual redress are the installation of pictures on the front door of the Arts and Social Sciences Building that depict Die Vlakte and the renaming of the HB Thom Theatre to the Adam Small Theatre in August 2018. A house owned by the University in Banghoek Road that was originally owned by the Okkers family was renamed the Piet Okkers House in November 2017. Restitution for the Die Vlakte community has continued to play a visible role in the visual redress activities of the University.

Opting for functional renaming is illustrated by the credible process to rename the JS Gericke Library to the Stellenbosch University Library in June 2017. The renaming was done to ensure that the University library remains a repository of the knowledge of the past and present. It is posited that the Library should, therefore, preserve its identity as a place of free knowledge accessibility. The Sasol Arts Museum was renamed by administrative fiat to the neutral Stellenbosch University Museum in November 2015.

A range of creative visual redress activities emerged across the main campus that emphasised a vision of inclusivity, dialogue and gender mainstreaming. For example, a set of bronze art depictions was installed on the grass of the Rooiplein in 2019. It features figures of 11 prominent women from diverse backgrounds sitting in a circle. According to its curator, SU Department of Visual Arts lecturer Stephané Conradie, the "idea came that if everyone could sit down in a circle and humble themselves and talk, then maybe we could move forward" (Paynter & Van Heerden, 2019:n.p.). A second example is the insertion of multilingual welcoming phrases on 30 benches across the Rooiplein, including braille, San and Moesliem Kaaps.

A final example is the installation of Perspex slates with the South African Constitution's Preamble engraved on it in front of the Ou Hoofgebou (Old Main Building).[23] The Faculty of Law is currently based in this building. This process was held up by the Stellenbosch Interest Group, a small group who has been raising legal questions and objections to renovations and changes to buildings on campus.

---

23 See Chapter 8 by Bradley Slade in this book for a discussion of developments relating to the Preamble installation.

Their putative purpose is to protect the heritage integrity of buildings. However, as in this case, their intervention caused a delay in the installation in a strategic place on campus, where it could elicit meaningful dialogue among students. The Preamble's installation challenges staff and students to embrace a radical break from the University's past commitment to an exclusionary judicial dispensation under apartheid and actively commit themselves to promoting human rights.

These visual redress initiatives were accomplished with the financial and logistical support and artistic advice of the institution. A key player in advising on the art dimension is Prof. Elmarie Costandius of the Department of Visual Arts.[24] Prof. Costandius has been active in University visual redress cultural activities for an extended period, first via her class teaching and research, and later through her work with her students in communities adjacent to the Stellenbosch campus. Her class teaching and student thesis supervision are also based on visual work. Prof. Costandius played a vital role in the University's visual redress work after 2015, which she did by positioning her work as part of the University's visual redress activities and providing advice to various visual redress processes at SU. Her visual redress activities are based on a critical citizenship educational approach that emphasises dialogue, relationship building and an appreciation of the potential of art to restore dignity and promote healing. This approach is visible in many of the visual redress projects that have been undertaken at SU after 2015.

The shifting institutional discourse from 2015 has given rise to visual redress activities, which, in turn, had an impact on the development of a visual redress policy led by the Transformation Office. Starting in 2017, the policy-writing process entailed writing several drafts and comprehensive consultation on campus. The policy texts contained a combined focus on visual cultural change and naming and renaming processes. Bringing the latter under visual redress policy is intended to encourage the initiation of naming processes in the various campus environments in addition to providing a unified platform of activity for these two – visual redress and naming – crucial transformation aspects.

---

24 See Costandius (2019) and Chapter 4 in this book for a description of her visual arts work on campus during the last 10 years.

Drafts of the policy were presented for input at SU's 10 faculties, and in Senate and Council. These consultations have influenced the drafting. The lessons learnt from the visual redress initiatives implemented after 2015 also played a role in shaping the draft. These lessons emphasised the decolonial underpinnings of visual redress[25] and the need to mainstream visual redress in curricula, teaching and learning, and research. The text regards the process of visual redress as important. Not only does the policy emphasise the importance of choices over the visual depictions of pictures, drawings, names and other symbols, but it also promotes the importance of processes for deciding on visual redress in specific University sites. The processes are intended to facilitate an appreciation of the violations caused by the symbols of the past, while having to display sensitivity to the need for restitutive and inclusive symbols adopted during current-day visual redress activities. The capacity to learn from participants and shifting perspectives is a crucial part of the visual redress process.

The policy drafting has therefore accommodated the need for processes that build an inclusive dialogue about, and compelling rationales for, choices made over visual culture at the University. Such an approach, I argue, is the outcome of what the policy-writers were able to learn from the policy consultations and those visual redress processes that took place in the institution. In other words, the policy text was written in conversation with the nature of the visual redress activities that have been taking place on campus.

Examples of a process approach have been highlighted by site-based visual redress processes on SU's campuses. Dialogical processes have been followed for a collage development process in the Mike de Vries Building by members of the Faculty of Science and the Faculty Charter development process embarked on by the Faculty of Medicine and Health Sciences on SU's Tygerberg campus.[26] Each of these initiatives ran via processes that involved members of the Faculty who may not have known one another well or have not collaborated on joint projects before.

---

25 The University issued a task team report on decolonising the curriculum in July 2017 (SU, 2017a).

26 Each of these visual redress processes is discussed in separate chapters in this book. See Faadiel Essop's chapter on the process of the Faculty of Science (Chapter 6) and Khairoonisa Foflonker's chapter (Chapter 7) on that of the Faculty of Medicine and Health Sciences.

Each process involved dialogue and learning. Building trust and respect among participating members were central to the visual redress praxis that emerged. This involved uncomfortable conversation that often stalled the process, yet returning to discussion after a period of reflection and time out helped to resolve conflict or to set aside differences.

The two processes succeeded in developing consensus-type visual redress perspectives among the members.[27] The visual cultural choices that were made represented a commitment to reconciliation, restitution and inclusion. Empathetic listening was cultivated in group discussions. Skilful chairing of sessions proved decisive in developing shared perspectives. Acquiring literacy and understanding about the artistic merits of initiatives provided a basis for informed discussion and decision-making. The process often elicited dispute and differing rationales for choice of words, design of artefacts or the use of colour. Their resolution often emerged later in the process once trust and understanding had developed, which facilitated the emergence of consensus. What these examples of a dynamic process reveal is that challenging, patient and consensus-building dialogue stands a good chance of producing broadly acceptable visual cultural activity on campus. Such an example of visual redress praxis is capable of developing a welcoming and inclusive institutional culture and campus environment for all students and staff on campus.

Conclusion

This chapter concentrated on visual redress at SU during the last 20 years. Emphasising a historicising approach, I discussed the changing discursive field of transformation at the University during the period. I suggested that the nature of visual redress activity can only properly be understood in the light of what the broader transformation discourse makes allowable on campus. In this light, I argued that visual cultural activity differed qualitatively in the period before, compared to the period after, 2015. Transformation struggled to find a foothold during the 2000–2015 period. The concomitant visual

---

27 The process of the Faculty of Medicine and Health Sciences culminated in the inauguration of the Faculty Charter in October 2019. The completion and installation of the collage developed by the Faculty of Science was interrupted by the onset of the Covid-19 pandemic. It is anticipated that it will be installed in 2021.

cultural adaptation reflected tactical adaptation to the new politics of the country and neutral renaming choices. The University's visual activities to engage the forcibly removed Die Vlakte community represents its first attempt at visual cultural redress, which is ongoing in current times.[28]

Visual redress emerged as an institutional imperative after the student protests of 2015. Subject to a decisive change in the institutional transformation discourses operative at the University, the post-2015 period witnessed the institutionalisation of visual redress in the structures and processes of SU. This gave rise to a range of redress-orientated visual cultural activities on the University's campuses, which, in turn, had an impact on the visual redress policy text development processes. A process-based visual redress praxis emerged during the period that is showing the way for ongoing visual cultural activity at the University and other campuses in the country.

References

Ball, S.J. 2006. *Education policy and social class: The selected works of Stephen J. Ball.* London: Routledge. https://doi.org/10.4324/9780203015179

Baumert, S. 2014. *University politics under the impact of societal transformation and global processes - South Africa and the case of Stellenbosch University, 1990-2010.* (Unpublished thesis, Stellenbosch University).

Biscombe, H. 2006. *In ons bloed.* Stellenbosch: African Sun Media.

Breyne, M. 2018. Sharing the past with our present/ce: Performing living sculptures in the traumascape of Stellenbosch, South Africa. *Liminalities: A Journal of Performative Studies,* 14(3):40-63.

Costandius, E. 2019. Fostering the conditions for creative concept development. *Cogent Education,* 6:1-10. https://doi.org/10.1080/2331186X.2019.1700737

---

28 See Chapter 10 in this book by Reneé Hector-Kannemeyer and Otto van Noie about the University's visual cultural activities with respect to the Die Vlakte community and the co-ownership initiative that is taking place at Lückhoff School.

De Sousa Santos, B. 2018. *The end of cognitive empire: The coming of the age of epistemologies of the South*. Durham: Duke University Press. https://doi.org/10.1215/9781478002000

DoE (Department of Education). 1997. *Education White Paper 3: A Programme for the Transformation of Higher Education*. Notice 1196 of 1997. Retrieved from https://www.gov.za/sites/default/files/gcis_document/201409/18207gen11960.pdf [Accessed 3 September 2020].

Fataar, A. 2018. Placing students at the centre of the decolonizing education imperative: Engaging in the (mis)recognition struggles of students in the post-apartheid university. *Educational Studies*, 54(6):595-608. https://doi.org/10.1080/00131946.2018.1518231

Foucault, M. 1982. *The archaeology of knowledge and the discourse on language*. New York, NY: Tavistock.

Hall, S. 1992. The West and the rest: Discourse and power. In: S. Hall & B. Gieben (eds). *Formations of modernity*. Cambridge: Polity Press, 275-331.

Jansen, J. 2020. 'It's not even past': Dealing with monuments and memorials on divided campuses. In: F. Freschi, B. Schmahmann & L. van Robbroeck (eds). *Troubling images: Visual culture and the politics of Afrikaner nationalism*. Johannesburg: Wits University Press, 119-139. https://doi.org/10.18772/22020024716.11

Lategan, B. 2001. Preparing and keeping the mindset intact: Reasons and forms of a theology of the status quo. *Scriptura*, 76:63-75. https://doi.org/10.7833/76-1-1183

NCHE (National Commission on Higher Education). 1996. *A framework for transformation*. Pretoria.

News24. 2015. Grandson welcomes removal of Verwoerd plague in Stellenbosch, 27 May. Retrieved from https://www.news24.com/News24/Grandson-welcomes-removal-of-Verwoerd-plaque-in-Stellenbosch-20150527 [Accessed 15 September 2020].

Nicolson, G. 2015. Stellenbosch: 'Luister' could lead to change. Daily Maverick, 1 September. Retrieved from https://www.dailymaverick.co.za/article/2015-09-01-stellenbosch-luister-could-lead-to-change/#.VehiOipVhBd [Accessed 15 September 2020].

Open Stellenbosch. 2015. *Statement after removal of Verwoerd plaque*, 28 May. https://www.facebook.com/openstellenbosch/posts/821179964597849 [Accessed 15 September 2020].

Paynter, A. & Van Heerden, L. 2019. SU honours women in the Rooiplein. *Die Matie.* Retrieved from https://diematie.com/2019/08/su-honours-women-on-the-rooiplein/ [Accessed 16 September 2020].

Pinkus, J. 1996. *Foucault.* Retrieved from https://www.massey.ac.nz/~alock/theory/foucault.htm [Accessed 2 September 2020].

Schmahmann, B. 2013. *Picturing change: Curating visual culture at post-apartheid universities.* Johannesburg: Wits University Press. https://doi.org/10.18772/12013045805

Schmahmann, B. 2020. Knocking Jannie off his pedestal: Two creative interventions to the sculpture of JH Marais at Stellenbosch University. In: F. Freschi, B. Schmahmann & L. van Robbroeck (eds). *Troubling images: Visual culture and the politics of Afrikaner nationalism.* Johannesburg: Wits University Press, 140-166. https://doi.org/10.18772/22020024716.11

SU (Stellenbosch University). 2000. *A strategic framework for the turn of the century and beyond.* Retrieved from http://www.sun.ac.za/english/Documents/Strategic_docs/statengels.pdf [Accessed 15 September 2020].

SU (Stellenbosch University). 2010. *Policy on the naming of buildings, venues and other facilities/premises.* Retrieved from https://www.sun.ac.za/english/Finance/Documents/Policies/NAAMGEWING%20EN%20VERNOEMING%20VAN%20GEBOUE%20ENG.pdf [Accessed 15 September 2020].

SU (Stellenbosch University). 2013a. *Task team on a welcoming culture at Stellenbosch University.* Retrieved from http://www.sun.ac.za/english/Documents/Rector/welcoming%20culture%20at%20Stellenbosch%20University.pdf [Accessed 15 September 2020].

SU (Stellenbosch University). 2013b. *Transformation at Stellenbosch: Future strategies.* Stellenbosch: Stellenbosch University.

SU (Stellenbosch University). 2015. Removal of the Verwoerd Commemorative Plaque. Event programme, 27 May.

SU (Stellenbosch University). 2016. *Language Policy of Stellenbosch University.* Retrieved from http://www.sun.ac.za/english/policy/Policy%20Documents/Language%20Policy.pdf [Accessed 19 September 2020].

SU (Stellenbosch University). 2017a. *Recommendations of the task team for the decolonisation of the curriculum at Stellenbosch University.* Retrieved from http://www.sun.ac.za/english/transformation/Documents/SU%20Decolonisation%20Task%20Team%20Final%20Report%20with%20Annexures.pdf [Accessed 14 September 2020].

SU (Stellenbosch University). 2017b. *Stellenbosch University Transformation Plan* (updated 2019). Retrieved from http://www.sun.ac.za/english/transformation/Documents/Transformation%20Plan%20(Update%20May%202019).pdf [Accessed 7 August 2020].

SU (Stellenbosch University). 2018. *Centenary message.* Retrieved from http://www.sun.ac.za/english/transformation/visual-redress/initiatives/a-centenary-message [Accessed 3 September 2020].

Chapter 3

Transforming the Stellenbosch University landscape(s):
The journey of visual redress[29] at Stellenbosch University

Leslie van Rooi

---

29 As indicated in this chapter, this term is used in the context of practice and policy at Stellenbosch University. Other terms are used to describe redress processes at other universities.

Introduction

The end of apartheid in South Africa also put an end to the segregated education system that unequally advanced the development of white South Africans over the development of other racial groups.[30] The Higher Education Act of 1997 ushered in a new phase in higher education. It integrated South African universities and advanced a new philosophy that focused on transformation and deliberately supported the reconciliation project prevalent, especially under the presidency of Nelson Mandela (DoE, 1997).

Currently, higher education planning and policy processes distinguish between historically white institutions (HWIs) and historically black institutions (HBIs) (Van Rooi, 2018:225). This distinction helps us to consider the historical realities of our institutions and the current challenges created by our historical inequalities and perpetuated by our current systems. Most South African universities remain on a transformation journey. Although these journeys show similarities, they play out differently at the various institutions.[31] The distinction between HWIs and HBIs is important for this chapter because the journey of visual redress at a HWI such as Stellenbosch University (SU) and the accompanying shift in institutional cultures follow a trajectory that differs from those of HBIs.

SU's transformation journey is currently guided by its Transformation Plan, which focuses on the three pillars of programmes, people and places (SU, 2017a).[32] Visual redress is part of the focus on places. However, it is not separate from the two other pillars. Indeed, any redress process should also find expression in teaching

---

[30] Due to its historical relevance, this chapter uses the racial categories used under apartheid, namely white, black, coloured and Indian. Unfortunately, these terms are still used in South Africa too often – also in an attempt to redress historical disadvantages.

[31] The public higher education sector in South Africa currently consists of 26 universities – 11 general academic universities (learning, teaching and research), 9 comprehensive universities and 6 universities of technology.

[32] This plan comes with a set of indicators that includes that of visual redress on institutional and environment-specific levels. These indicators are used in the annual Transformation Report shared with the Department of Higher Education and Training (DHET) and with SU institutional structures.

and learning as well as research (programmes), and it should enhance and renew the institutional culture (people) (SU, 2020b:2).

Some of the ways in which universities express changing campus cultures and contexts linked to transformation is through changing building and venue names as well as through removing and/or adding public symbols, including statues and art. At SU, this process is guided by the work of two institutional committees, namely (i) the Committee for the Naming of Buildings, Venues and Other Facilities/Premises[33] and (ii) the Visual Redress Committee.[34] Both of these committees report to the rectorate, and membership is shared to align and link the work of the committees deliberately.

SU (2020b:3) defines visual redress as follows:

> … an attempt to right the wrongs of former and current powers by removing hurtful symbols (e.g. of apartheid), social injustice and misrecognition; and by remedying the harm that has been caused by these visual symbols that should have African centrality as an outcome and that should allow for the inclusion of a variety of expressions, stories, identities and histories.[35]

From 2017 to 2020, SU has changed various names, added a range of campus symbols and other visual objects and also contextualised building names and statues. Initiatives included the following:

- The commissioning of an art installation called The Circle[36]
- The installation of the SU 2018 Centenary Restitution Statement[37] as a reminder of where we were and where we are heading

---

33 This committee is guided by SU's policy for the Naming of Buildings, Venues, Facilities and Other Premises (SU, 2010). The principles of this policy have been integrated into the Visual Redress Policy (SU, 2020b), currently in draft format.

34 This committee is guided by the Visual Redress Policy (SU, 2020b).

35 This definition is part of the current draft Visual Redress Policy (SU, 2020b) and was developed by me and Prof. Elmarie Costandius, both members of the Visual Redress Committee.

36 Photos available at http://www.sun.ac.za/english/transformation/visual-redress/initiatives/the-circle.

37 Photos available at http://www.sun.ac.za/english/transformation/visual-redress/initiatives/a-centenary-message.

- Welcome messages in 15 languages,[38] including braille, South African Sign Language and San, carved onto benches in public areas on the Rooiplein
- The installation of a map[39] of Die Vlakte at the entrance of the Arts and Social Sciences Building, a structure built on the grounds from where families were evicted under the Group Areas Act in the 1960s, linking with work already done in the Arts and Social Sciences Building as well as at the Old Lückhoff School in Banghoek Road.

At the time of writing this chapter, SU was in the middle of another name change process for the former RW Wilcocks Building, which was expected to be concluded by the end of 2020.[40] Various other projects will be rolled out in the coming year (2021) through the work of the Visual Redress Committee as well as various SU environments. These initiatives will be aligned with the SU Transformation Plan, the key performance indicators for transformation for each SU environment and the draft Visual Redress Policy.

As is the case at other universities, SU is continuously learning and adjusting its processes accordingly. An important lesson learned is that visual redress processes should foster an inclusive environment where people meet, talk and share ideas, and where identities and lifestyles are shared to enable people from diverse cultural backgrounds to co-create new ideas and perspectives. Public engagement and heritage-related processes, as well as the concepts addressed, ask for long and deep consultation. As the Stellenbosch campus of SU is an open campus, we are also continuously reminded that conversations should not only occur within the various campus communities, but also include stakeholders in the broader town. This principle is true for visual redress and naming/renaming processes.

Over the years, SU has learned that the naming/renaming processes and those of visual redress are interlinked, as expressed in the draft Visual Redress Policy (SU, 2020b:2). The policy combines visual redress and naming processes in one document, albeit with two implementation structures, as explained above.

---

38 Photos available at http://www.sun.ac.za/english/transformation/visual-redress/initiatives/the-benches.
39 Photos available at http://www.sun.ac.za/english/transformation/visual-redress/initiatives/die-vlakte-map.
40 For the rationale and process behind the renaming of the RW Wilcocks Building, see SU (2020a).

Movements such as Open Stellenbosch, #RhodesMustFall and #FeesMustFall, as well as their outcomes, had a direct impact on the formalisation of SU's visual redress processes. Susan Booysen (2016:2–3) states the following about these movements:

> The students themselves used the term 'movement' in relation to their multi-campus, cross-province and international action under the banner #FeesMustFall – and several derivatives of Fallism over time, including #RhodesMustFall in early 2015, #RhodesSoWhite, #OpenStellenbosch, #TransformWits, #KingGeorgeMustFall, #TheStatueMustFall, #FeesMustFall, #NationalShutdown, #FeesWillFall, #ANCMustFall, #FeesHaveFallen and #PatriarchyMustFall. The ideologies of feminists, the intersectionality of continued social injustice, black-African consciousness and identity, and dismissal of liberalism and neoliberalism were the core of the combination of more immediate targets for non-negotiables in the mix of targets for Fallism.

This chapter focuses on and shares SU's visual redress journey. Even though visual redress processes have been underway at SU, the chapter argues that the #RhodesMustFall movement acted as a catalyst that led to a clear, deliberate shift that guided the University to better formulate what it understands visual redress to be. It discusses the link between transformation and visual redress at SU and shares the motivation and key drivers behind visual redress at SU. Remarks are made about ongoing processes, and lessons learned are highlighted. The concluding remarks point to the way forward.

SU at the turn of the century and beyond[41]

Since the advent of democracy, SU's ongoing journey of transformation has resulted in several changes that relate to policies, demographics and structures. These changes have primarily been driven by key strategic documents, including the following:

---

41 For a brief historical overview of SU, see SU (2018).

- SU's strategic framework for the turn of the century and beyond[42] (SU, 2000)
- The SU Task Team on a Welcoming Culture at Stellenbosch University (SU, 2013b)
- The current SU placement policy (SU, 2013a)
- The current SU Language Policy (SU, 2016)
- The current SU Admissions Policy (SU, 2017a)
- The current SU Transformation Plan (SU, 2017b).

Because SU was an institution that actively participated in creating and celebrating apartheid ideology and Afrikaner nationalism, it is not surprising that the institution, like other historically Afrikaans universities, celebrated these ideologies in and through its symbols, statues and building names. As Albert Grundlingh (2020:23) points out, it left its mark on the visual culture of the institution.

The documents and policies mentioned above, as well as their strategic foci, point to a clear shift away from an institution steeped in apartheid ideology and Afrikaner nationalism. However, polices must be linked to practices, and SU had to continue to break free from the shackles of its apartheid past. This point was highlighted by the Open Stellenbosch movement during the #FeesMustFall protests. Because of the slow pace of transformation, SU management had to appear before the parliamentary portfolio committee for Higher Education and Training in 2015 and 2017.[43]

Perhaps the most painful outcry from some members of Open Stellenbosch came through the *Luister*[44] video. Through this video, students from SU and the Elsenburg Agricultural College shared painful allegations of racism as experienced by them on the two campuses as well as in the town of Stellenbosch. The video led to a national conversation on the topics shared in the video and initiated internal and external processes to review the SU institutional culture. It was perhaps the strongest catalyst for what transpired at the meeting between SU and the portfolio

---

42 This document was finalised and approved in 2000 when Prof. Andreas van Wyk was the rector of SU. It can be argued that the document influenced the strategies of the two rectors to follow, namely Prof. Chris Brink and Prof. Russel Botman (Botha, 2007; Grundlingh, Landman & Koopman, 2017).

43 For an overview of the meeting as well as the full presentation from SU, see SU (2017c).

44 'Luister' is an Afrikaans word that means 'listen'. For the full video, see Contraband Cape Town (2015).

committee in 2015. SU's institutional response to the video focused on an assurance that transformation was being prioritised and that the University sympathised with the pain of black students in particular (SU, 2015).

Visual redress became a focused part of transformation following the #FeesMustFall protests. It includes the ongoing process of changing the names of buildings and venues, removing contentious and hurtful symbols and adding new symbols. Although the term 'visual redress' has only been used in a formalised manner since 2016, SU has been undertaking processes that align with the current interpretation of the term since at least the late 1990s. Some of the most notable name changes on campus in the 1990s and thereafter are the HF Verwoerd Building (name changed in 1992), the BJ Vorster Building (2002) and the DF Malan Building (2005)[45] (Cloete, 2018). Busts and other memorial symbols that depicted some of the prime ministers of the apartheid era, most of whom were also chancellors of SU,[46] were also removed.

Despite these developments, the University continued to receive criticism for its apparent slow pace of change and for its apparent non- or semi-participatory processes of visual redress that did not represent deep-rooted institutional change. An important criticism was the view that SU's visual redress processes did not allow for intensive participation of the campus community and the communities around the institution.

The removal of the Verwoerd plaque

The impact of the #RhodesMustFall, the Open Stellenbosch and the national #FeesMustFall movements led to a more focused and deliberative process of visual redress at SU. This process started with the removal of the Verwoerd plaque[47] on 27 May 2015. Although visual redress at SU did not start at this time, the removal of

---

45 This building is in Merriman Avenue and is currently known as the Mike de Vries Building. It should not be confused with the former DF Malan Centre renamed as the Coetzenburg Centre in 2014.

46 For a list of the chancellors, rectors and vice-chancellors between 1918 and 2018, see the SU Transformation Plan (SU, 2017b).

47 For a brief overview of the life and work of HF Verwoerd, see South African History Online (2019).

this plaque in the former HF Verwoerd Building led to a formalised focus on visual redress at the University.

The HF Verwoerd Building was officially renamed the Accounting and Statistics Building in 1992 (Cloete, 2018:45). However, the plaque commemorating the opening and naming of the building in honour of HF Verwoerd was left in the corner of the building close to the main entrance. In 2015, attention was called to this plaque with calls from the Open Stellenbosch movement to have it removed for SU to break free from its apartheid past through accelerating transformation.

The removal of the plaque formed part of an official SU ceremony where, among others, Verwoerd's grandson, Wilhelm Verwoerd, delivered a speech indicating that he hoped that the removal of the plaque would convey a sense of healing (News24, 2015). During the event, members of the Open Stellenbosch movement protested in silence by waving placards of the old South African flag covered with an x. The plaque was replaced by a portrait of the national flag of the Republic of South Africa.

Figure 3.1: The Verwoerd plaque in the Accounting and Statistics Building days before its removal (photo by the author)

Figure 3.2: Members of Open Stellenbosch protesting during the official ceremony that marked the removal of the Verwoerd plaque in 2015; in the front row is Dr Wilhelm Verwoerd, grandson of the late HF Verwoerd, and Prof. Wim de Villiers, rector of SU (photo supplied by SU)

Figure 3.3: The national flag covers the area where the Verwoerd plaque once was (photos by Masa Kekana/EWN)

From my perspective, the call for the removal of the Verwoerd plaque as well as its subsequent removal was a turning point for visual redress at SU. Not only did it compel SU management to understand that visual redress should be deliberate and formalised, but it also underscored that visual redress processes should incorporate direct student input and engagement. This event[48] had a strong impact on my own thinking about visual redress, informed my perspectives and guided me in my current role as an institutional leader of transformation and visual redress at the University.

Jansen (2020:135) reminds us that reason should guide decision-making discourse and processes at universities and that a good crisis should not be wasted. This is exactly what the removal of the Verwoerd plaque allowed at SU. An event that started with anger and high emotion offered the University an opportunity to reflect on its processes. Embedded in the ambit of the #FeesMustFall protests, it guided the University in formalising a platform for processes of visual redress that would enable the deliberate and ongoing change of the visual landscape on and around its campuses.

#RhodesMustFall

The symbolic removal of the Verwoerd plaque took place on 27 May 2015, just more than a month after the statue of Cecil John Rhodes was removed from the university campus of the University of Cape Town on 9 April 2015.

The #RhodesMustFall movement and later the national #FeesMustFall movement in 2015 and 2016 were catalysts for formalising visual redress at SU. Protests, engagements and conversations linked to the work of Open Stellenbosch during the #FeesMustFall period focused on debates on language (the prominence of Afrikaans at SU), identity, institutional culture and statues and other public symbols on the SU campuses – important markers and influences of institutional culture in the context of a university.

During this period in 2015, students with the support of, among others, Elmarie Costandius, a professor in Visual Arts at SU, started to propose new statues and

---

48 During this period, the author served as the head of the Frederik Van Zyl Slabbert Institute for Student Leadership Development at SU.

symbols as well as engagement with some of the most prominent statues and symbols on campus (see Schmahmann, 2020:148–150). These suggestions were later some of the first visual redress initiatives of the first phase of the visual redress project.

As is the case with statues at other universities, in particular HWIs, the Jannie Marais statue on the central Rooiplein of the Stellenbosch campus of SU came under increasing scrutiny. During the height of the #FeesMustFall period in 2015, student groups on various occasions showed discontent towards the statue, including by starting fires around the pedestal of the statue. In return, students from Afriforum Youth attempted to wash the pedestal as a way of signalling their support for the preservation of this statue. On a particular day, as Afriforum students were cleaning the pedestal, other students, including representatives from Open Stellenbosch, threw clay and sand on the pedestal to show their dismay. A tense stand-off arose that luckily did not turn into a serious incident.

The Jannie Marais statue remains contested, and the tension around the statue has to be continuously managed, as is the case with other statues on the SU campuses. Three other prominent statues on the Stellenbosch campus that have also been contextualised as part of the ongoing visual redress process are those of Danie Craven (in front of the Marais House, Coetzenburg), Johannes du Plessis (the so-called Pink Piet statue) and John Murray (the first professor of the Theological School at SU), the latter two both in front of the Faculty of Theology in Dorp Street.

Figure 3.4: The author with various students, colleagues and workers next to the Jannie Marais statue during a tense stand-off between Afriforum Youth supporters and supporters of the Open Stellenbosch movement (photo owner – Leslie van Rooi)

SU understands the process of visual redress as a continuous and ongoing process without an end date. As indicated in the draft Visual Redress Policy (SU, 2020b:5–6), the process will also continue to be proactively managed, whether through engaging with internal and external stakeholders on visual changes or through prompt visual redress processes, when necessary.

The establishment of a task team for visual redress at SU

When I started in my current role as senior director for Social Impact and

Transformation at SU[49] in 2018, one of my first responsibilities was to join a University task team meant to oversee visual redress. The task team was chaired by Prof. Nico Koopman, Vice-Rector: Social Impact, Transformation and Personnel. The task team had the mandate to:

- structurally formalise visual redress through the development of an institutional policy to govern visual redress at the University, and
- guide visual redress processes at SU by, among other things, advising the rectorate on visual redress matters and implementing processes in collaboration with other internal SU environments and stakeholders, e.g. faculties, professional and administrative support services (PASS), the Students' Representative Council, etc.

It was soon realised that the process of visual redress could not be managed on an ad hoc basis through a temporary task team. It needed to be overseen by a full-time committee whose functioning would incorporate the tasks intended for the original task team. Therefore, the Visual Redress Committee was established to oversee the implementation of visual redress at the University.

The committee currently consists of ex officio members from the SU transformation portfolio and various senior managers from faculties and PASS environments. Via its membership, it links directly with Facilities Management as well as the Corporate Communications and Marketing Division. These two SU environments are central for consultation about and implementation of visual redress initiatives across the University. The committee meets at least four times per year and reports to the rectorate.

A 'sister committee' of the visual redress committee is the SU Committee for the Naming of Buildings, Venues and Other Facilities/Premises. This committee is responsible for reactively receiving and processing requests for the naming and renaming of buildings, a process guided by SU's policy for the Naming of Buildings, Venues, Facilities and Other Premises (SU, 2010), which was accepted and implemented in 2010. The two committees deliberately have shared members

---

49 One of my responsibilities in this position is to lead the visual redress portfolio.

to align their functions and processes. The functions of the two committees will be guided by the draft Visual Redress Policy (SU, 2020b:2–3) as soon as it is approved to facilitate even greater cohesion between these two related and important transformation activities.

Towards a visual redress policy for SU

At the time of finalising this chapter, SU's draft Visual Redress Policy was undergoing final approval processes via the various SU committees and statutory bodies, as required by the approval process of policies at SU. It had already undergone a full round of consultation with, among others, all faculty committees, the SU Institutional Forum and the SU Council. The consultation process also included a full public participation process that lasted 30 days, during which numerous proposals were received. Through this consultation process, the policy wants to signal a deliberate and deep engagement with various internal and external stakeholders.

The draft policy acknowledges its embeddedness in SU's Vision 2040 and Strategic Framework (SU, 2019) as well as the catalytic effect of #FeesMustFall on the eventual formalisation of processes and a policy for visual redress at SU (SU, 2020b:1–2). It calls for active and deliberate integration of visual redress processes with the core functions of SU.

The vision of the Visual Redress Policy and the implementation of the various projects resulting from it are intended to inform teaching and learning at SU. The policy provides impetus for disciplinary and interdisciplinary conversations about visual redress activities on campus concerning the University's curricular as well as its co-curricular offerings. Dialogue in teaching and learning environments about the policy and its implementation is meant to elicit critical awareness about visual redress projects being undertaken on campus and it is foreseen that this will be a continues process. The Visual Redress Policy is also intended to stimulate research possibilities and outputs at SU in collaboration with other universities, both local and global.

The Visual Redress Policy links directly with the SU Transformation Plan, specifically the plan's description of 'place' (SU, 2017b:6). Linked to the SU Transformation Plan is the ongoing process of developing key result areas for transformation at SU, including visual redress. As such, the plan will find impetus in the broader, ongoing transformation processes at SU to further stimulate visual redress.

The process of finalising the policy has allowed SU to think about and engage academically with the underlying scholarly aspects that inform visual redress and naming/renaming processes. In this regard, the policy followed an approach to visual redress that is informed by discourse that promotes deep-rooted change. Jansen (2020) warns that the lack of discourse might have a negative impact on social cohesion in the sense that redress processes might lead to nothing but displacement. As Jansen (2020:136) states: "It would become clearer during the course of debates on Afrikaner statues that what was demanded by many black protesters was displacement – the erasure of one set of nationalist symbols (white) and its replacement by another (black)."

The principles of the policy provide an understanding of visual redress at SU in the context of a philosophy that allows for engagement, enrichment, social cohesion and a sense of belonging (SU, 2020b:5–6). Through its policy process, SU reminded itself about the foundations from which it executes visual redress. It affirmed that visual redress processes must consider the complex interaction and impact of local, national and international imperatives. Given the nature of universities and the fact that they consciously strive to make a positive impact on society, universities cannot but engage with societal role players linked to changes about their symbols, statues, building names, etc. This engagement must allow for deep reflection and enhance conversations about the mentioned matters in society at large. These conversations should also have a direct impact on ongoing engagements and decisions on campuses.

Transformation on our University campuses must also allow for engagement with and a direct impact on society at large. Just as the #RhodesMustFall movement had an impact on South African society at large, our redress processes should also show a commitment towards engaging in questions of social cohesion in our communities.[50] As the Transformation Plan (SU, 2017b:5–6) puts it:

> The theme of "place" refers to social inclusion and changes in both the physical spaces and the foundational institutional culture that facilitate a sense of belonging among students and staff. The theme includes visual redress, welcome culture interventions, and the design and organisation of spaces that enable access to students and staff living with a range of disabilities. The focus on "place" also includes the way in which the visual identity and celebrations of SU are expressed as an institution rooted in Africa.

Given the nature and the positioning of the SU campuses, e.g. the Stellenbosch campus within the town of Stellenbosch, this university cannot but engage with communities in and around its campuses. The impact of SU's policies and processes, including that of visual redress, is not limited to its campuses. Through its policies and processes, SU should attempt to make a positive impact on society by promoting social cohesion.

Visual redress and higher education in South Africa

Although it has a particular expression at SU, the visual redress journey at this university is not unique. The University of the Free State followed a similar journey, not only in terms of how processes played out, but also in the involvement and role of the media, alumni and other parties in these campus processes (Jansen, 2020:127–128).

My interaction with colleagues at other institutions gave me the sense that other HWIs experienced similar journeys. Deliberate conversation with one another as well as with HBIs must be encouraged to share lessons and experiences and to engage on the topic. Considering the public role and social impact of universities, these conversations should also not be limited to the higher education environment. University communities should be encouraged to actively participate in national debates on public statues and symbols.

---

50 For an overview of the impact of the #RhodesMustFall movement on statue-linked discourses in South Africa at large as well as the neglect of specifically post-apartheid statues and symbols in South Africa, see Nettleton and Fubah (2020).

Universities do not only have to grapple with the nuances of art and visual identities on our campuses from the past. They also have to navigate the complexities of identity in terms of new and additional art that forms the backbone of current, sometimes harsh and silencing, conversations on and around campuses. As Schmahmann (2013:12) states:

> In addition to shaping concerns with images of the past, the question of transformation underpins increased sensitivity towards instances in which new art, acquired, produced by or shown at universities, may violate the dignity and standing of one or other group. It seems, in fact, that in the post-apartheid period, South African universities have developed a heightened awareness of the visual domain.

Universities will almost certainly continuously be confronted with, on the one hand, the need and, in some instances, the pressure to change campus cultures and identities, and, on the other hand, the complexity and non-neutrality of art, symbols, signs and names prevalent on our campuses. Given the lack of clear guidance and guidelines from the DHET, universities will most likely have to navigate this space through practice, experience, learning, unlearning and continuous engagement among themselves and with the broader South African society.

One of the lessons we can learn from the current Black Lives Matter[51] debates is that struggles linked to identity often flow over to the existence and non-existence of identity markers that include the look and feel of public spaces, museums and campuses. It should therefore be no surprise that, during the height of this movement in 2020, symbols and statues honouring slave traders where defaced and toppled in several countries. As such, the South African debate should also be read and interpreted as fully part of ongoing international debates and processes (Van Rooi, 2020).

Closing remarks

Although off to a relatively slow start, the visual redress project at SU is well on its way to impact the visual identity, institutional culture and cultural landscape of this

---

51 For an overview of the link between the Black Lives Matter movement and statues, see Grovier (2020).

university. Over the next few years, the project will, among others, link with the rebranding processes at SU and will enhance the principles and outcomes of SU's Transformation Plan and its institutional and environmental key result areas. It is foreseen that visual redress at SU will not only take on an institutional character, but will also increasingly be driven by departments, faculties, PASS environments and the student body.

Universities are not islands removed from the various contexts around them. The visual landscape of universities will be influenced by national identity as well as historic and heritage-linked discussions. Conversely, it will also influence debates, policies and practices linked to our nation's cultural heritage.

Debates at our universities can, however, not be carbon copies of those in wider society. It should reflect the critical and contingent nature of spaces where diversity is celebrated and should be influenced by the relevant academic, historical and identity nuances. Debates should engage with the complexity, multi-faceted nature of histories. Schmahmann (2013:16) states in this regard:

> Discussion about institutional culture and its prejudices can be very helpful in considering how the visual realm may be affected by and bound up with, for example, imperialist early histories as well as how visual culture might reinforce and perpetuate inequalities of race, gender or class. But while recognising how imagery and objects may be informed by and related to prejudicial practices and histories, it seems important that art and imagery inherited from earlier eras not be interpreted *only* as the unfortunate and embarrassing outcome of unhealthy alliances and allegiances in the past. Images are almost invariably more complicated than such readings suggest.

Given South Africa's continued struggle with its past and current realities, and specifically how it plays out in the context of statues, names and symbols in our towns, cities and public spaces, universities should fervently participate in these critical debates and discussions. This participation should facilitate deep reflection that allows for an understanding of history, our various outlooks and identities as well as the social compact enshrined in and through the South African Constitution. Should this not be the case, we run the risk of chipping away at some of South

Africa's hard-earned democratic gains and freedoms.

As Jansen (2020:137) notes:

> It might well be that the indiscriminate assault on the visual imagery of universities in 2015–2016 contributed to changing campus cultures in ways that are likely to be intolerant and anti-educational in relation to engaging difficult subjects. In that sense, far more fell than Cecil John Rhodes alone.

To prevent this from being the case, universities must continuously reflect on and engage with the nature, motivations and underlying rationales for their visual redress processes and outcomes. This is best done within a framework that allows universities to play a meaningful part in enhancing social cohesion in South Africa.

References

Booysen, S. 2016. Introduction. In: S. Booysen (ed). *Fees Must Fall: Student revolt, decolonisation and governance in South Africa.* Johannesburg: Wits University Press, 1-20. https://doi.org/10.18772/22016109858.5

Botha, A. 2007. *Chris Brink: Anatomie van 'n omvormer.* Stellenbosch: African Sun Media. https://doi.org/10.18820/9781920689360

Cloete, E. 2018. *Geboue van die Universiteit Stellenbosch.* Stellenbosch: African Sun Media.

Contraband Cape Town. 2015. *Luister.* Retrieved from https://www.youtube.com/watch?v=sF3rTBQTQk4&ab_channel=ContrabandCapeTown [Accessed 20 October 2020].

DoE (Department of Education). 1997. *Higher Education Act, No. 101 of 1997.* Retrieved from https://www.gov.za/sites/default/files/gcis_document/201409/a101-97.pdf [Accessed 20 September 2020].

Grovier, K. 2020. Black Lives Matter protests: Why are statues so powerful? BBC, 12 June. Retrieved from https://www.bbc.com/culture/article/20200612-black-lives-matter-protests-why-are-statues-so-powerful [Accessed 20 October 2020].

Grundlingh, A. 2020. The trajectory and dynamics of Afrikaner nationalism in the twentieth century: An overview. In: F. Freschi, B. Schmahmann & L. van Robbroeck (eds). *Troubling images: Visual culture and the politics of Afrikaner nationalism.* Johannesburg: Wits University Press, 23-39. https://doi.org/10.18772/22020024716.6

Grundlingh, A., Landman, R. & Koopman, N. 2017. *Russel Botman: 'n Huldeblyk 1953-2014.* Stellenbosch: African Sun Media. https://doi.org/10.18820/9781928314264

Jansen, J.D. 2020. 'It's not an even past': Dealing with the monuments and memorials on divided campuses. In: F. Freschi, B. Schmahmann & L. van Robbroeck (eds). *Troubling images: Visual culture and the politics of Afrikaner nationalism.* Johannesburg: Wits University Press, 119-139. https://doi.org/10.18772/22020024716.10

Nettleton, A. & Fubah, A. . 2020. *Exchanging symbols: Monuments and memorials in post-apartheid South Africa.* Stellenbosch: African Sun Media. https://doi.org/10.18820/9781928480594

News24. 2015. Grandson welcomes the removal of Verwoerd plaque, 27 May. Retrieved from https://www.news24.com/News24/Grandson-welcomes-removal-of-Verwoerd-plaque-in-Stellenbosch-20150527 [Accessed 27 September 2020].

Schmahmann, B. 2013. *Picturing change: Curating visual culture at post-apartheid universities.* Johannesburg: Wits University Press. https://doi.org/10.18772/12013045805

Schmahmann, B. 2020. Knocking Jannie off his pedestal: Two creative interventions to the sculpture of JH Marais at Stellenbosch University. In: F. Freschi, B. Schmahmann & L. van Robbroeck (eds). *Troubling images: Visual culture and the politics of Afrikaner nationalism.* Johannesburg: Wits University Press, 140-165. https://doi.org/10.18772/22020024716.11

South African History Online. 2019. *Hendrik Frensch Verwoerd.* Retrieved from https://www.sahistory.org.za/people/hendrik-frensch-verwoerd [Accessed 20 October 2020].

SU (Stellenbosch University). 2000. *Stellenbosch University's strategic framework for the turn of the century and beyond.* Retrieved from http://www.sun.ac.za/english/documents/strategic_docs/statengels.pdf [Accessed 19 October 2020].

SU (Stellenbosch University). 2010. *Naming of Buildings, Venues Facilities and other Premises.* Retrieved from https://sunrecords.sun.ac.za/controlled/C4%20Policies%20and%20Regulations/Naming%20of%20buildings,%20venues,%20facilities%20and%20other%20premises.pdf [Accessed 19 October 2020].

SU (Stellenbosch University). 2013a. *Placement in residences, and in listening, learning and living houses, as well as allocation to PSO wards and clusters.* Retrieved from https://sunrecords.sun.ac.za/controlled/C4%20Policies%20and%20Regulations/Placement%20in%20residences,%20and%20in%20Listening,%20Learning%20and%20Living%20Houses,%20as%20well%20as%20allocation%20to%20PSO%20wards%20and%20clusters.pdf [Accessed 20 October 2020].

SU (Stellenbosch University). 2013b. *Task Team on a Welcoming Culture at Stellenbosch University.* Retrieved from http://www.sun.ac.za/english/Documents/Rector/welcoming%20culture%20at%20Stellenbosch%20University.pdf [Accessed 19 October 2020].

SU (Stellenbosch University). 2015. *Stellenbosch University's response to the Luister video.* Retrieved from http://www.sun.ac.za/english/Documents/Verklaring%20-%20Luister-video-%20English%20(Friday%2021%20Aug).pdf [Accessed 15 September 2020].

SU (Stellenbosch University). 2016. *Language Policy.* Retrieved from https://sunrecords.sun.ac.za/controlled/C4%20Policies%20and%20Regulations/Language%20Policy.pdf [Accessed 20 October 2020].

SU (Stellenbosch University). 2017a. *Admissions Policy.* Retrieved from https://sunrecords.sun.ac.za/controlled/C4%20Policies%20and%20Regulations/Admissisions%20Policy_2017.pdf [Accessed 19 October 2020].

SU (Stellenbosch University). 2017b. *Stellenbosch University Transformation Plan.* Retrieved from http://www.sun.ac.za/english/transformation/Documents/Transformation%20Plan%20(Update%20May%202019).pdf [Accessed 19 September 2020].

SU (Stellenbosch University). 2017c. *SU in Parliament*. Retrieved from https://www.sun.ac.za/english/Lists/news/DispForm.aspx?ID=4933 [Accessed 20 October 2020].

SU (Stellenbosch University). 2018. *Stellenbosch University 100: 1918-2018*. Retrieved from http://www0.sun.ac.za/100/en/timeline/1859/ [Accessed 20 October 2020].

SU (Stellenbosch University). 2019. *Vision 2040 and Strategic Framework 2019-2024.* Retrieved from http://www.sun.ac.za/english/about/Pages/Strategic-Documents.aspx?TermStoreId=d4aca01e-c7ae-4dc1-b7b2-54492a41081c&TermSetId=7989b2c1-6fd7-4cbf-a8ae-07ebb77dc18b&TermId=5b45c78b-1f53-4676-b8de-457df7a28c29 [Accessed 20 October 2020].

SU (Stellenbosch University). 2020a. *SU's RW Wilcocks Building to be renamed*. Retrieved from http://www.sun.ac.za/english/Lists/news/DispForm.aspx?ID=7537 [Accessed 20 October 2020].

SU (Stellenbosch University). 2020b. *Visual Redress Policy Draft*. Retrieved from http://www.sun.ac.za/english/transformation/Documents/Visual%20Redress%20Policy%20draft_eng.pdf [Accessed 19 September 2020].

Van Rooi, L.B. 2018. Decolonising knowledge: Current conversations on racism, identity and decolonisation within the higher education sector in South Africa. In: C. Jones (ed). *Justice-based ethics: Challenging South African perspectives.* Cape Town: AOSIS, 223-246. https://doi.org/10.4102/aosis.2018.BK77.09

Van Rooi, L.B. 2020. Wat het nou eintlik verander? *Vryeweekblad*, 25 June. Retrieved from https://www.vryeweekblad.com/menings-en-debat/2020-06-25-proteste-teen-standbeelde-wat-het-nou-eintlik-verander/ [Accessed 27 September 2020].

Chapter 4

Visual redress at Stellenbosch University: A reflection on practice from 2010 to 2021

Elmarie Costandius

Introduction

The current situation in the world with the Covid-19 pandemic has brought new light to uneven power relations and injustices regarding social class, race and gender. In South Africa, with our large discrepancy between rich and poor, these realities are experienced on an even deeper level. The financial and emotional strain because of the injustices of the past are reopened in the unsure and unstable circumstances of the pandemic. Higher education institutions went through huge adjustments in 2020 because of the pandemic, where students' learning was disrupted because of unsuitable learning spaces for many students in South Africa to continue learning away from institutions.

At Stellenbosch University (SU), learning has continued for most students, with the financially stable students (mostly white students) finding the transition to online learning much easier than poor students (mostly black, coloured and Indian [BCI] students). At SU, the main campus is currently mostly deserted and when one walks through campus, it is as if one sees the buildings and structures in a new light. The marble statue of JH Marais,[52] standing on its high pedestal on the brick and concrete surface on the Rooiplein, stands out even more without human bodies cancelling out its prominence. On the other side of the Rooiplein, the grass between the sculptures of the eleven sitting women has grown high – it is as though they continued their fruitful group conversations and the grass just kept growing. These two symbols are taken as metaphors for this chapter. The past is still with us, as the Marais statue reminds us, but there is an opportunity to collaborate and to engage on a more conducive level, as the sculpture of the eleven women reminds us.

Buildings, statues, sculptures or any kind of visual symbols have the potential to influence thinking and actions: The environment has an effect on us, even though we are not often aware of it. According to Lefebvre (1991), spaces shape those who

---

52 JH Marais was a businessman who funded the start-up of the University in 1818.

inhabit and move through them, naturalising behaviour and privileging certain modes of being over others. Universities, and particularly,

historically white universities, often take their visual landscapes for granted – viewing them as neutral and natural. The spaces on the SU campus largely represent an inclusive colonial history. The physical landscape of higher education institutions must be seen as an important aspect if transformation is to occur. Research (Clark & Costandius, 2020; Schmahmann, 2013) shows that visual redress may provide a means to attend to underlying, unspoken and unconscious expressions of exclusion that remain in higher education institutions on South African campuses today.

This chapter will elaborate and reflect on my own practice of the last ten years, where I aimed to facilitate art-based transformative projects in collaboration with various stakeholders on the SU campus and communities. The art-based projects during this time aimed to utilise the critical and social potential of the arts to probe issues in an open-ended way – aimed to create scaffolding for students, lecturers and me to explore sensitive issues with peers and members of the Stellenbosch community. The theme of social transformation invited varying intensities of interest – from activism to curiosity to distance and fear, but also for some a sense of welcoming. In the following sections, theoretical perspectives on art-based methods will be discussed as a lens for the reflection on practice that will follow. The reflection on practice will be chronologically divided into three parts, namely 2010 to 2014, 2015 to 2017 (including the student protests during 2015 and 2016) and 2018 to 2020. In the discussion and conclusion, the most prominent issues and insights that emerged will be summarised.

Art-based methods

In this section I will elaborate on art-based processes as a potential transformative method. Related perspectives, such as new materialism, which includes concepts such as entanglement, embodiment and relationality, will also be discussed. According to Barrett and Bolt (2007), art-based practice is a different form of creating knowledge. It is a valid alternative mode of enquiry to traditional learning and research. Deleuze and Guattari (1997:198) refer to ways of thinking that can take place through concepts such as philosophy, or functions, as in natural science, or as sensations in the form of art practice. Barrett and Bolt (2007) explain that knowledge is produced through engagement between self and material in the artistic process. Golańska (2020:6) sees the artistic process as an "integration of different modes of thinking/knowing – intuitive-rational, bodily-intellectual and material-semiotic".

Art affects us and creates sensations that work as "triggers for a more critical inquiry or forcing affective-emotional engagement with what is encountered" (Golańska, 2020:19). Dolphijn and Van der Tuin (2012:19) describe affect as the in-between: "it is a folding-in of external influences and a simultaneous unfolding outwards of affects." The affective turn requires a shift in thought because of the "complex interrelations of discursive practices, the human body, social and cultural forces, and individually experienced but historically situated emotions and affects" (Zembylas, 2014:379). Affect is seen as a process of constant social production, rather than a final product that can be coded (Clough, 2007). It is not only what the artwork represents that can affect us, it is also what it triggers in ourselves and what other connotations we create because of that trigger. The affective reactions are entangled with the cognitive understanding. The body often reacts and the brain afterwards tries to interpret the bodily reaction. Merleau-Ponty (2002) specifically emphasises the role of the body in human experience and states that the way in which we experience and perceive the world is influenced by our embodied experiences. Descartes' dualism approach to the body hugely affected Western thinking, as the body was considered "distinctly inferior and its perceptions considered unreliable and illusory" (Murphy & Murphy, 1969, cited in Johnson, 2017:88). However, we know that when we pass a statue or walk into a space, it affects us. Our bodies tell us that we are affected because we, for instance, start to sweat, and it is only afterwards that the brain reflects on the sudden reaction of sweating. Our body is therefore also a source of knowledge and has the potential to produce knowledge. Artworks, statues and buildings are not innocent and separate from humans. Therefore, a more relational, embodied/material/discursive type of engagement is needed in our interactions with the human and non-human.

According to MacLure (2013:662), sense is crucial for its "potential to trigger action in the face of the unknown". Deleuze and Guattari (2004:169) argue that "[t]o the extent that events are actualised within us, they wait for us and invite us in". MacLure (2013:662) refers to Deleuze's concept of 'sense' that is "pre-personal and pre-conscious", and it is only by chance that certain connections are made; at certain times and under different conditions other connections will be made. We are entangled and in an assemblage (Deleuze & Guattari, 1997) relation to things around us: self, others, body, mind, political, social, historical, the spaces that we are in, buildings, signs, what you read or do, family, etc. The relations between the components in an entanglement are relevant, as they affect one another, and the aim is to rethink these relations so that the basis of how we think and act is influenced and adjusted.

In the next section I will elaborate on a few selected art-based projects and processes that took place during the last ten years as part of my own teaching and learning engagements with students, lecturers and communities outside of SU.

Critical citizenship projects between 2010 and 2014

As part of my Visual Communication Design (VCD) course, I included critical citizenship education. I used the definition of Johnson and Morris (2010:77–78) as a guideline, namely that citizenship education is based on the promotion of a "common set of shared values (e.g. tolerance, human rights and democracy), which prepare young people to live together in diverse societies" and that critical citizenship has the potential to contribute to the "promotion of social justice, social reconstruction and democracy". The word 'critical' is added to citizenship education and therefore includes critical thinking and critical pedagogy (Johnson & Morris, 2010:77–78). Even though the VCD course in the past addressed social issues, my previous projects were imaginary projects, and students and I did not engage with other students and communities outside of the University. Social and political issues were implicitly addressed, but not explicitly included and discussed. During my first years of teaching full-time at SU between 2006 and 2009, it became clear that social issues cannot be addressed only through imaginary projects. This is why I decided to take the projects outside the visual arts building on campus and to communities around campus. As one of the students remarked: "Some things you only learn from actively doing and all lessons cannot be learnt in the studio." The change from studio to public changed the dynamics of the projects. These projects and the new insights that I gained from taking the projects outside the studio space made me realise that practically engaging in critical citizenship education, physically and mentally, was a crucial component for any curriculum.

In 2010 I started to work with a non-governmental organisation in Kayamandi, and students and Grade 11 learners worked on projects where the students needed to gather information from the learners to be able to pass their projects. This is different from the traditional community interaction projects where students would teach learners a skill or help them with their school work – which was more a helping behaviour reaction. The projects were named by the students and learners: "See Kayamandi, see yourself" and "Learning life skills in Kayamandi." The information students collected from learners were visually expressed in typographical layouts (see Figures 4.1 to 4.6). Reflective writing was used at the start and end of the two-week projects, where students contemplated on actions and reactions in the community exchanges. The aim of the projects was to facilitate deep learning through themes such as stereotyping, power relations, blackness/whiteness, discrimination and helping behaviour. These projects were examples where socio-political issues were explicitly addressed and where students were exposed to and negotiated relations with different communities outside SU.

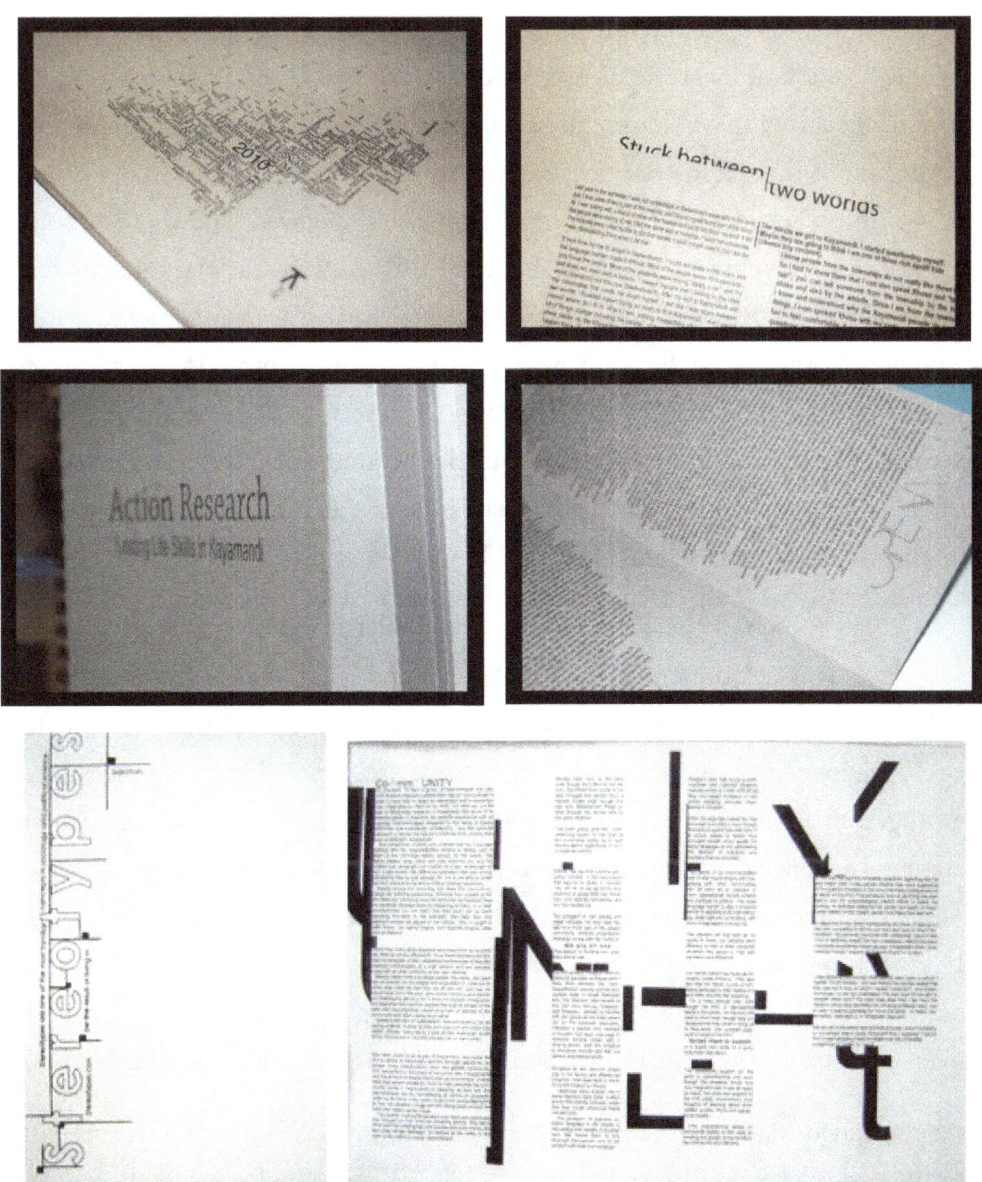

Figures 4.1–4.6: Typographical layouts, 2010. (photos by Karolien Perold and author)

In my research in 2010 to 2012 for my PhD dissertation, I identified certain barriers to citizenship education, namely "power relations and structures, stereotyping and prejudice, and whiteness", but also identified strategies that could facilitate critical citizenship, namely "dialogue, community interaction, reflection and design as a medium of learning" (Costandius, 2012:21). Power relations are evident in all our actions in a teaching and learning environment. In the community interactions I specifically became aware of students and my own stereotypical views of ourselves and of the people with whom we interacted. The creation of spaces for open dialogue became one of the main strategies that we utilised in the projects. Students and I were writing reflections on the projects in which we engaged, and these became a steep learning curve for me, especially when I realised what various students really thought about the projects. I often considered giving up teaching, as the critique of students in the open reflections were a lot for me to absorb. However, it forced my own confrontation with my whiteness to become a long journey of continuous reflection. During that time, I received much encouragement from specifically Dr Brenda Leibowitz from the Centre for Teaching and Learning and she involved me in many projects that were launched at SU during that time.

In 2011, as part of the HOPE Project[53] of the late rector and vice-chancellor of SU, Prof. Russel Botman, Brenda Leibowitz and Linda Smith from the Centre for Teaching and Learning investigated the possibilities of having a Signature Learning Experience programme for all first-year students. The group investigated the programmes that were implemented in America, Australia, Canada and New Zealand. The aim of this signature learning was to facilitate citizenship education, civic engagement and education for the public good, with the requirement that this programme also address the goals of the HOPE Project (Smith, 2011). The groundwork that was laid by the signature learning investigation later led to the implementation of the graduate attributes[54] at SU.

I continued the critical citizenship projects for my VCD students during 2011. A group of students decided to install a mobile toilet on the Rooiplein, because the group felt that the SU students needed a safe space to communicate. The project was titled "I am the collective Matie: Making your private thoughts public" (see Figure 4.7). In the reflection that one of the students in the group wrote, he said:

---

53 SU's HOPE Project was about "doing world-class research on local, regional and African challenges in state-of-the-art facilities with the best expertise available, while providing the best opportunities for learning and the growth of a new generation of thought leaders" (SU, 2013b:n.p.).

54 The development of graduate attributes aims to form an integral part of SU's student-centred teaching and learning strategy. The graduate attributes that were developed include an enquiring mind, an engaged citizen, a dynamic professional and a well-rounded individual (SU, n.d.(b)).

On Friday 22 February our group placed a portable toilet on the Rooiplein. Our concept in short was to create a space where students and the surrounding public could share their thoughts, opinions and be heard in an anonymous, private yet public manner. We wanted people to take up the challenge, which is to let their honest voice and thoughts be heard in public. The concept of having a space such as a toilet on the Rooiplein was therefore birthed. It became a slightly awkward space because it should be private yet was placed in the most public of settings. We wanted to empower and encourage students to step out of the private box within which they hold their true opinions and thoughts and build courage to share them in public. We believe honesty, individuality and diversity in opinions will be the starting block for creating a welcoming culture.

Figure 4.7: "I am the collective Matie: Making your private thoughts public", 2011. (photos by students)

The students were given the opportunity to decide for themselves which issues they wanted to address, in this case on the SU campus. Because these projects were not imaginary projects (as done mostly in the Department of Visual Arts), the learning was a more engaged and embodied experience. Together with the practical implementation of the project, the students had to do research on the topics that they have chosen and write a reflection on learning, and in that way the theory, practice and reflection were happening simultaneously and relationally.

In 2012, Prof. Botman contacted me after he heard about the previous toilet installation, and asked whether the students would put the toilet up again (see Figure 4.8), because he thought it was important to give the students a chance to voice their concerns and an opportunity for management to see what students' concerns were at that stage. Examples from students' writings are "One day your children will despise you for your homophobia", "We need each other", "Don't judge me. There is a story behind who I am!", "It is not our darkness that frightens us but our light" and "We are all equals, we just don't always realize or act on that knowledge".

Figure 4.8: Toilet and examples of text written on the toilet, 2012. (photos by students)

One of the initiatives that Prof. Botman started was the establishment of a Transformation Office and my students collaborated on several projects with the Office, specifically with Monica du Toit, who was the head of the Transformation Office at the time. One of the collaborative projects done on Women's Day in 2013 was a project titled "ONE IN 3: Stick together, beat abuse", which aimed to create awareness and support for abused women. Another project, "Alteration", was done by a group of students that suggested a scaffolding in front of the JH Marais statue on the Rooiplein to enable everyone (especially women) to be on the same level as the raised statue. The aim of the scaffolding was to "confront the status and power that are present on campus" and to alter the current power relations by putting them on the same level.

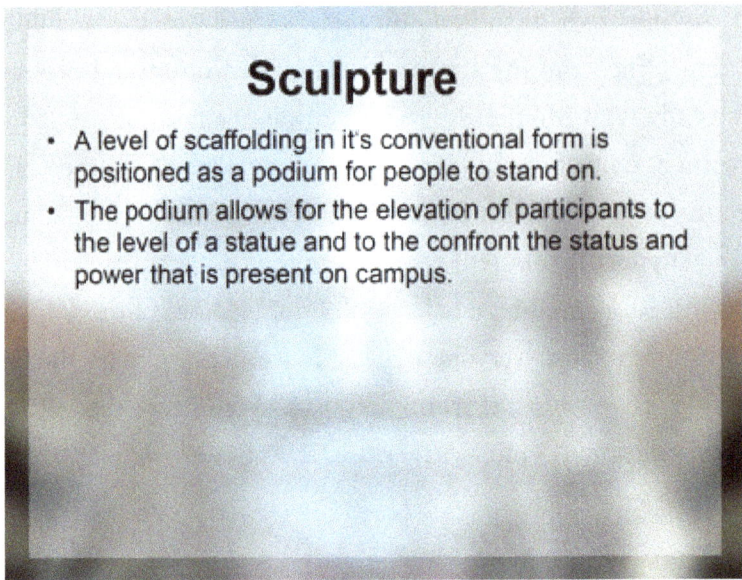

Figure 4.9: "Alteration", 2013. (photos by students)

In 2013, Prof. Botman also appointed a task team, of which I was a member, to draft a concept document on the creation of a welcoming culture at SU (2013a). The role of the task team was to create a document that i) defines a welcoming culture and ii) sets out principles that enable units to implement and align the said strategy with the overarching strategies of the University, and to create a draft policy. A survey on a welcoming culture (SU, 2013c) was launched and more than 963 students, staff and lecturers responded. The report on the results of the survey states: "What is clear is that much contestation still exists, around areas like language, diversity, symbols and even art. How the University deals with these contestations will determine its ability to build a welcoming environment" (SU, 2013a:n.p.). Some of the activities that were implemented were the Muslim prayer room, a cluster and mentor programme for first-years, a faculty-led bursary scheme to diversify the student body and workshops for students led by an international expert on diversity. The practice of race-based room placements at hostels, where race was the main factor taken into account when determining roommates and students of colour were placed with students of colour, was changed during 2012/2013.

The recommendations from the report were divided into sections and the one section, titled "Intercultural interaction and inclusion", highlighted for instance the following aspects: Accommodate various language needs (ten mentions), cater for every culture on campus/respect diversity (eight mentions), promote intercultural events/contact/experience/workshops (six mentions), more open discussions/critical engagement (five mentions), multilingual signage (four mentions) and rename buildings/visual redress[55] (three mentions) (SU, 2013a:n.p). In 2013, in reaction to the survey's recommendations, I gave a welcoming culture project to my students. One group of students decided to do a graffiti wall, where they asked the question: What is South Africa becoming? It is interesting to see that the words 'restless', 'less ignorant' and 'ripe for change' were written on the walls by students in 2013 already.

Figure 4.10: Graffiti wall, 2013 (photos by students)

---

55 The term 'visual redress' was first used in conversations between the Transformation Office, the Centre for Teaching and Learning, people involved in the art projects and me in 2013 to refer to the physical spaces that needed to be changed to enable more inclusive and welcoming spaces at SU. It was used here (as far as I know) for the first time in an official document (SU, 2013a).

There were also other welcoming projects by other students, such as a project on signage. One of the students, who was from Botswana, did a project on her struggles with finding examination halls because the signage was mostly in Afrikaans. She commented: "Finding exam or test venues outside my department was a nightmare. Thank God for [name of fellow student] for being my exam venue-finder. It was so much effort that psychologically I panicked every time before an exam." The SU Security Office and Library were some of the buildings on which she commented: "The USBD [Stellenbosch Campus Security], the most important organisation for a student, especially in terms of protection, it took quite a while for me to locate their building, and [the] funny thing is I walked past it every day." The student also commented that "[i]n my fourth year I realised that there was no sign in English for the library on the whole campus". This was later corrected and the Library's name was changed in 2017 to the Stellenbosch University Library.

Figure 4.11 and 4.12: Stellenbosch Campus Security, 2013 and Stellenbosch University Library, 2013 .
(photos by students)

Another art project that was organised with the Transformation Office and my VCD students in 2013 as part of the Diversity Week activities was tablecloths and a washing line above the Library, on which students could write and express their opinions openly (see Figures 4.13 and 4.14). Some of the examples that were written on the cloths were: "What we have in common is more important than the difference", "the world = diverse #believe it" and "Inter-racial couples rule." The washing line idea was to 'air out dirty laundry' and it gave students an opportunity (as in the toilet installation) to express their feelings openly. Students were invited to confess anonymously and acknowledge some hurt that a person might have caused another person.

Figure 4.13: Diversity Week: Beaded arm bands and the table cloth writing spaces, 2013. (photos by students)

Figure 4.14: Diversity Week: Washing line, 2013. (photo by student)

These projects continued in particular by using the Rooiplein as a space to interact with other students on campus. In 2014, a postgraduate student also wrote her master's thesis on art as a transformative agent. The aim of the research was to explore whether interactive public art on campus can lead to conversations and actions to bring about transformation and social justice (Figure 4.15).

Figure 4.15: We belong here by Anika van den Berg, 16 May 2014 . (photo by student)

In a project during 2014, a group of students also suggested projections on the building on the Rooiplein, especially on public holidays such as Workers' Day (see Figure 4.16) and of prominent leaders (see Figure 4.17) to counter the prominence of the JH Marais statue in the middle of the Rooiplein. A student also suggested adding poems of Adam Small on benches on campus (see Figure 4.18). This idea was later used and implemented in 2019. This will be discussed later in the chapter.

Figure 4.16 and 4.17: Workers' Day projections, 2014, and projections of prominent leaders, 2014. (photo by students)

Figure 4.18: Bench suggestion, 2014. (photo by student)

Later in 2014, a PhD student, Gera de Villiers, and I also reacted by designing a multilingual (Afrikaans, English and isiXhosa) signage system on campus that was presented to Facilities Management (see Figures 4.19 and 4.20). The decision was then taken by Facilities Management and the Rector's Management Team to add English to the signage system, but not isiXhosa. It was only in 2018 that isiXhosa was added to some of the signage on campus. The question also arose which language should be used first. The current order of the languages are: first Afrikaans, then English and then isiXhosa. There were many discussions regarding adding three languages, because of the short time available when driving past a sign in a moving car when you only have a few seconds to read the signage. Our suggestion as a solution for readability while driving was to have only English, but this was rejected by Facilities Management. Another idea for the signage on the buildings for visitors on foot was to add a QR code on the signage that gives a map of campus and information on the buildings that could form part of a walking route.

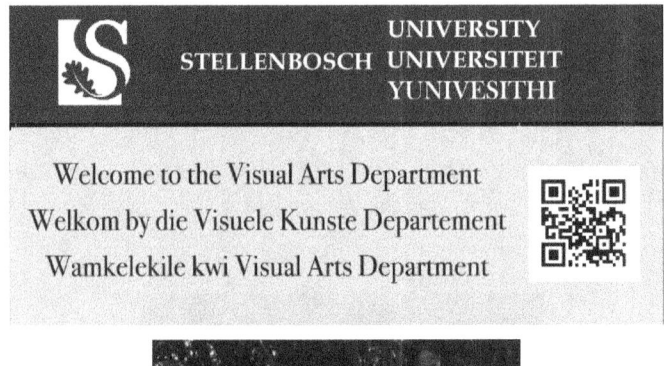

Figures 4.19 and 4.20: Suggestion to Facilities Management, 2014 and example where isiXhosa was added, 2018 (presentation by Gera de Villiers and photo by student)

In 2015, a survey was done by PhD student Gera de Villiers on new artworks on campus. The first question of the survey was: "If new statues or forms of visual were to be introduced on campus to include a diverse culture, who or what would you suggest?" Most students chose to have a sculpture of Desmond Tutu or Nelson Mandela. Their next choices were Adam Small and Boetie Kannemeyer, a resident of Die Vlakte. Other suggestions were Thuli Madonsela and Russel Botman.

Some of the responses from students to Question 1 under "Other suggestions" were as follows:

- No political icons
- Should be someone who was born/is famous for work done in and around the Stellenbosch/Western Cape area
- Art which presents diversity and science
- Statue of a farm labourer and a domestic worker on the Rooiplein
- I prefer no statues at all as first choice
- Save the money and use it towards student bursaries.

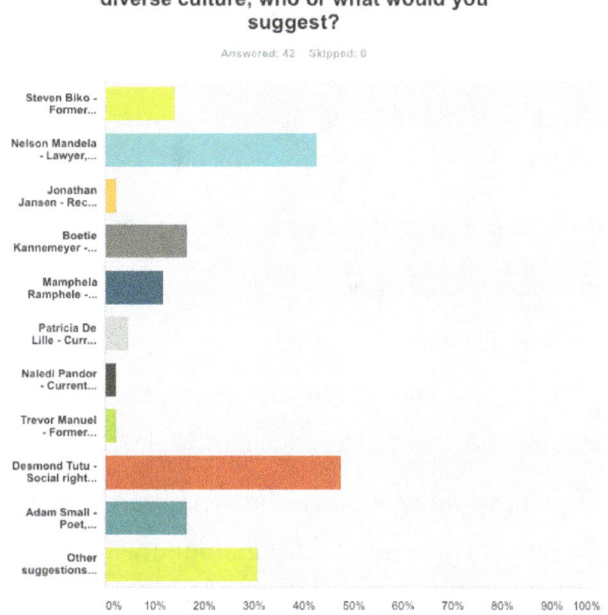

Figure 4.21: Visual redress on SU campus survey, data collection, 17 August 2015 (presentation by Gera de Villiers)

Question 2 was: "If another statue were to be erected, would you prefer a more traditional statue or a contemporary sculpture?" Responses to Question 2 under

"Other suggestions" included the following:

- Both types pls – who will pay? Lotto.
- I prefer no statues at all. Rather, create a garden or plant a tree or start a recycling plant and name that after someone or in the memory of someone (if you have to).
- Waste of money. Give bursaries to black students instead of this!
- Save the money and use it towards student bursaries.
- A form of interactive public art.

There was also a space in the survey for general comments. Here are some examples of such comments from students:

- Let's not erect statues for people who are already widely celebrated. Let's memorialise the lesser-known people who deserve it.
- Completely do away with buildings named after individuals – name them after disciplines.
- Statue and bust of Russel Botman as a champion of hope and inclusivity.
- Plant trees and create water-wise indigenous gardens. Name the garden after some significant person.
- I would like to see signage by the Arts and Social Sciences Building acknowledging Die Vlakte, its residents and the history.
- Get the University more inclusive by giving more bursaries and changing the language policy instead of faffing around with window dressing. Then the visual change would be more students of colour.
- Stay away from people who are still living. They still have time to [f...] things up. Think Robert Mugabe: He was a hero in the 80s, but became a tyrant. Wait until they have died …
- Multilingual signage.

This section discussed projects from 2010 to the beginning of 2015. I believe that the frustrations that many students experienced on campus were expressed in the events discussed above, but it was only during the student protests in 2015 and 2016 that students' voices came strongly to the fore and SU management seriously reacted to calls from students to be included and accommodated. In the next section, projects and processes will be discussed that took place in 2015 to 2017.

Projects in 2015 to 2017

Early in 2015, Louise Green and I decided to do a project with second-year VCD students together with English honours students. The challenge was to memorialise the history of the Arts and Social Sciences Building which was built on the same place where 'coloured' people were forcefully removed starting in 1964. The area was called Die Vlakte. In addition to the 3 700 coloured inhabitants, six schools, four churches, a mosque, a cinema and ten businesses were affected by the forced removals. The aim of the project was to make students and lecturers aware of and allow them to reflect on the history and the current consequences of that history in the present. Three community members who lived in Die Vlakte or had family who lived there were invited to tell the students about their experiences. Students were also asked to conduct interviews with other students in the Arts and Social Sciences Building to find out how many people know about the history, and they were also required to write reflections on their learning. The final presentations were made to a group of lecturers and the dean of the Faculty of Arts and Social Sciences. At the presentation to the dean, the students mentioned that Mr Abels, one of the Die Vlakte community member participants, suggested a bursary for Die Vlakte descendants. This was communicated to the rector and is now implemented at SU. The University took credit for initiating the bursary, but the credit should in fact have been given to Mr Abels, which would have improved relations between SU and the Die Vlakte community. See examples of the projects from students in figures 4.22 to 4.25. The "House installation" and the "Reconstruction month" student projects will be a starting point for the Die Vlakte garden that is planned for 2021 next to the Arts and Social Sciences Building. This process will not be possible without the important input of the Die Vlakte community.

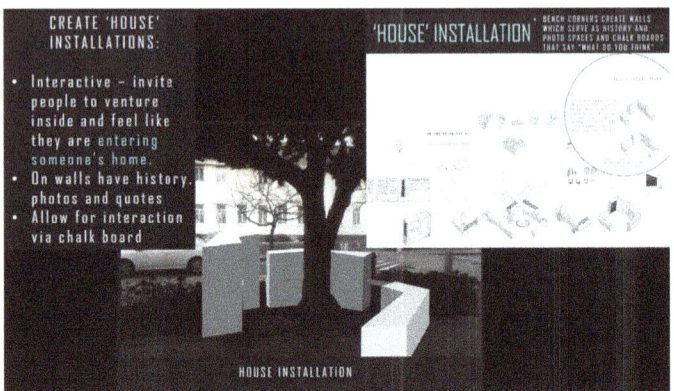

Figure 4.22: "House installation", 2015. (presentation by students)

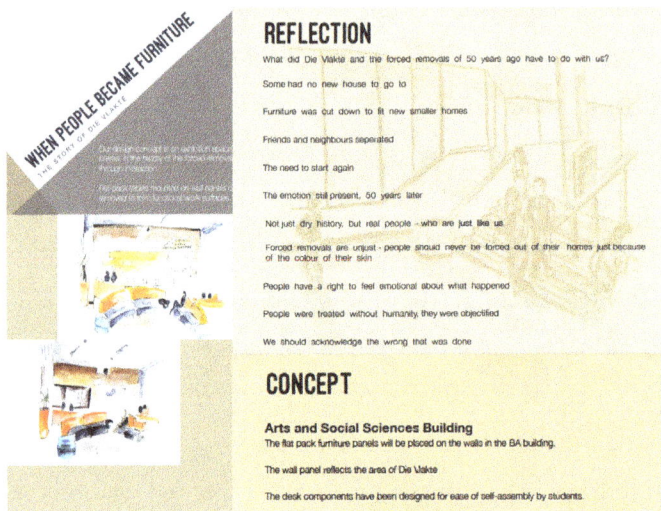

Figure 4.23: "When people became furniture", 2015. (presentation by students)

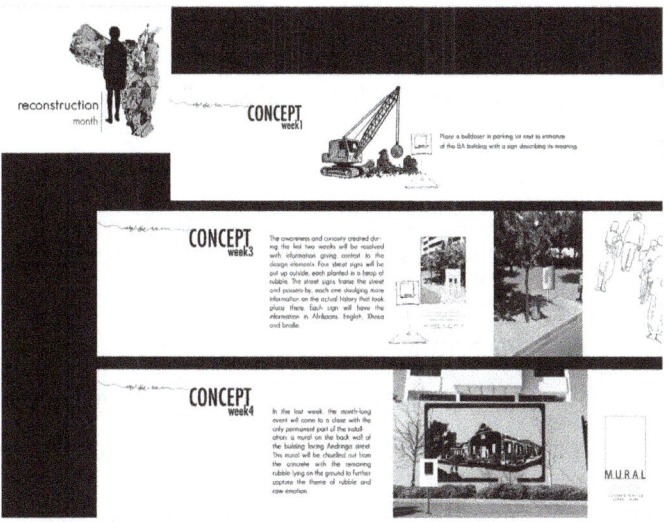

Figure 4.24: "Reconstruction month", 2015. (presentation by students)

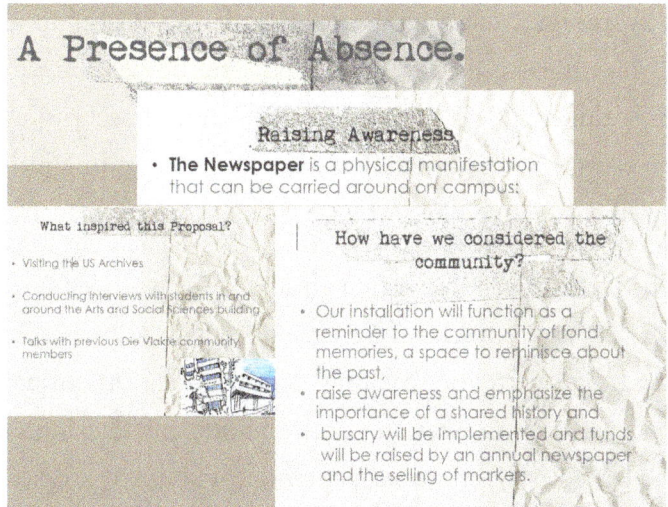

Figure 4.25: "A presence of absence", 2015. (presentation by students)

Some of the students' reflection on the Die Vlakte project included the following:

> It is easy to disregard paper and to disregard things written on paper, posters and objects, but you cannot ignore stories on people's faces and the passion of their experience. … We were informed that after 32 years, the hate and the heart-felt [are] still there[,] that the moment you start talking, it starts barrelling.

> Personally I feel completely unequipped for such a task and even other older students can't believe we were given such a huge project. … It is a loaded topic with months of research required to understand the full scope of emotions, wrongs, benefits, disadvantaging and joys that all formed part of the history.

Another student strongly resisted the project and reacted in this way: "I wanted to get up and say what I think, I didn't want to do this project." This project again confirmed that community interaction is not only a mental experience, but also a bodily experience, and critical thinking can only be internalised when in practice. Experiencing mental and bodily discomfort when dealing with sensitive issues such as racism or sexism is a good space for starting critical self-reflection and change.

In March 2015, the #RhodesMustFall student protest started and the Rhodes statue at the University of Cape Town was removed in April. During that time, the #FeesMustFall protest started and the Open Stellenbosch movement was formed on the SU campus. During the student protest, the need to redress learning environments became more urgent. The Marais statue became a focal point for student resistance during 2015. Because of the increased security on campus, my own projects on campus were limited. Permission to use the Rooiplein as a space to organise or implement interventions was not possible during that time.

I started a critical citizenship research group in 2012 with lecturers from various races and genders from the faculties of AgriSciences, Arts and Social Sciences, Science and Theology and the Centre for Teaching and Learning. This group discussed and reflected on concepts and practices on transformation and decolonisation for about six years and collaboratively presented papers and published articles and chapters. The group also did a research project in 2015 to 2016, where photographs of the student protests (see Figure 4.26) were shown to lecturers on campus and they were asked for their reaction.

Figure 4.26: Pamphlet with photographs of the student protests given to students and lecturers (presentation by author)

Examples of data collected from students and lecturers regarding the #FeesMustFall protests include the following:

- These events place stress on my relationship with lecturers, as I want to see them actively partake in solving these issues and oftentimes this is not the case or they are not as involved as they should be. Sometimes it even appears that they do not care at all.

- Frustrated that we are blinded by our feelings, which does not allow us to gain perspective on the situation.

- The images have different effects on me, both bodily and cognitively. I feel tension and fear, but also sympathy and pain for the people who had to protest to make their voices heard.

- I feel anger towards both the protesting students and the institutional powers. The experience of not hearing, listening and understanding is a huge cognitive challenge. It seems as though the rational competencies of academic training are of no help in developing a way forward.

- That I am dealing with students who are determined to challenge even my position as a lecturer. My attitude to them is one of respect, but also fear.
- I suddenly feel that my words are not compatible with the experiences and world around me.

These reactions of the students and lecturers gave the critical citizenship group a broader understanding of how students and lecturers experienced the student protests. This also led to the group becoming involved in other projects, such as collecting information on sensitive areas (see Figures 4.27 to 4.29) that BCI students experienced on campus. One of my master's students, Stephané Conradie, who was part of the Open Stellenbosch movement, collected information and came up with concepts for artworks on how to react to the requests from students regarding feeling welcome on campus.

Figures 4.27–4.29: Sensitive spaces and places identified by the Open Stellenbosch movement: Names of certain buildings, library Special Collections division and Voortrekker woodcut at the Administration Building, 2016 (photos by Stephané Conradie and author)

Also in 2015, I initiated a project with a sculpture lecturer and students to also make suggestions for visual redress on campus. I shared with them some of the previous ideas and one of the students, Nicolene Burger, decided to actually build the steps (see Figure 4.30) that the students suggested back in 2013. The JH Marais statue has been the centre of attention during the 2015–2016 student protests. Making the 2013 staircase suggestion real became more urgent because of the student protests. The difference between the 2013 and 2015 staircase was that the 2013 students built it to be on the same level as the statue and the 2015 staircase asked the question whether it was time for JH Marais to step down. After that performance and installation, the SU management and the Transformation Office discussed the issues regarding statues and plaques and decided to remove the Verwoerd plaque, but to keep other statues such as the JH Marais and contextualise the statues so that conversations could be opened up about the history and how that informs the present and future artworks on campus.

Figure 4.30: Flight, Nicolene Burger, 2016
(https://openforumresidency.wordpress.com/2016/11/04/featured-content/)

One of the artworks that was developed by Stephané Conradie and the students from the Open Stellenbosch movement was called *The Circle* (see Figure 4.31). This was the description that was given as a motivation for the artwork:

When we think of bronze monuments, we normally associate them with towering statues, larger-than-life figures and idolised/immortalised figures to which no one can relate. They are also positioned in heroic poses that give them a sense of grandeur, isolated in time and space. *The Circle* will be based on a sculptural project that would bring many of our historical or present/future leaders together on the floor in a seating position as if in discussion or casual conversation with one another. This idea would be to symbolise the need for humility and to practically sit down and listen to one another. The figures could also be the students themselves, as they symbolise the future of our nation and leadership in the past and presently as well as leaders to come. These circles could be positioned on many different open spaces on campus such as the grass on the Rooiplein where many students sit and relax while having conversations. By placing the sculptures there, they would represent becoming part of the day-to-day conversations that take place on campus.

Figure 4.31: Visual representation of The Circle, 2016 (photo by Stephané Conradie)

Another artwork suggested by Stephané Conradie in collaboration with the Open Stellenbosch movement was called *The Deliberation Bridge: Sound Installation* (see Figure 4.32). The artwork was described as follows.

This sound installation would take on the format of two speakers installed on the bridge linking Admin A and Admin B. The position is key, as the Rooiplein has become an impromptu meeting place over the years, specifically in 2015, when it has seen many students and staff meet to discuss current political and social issues taking place in South Africa and on the Stellenbosch University campus. Once a week, a pre-recorded conversation would be broadcast from these speakers. These conversations could be historical speeches or current topics that have sparked conversations on campus. The installation therefore also becomes a participatory installation where different societies and/or departments in the faculty could potentially be responsible for a specific week's recording/deliberation/conversation.

Figure 4.32: Visual representation of The Deliberation Bridge: Sound Installation, 2016. (presentation by Stephané Conradie)

Other suggestions from the Open Stellenbosch movement regarding statues and busts included the following:

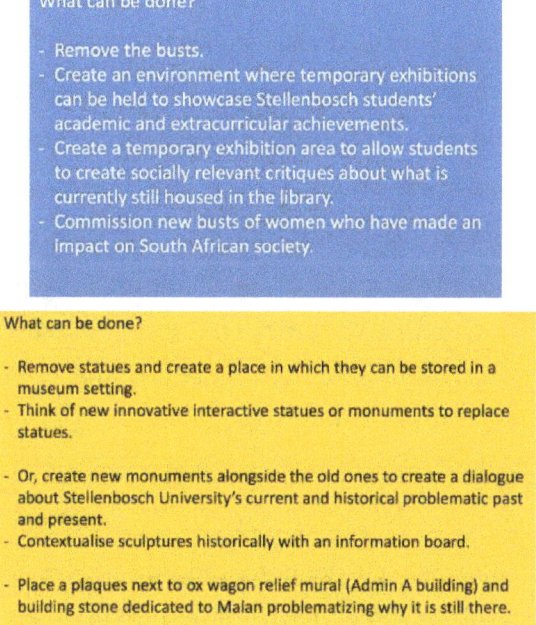

Figure 4.33: Suggestions from students, 2016

In 2017, during the discussions on various artworks that were developed (also in collaboration with the Transformation Office), it became clear that the Student Representative Council (SRC) members should also be involved in suggesting and voting for artworks (see the voting results from the 2017 SRC in Figure 4.34).

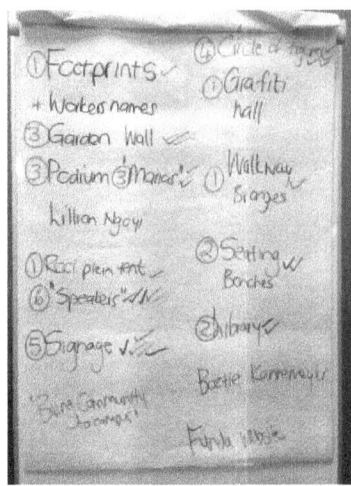

Figure 4.34: SRC voting for projects to be implemented, 2017. (photo by author)

In my own teaching, I realised that students are hardly ever exposed to art and artists in their own communities that are not mainstream. In 2017, I started collecting art in previously disadvantaged communities around Stellenbosch to include local knowledge in my art curriculum. The "Reimagine the socio-political history of the Arts and to Decolonise the Arts curriculum (RADA)" project is geared towards the documentation of material culture, namely objects, traces and/or events among local communities that can be described as textual (such as poetry, literature, art, craft and design), spatial (architecture and landscape), performative (theatre and dance) and sensory (with interests such as food, games and sport) (see Figure 4.35 and https://art.sun.ac.za). Fataar (2018:7) claims that that "[t]he call for decolonising education is nothing less than the full incorporation of humanity's knowledge systems into the curriculum and knowledge selection systems of universities and schools". This highlights the importance of including previously excluded indigenous knowledge in the curriculum. Le Grange (2016) states that one of the ways to decolonise the curriculum would be to explore ways to include local and regional content in the curriculum, especially in areas where Eurocentric knowledge systems continue to dominate. The purposes of the RADA project was to decolonise the arts curriculum, which refers to collaboratively sharing, constructing and disrupting existing knowledge.

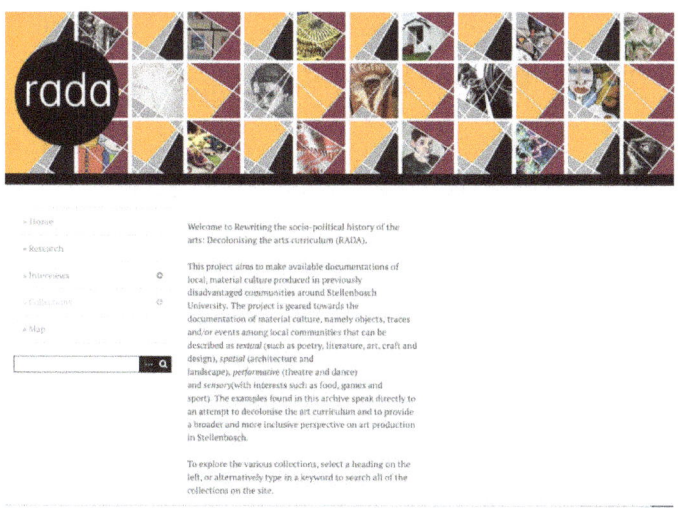

Figure 4.35: RADA homepage (https://art.sun.ac.za)

In 2017, Prof. Schoonwinkel, Vice-Rector: Teaching and Learning, established the Decolonisation of the Stellenbosch University Curriculum task team, of which I was also a member. I contributed specifically regarding spaces:

> Spaces that need to be decolonised include physical and discursive spaces, the mind and classroom spaces/curricula. Approaches to these spaces can be to erase, replace or re-interpret them. We need to realise that some spaces are inherently unsafe due to unequal and discomforting power relations. The transformation of buildings and public spaces is vital for decolonisation. Virtual spaces, symbols, offices, buildings, architecture, artefacts, photographs and statues should also be considered. … It is therefore recommended that both physical and discursive spaces, as well as the mind space of those teaching the curriculum, should be decolonised. It is further recommended that the classroom space and curriculum be expanded by the open discussion of what social justice may mean in relation to decolonisation (SU, 2017:17, 19).

The data that were collected during the student protests were especially valuable to inform future projects on campus. They also informed the Visual Redress Plan, which I compiled in 2017 and which was the basis for the presentations that were done to the Rector's Management Team to motivate for strategic funding for implementing some of the artworks that were suggested during the last ten years, but especially during the student protests. The next section will focus on 2018 to 2020, during which strategic funding was made available from the Rector's Management Team for implementing artworks and contextualising statues on campus.

Stellenbosch campus in 2018 to 2020

A presentation was delivered by Prof. Nico Koopman (Vice-Rector: Social Impact, Transformation and Personnel), Dr Leslie van Rooi (Senior Director: Social Impact and Transformation) and me to the Rector's Management Team, suggesting visual redress artworks and processes on campus, upon which they decided to make strategic funding available for visual redress on campus. The ideas that were collected since 2010 from student projects and specifically during the 2015–2016 student protests were put in place to implement some of those ideas. A Visual Redress Committee was also called together by Prof. Koopman. These projects and processes will be discussed in the following paragraphs.

In 2018, I became part of a dedicated group that developed the centenary commemorations of SU. The process had already started when I joined and the slogan for the commemoration campaign that was suggested was "100 years of excellence". I immediately raised a flag and said that there were many incidents during the last 100 years that were not excellent and using that slogan would be an insult to the people who were emotionally and financially disadvantaged during the last 100 years. My suggestion was to choose a slogan that acknowledged the past and included a commitment to the future. The slogan was then changed to: "100 years of learning, growing and moving forward together" (SU, n.d.(a)). It was then a natural progression to also have a centenary message, the Centenary Restitution Statement, permanently put up as a reminder of the past injustices and a commitment to the future, as seen at the entrance of the Stellenbosch University Library (see Figure 4.36).

Figure 4.36: Centenary Restitution Statement: "In its 2018 Centenary Year, SU celebrates its successes and achievements. We also acknowledge, with deep regret, our role in the injustices of our country's past. SU commits itself to the ideal of an inclusive, world-class university in and for Africa. Forward together", Prof. Wim de Villiers, Rector and Vice-Chancellor, 2018. (photo by author)

The sculpture of the eleven women in a circle (see Figure 4.37) on the Rooiplein was inspired by the previously mentioned suggestion in 2016 by Stephané Conradie and the Open Stellenbosch movement. The difference between the 2016 and 2019 suggestions was that only women were chosen for the circle because of the underrepresentation of women on campus. The women represented are Krotoa/Eve, Prof. Thuli Madonsila, Winnie Madikizela-Mandela, Fatima Meer, Lillian Ngoyi, Quanita Adams, Antjie Krog, Kgothatso Montjane, Zanele Muholi and Dope Saint Jude (see Twitter link in Figure 4.38). The eleventh anonymous woman represents all other women's voices who are invited to participate in the discourse. A survey was launched on campus where approximately the same amount of BCI and white students were asked to vote for women whom they see as leaders in the South African society. It was interesting to note that Winnie Madikizela-Mandela received the most votes, even though she was considered as a controversial figure to some people. The following nominated women, and in the case where they were deceased, their families, were contacted to ask permission to put up an image of them in the circle sculpture. The outline of the women and a suggestion for the wording were included in the formal invitation to the women. Some of the women or families decided to adjust their outlines of their figures (such as Quanita Adams, who asked for bigger hair, as that is her trademark) or text (such as Fatima Meer, whose daughters decided to add some text) and their wishes were adhered to.

Figure 4.37: The Circle, curated by Stephané Conradie, 2019. (photo by author)

Figure 4.38: Dope Saint Jude, Twitter page, 2019.
(https://www.facebook.com/dopesaintjude/posts/2469597393091096)

It was also interesting to hear a comment from a colleague, who argued that from his perspective, the fact that the women are sitting and the Marais statue is standing on a pedestal perpetuates the concept that women are subservient to men. It is exactly these socially constructed ideas that we would like to open up for discussion, as we believe that a sculpture of women sitting in a circle is a far better symbol for positive engagement, and the perception that a man standing on a pedestal represents power is a constructed image that needs to be re-evaluated. Reacting to the Marais statue by making another statue is to some extent buying into the type of symbolism that was used in the West to honour mostly white men. The type of symbols that we choose need to be reflected on as well.

Welcoming messages on benches on the Rooiplein in 16 languages (Afrikaans, Braille, English, isiNdebele, isiXhosa (see Figure 4.39), isiZulu, Kaaps, Moesliem Kaaps, San, Sepedi, Sesotho, Setswana, South African Sign Language, SiSwati, Tshivenda and Xitsonga) were installed. This idea was inspired by the student project of 2014. A lecturer from General Linguistics, Sima Mashazi, was asked to gather all the African languages and English welcoming messages and community members were consulted for the Afrikaans, Kaaps (Simon Witbooi) and Moesliem Kaaps (Aslam Fataar). On Heritage Day in 2019, a student dressed up in her traditional clothes and took a picture of herself in front of the bench with her own language (see Figure 4.40). The Kaaps message "Koppel 'n lyn" (see Figure 4.41) attracted a lot of attention, because the meaning of the phrase differs depending on the geographical area in the Western Cape. It could mean either making a connection with someone, or it refers to someone using drugs. Some students were very offended, because they felt that SU associates Kaaps with people using drugs. This issue also opened up other conversations about language and the use and place of Kaaps as a language at SU.

*Figure 4.39: isiXhosa bench: Isandla sihlamba esinye
(The one hand washes the other / Hands wash each other), 2019. (photo by author)*

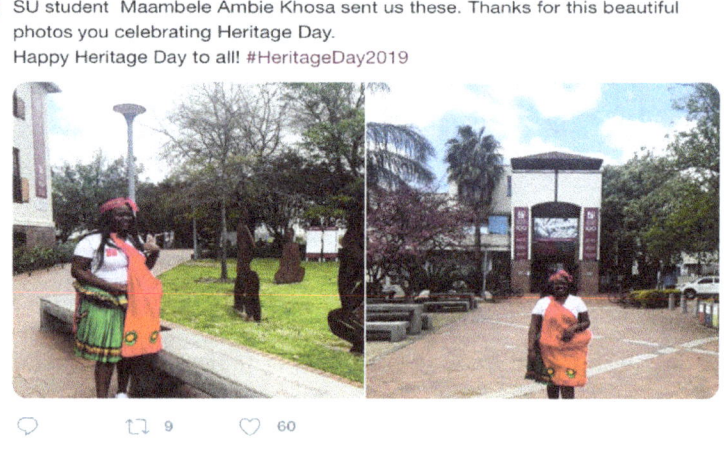

*Figure 4.40: a) Student at the bench with the Tsonga message, 2019.
(https://twitter.com/stellenboschuni/status/1176390936806535168)*

Figure 4.41: Bench with the message in Kaaps: "Koppel 'n lyn", 2019. (photo by author)

One of the comments that also emerged from the welcoming messages collected for the benches was that the people of Stellenbosch are still divided to a great extent (emotionally and physically). The idea of having maps showing different areas of Stellenbosch emerged in the discussions with lecturers and members of the Visual Redress Committee. The discussions were complex, because some of the areas, such as Pniel and Jamestown, see themselves as towns on their own, while others, such as Idas Valley and Kayamandi, are considered part of Stellenbosch. Bridges were placed between the maps to encourage better relations between the different communities.

Some of the other projects that were implemented by the Transformation Office and me were the contextualisation of statues, for instance at the Faculty of Theology (see Chapter 9), a special collection space in the Stellenbosch University Library (see Chapter 5), the establishment of gallery space on the Rooiplein and a Die Vlakte map that was installed at the Arts and Social Sciences Building. Apart from these implementations, workshops were held at various faculties and departments, because there was a realisation that lecturers and students of these faculties and departments need to be involved themselves in the processes of transforming their own visual spaces to make it a more welcoming and inclusive space.

Discussion

The projects that were described in this chapter aimed to include embodied, material and discursive engagements, and the processes that were followed in which students, lecturers and communities were involved were an important part of the learning for all involved. New materialist thinking focuses on ontologies, ways of being, truths and realities, not simply epistemology (knowledge and meaning making). New materialist ways of inquiry give space to consider not only epistemology (knowing), but also being (ontology) and doing/making (axiology) – the relational ways we come to be and know in the world entangled not only with humans, but also with the non-human (materials such as art, statues, animals, books and so forth). We are part of the entanglement in the visual redress process ourselves and of the research methods that we are using – we are part of what we seek to understand (Barad, 2007).

The product that is presented in this chapter is also a small cut of the reality of what is really involved in the entanglement. Barad (2007) calls this the 'agential cut'. We make cuts because certain aspects glowed and we believe that we reacted objectively by choosing these cuts. Yet the cuts in fact chose us. In the same way, if we chose to write for instance about a statue, the statue started to glow for us because something in ourselves was triggered. These affective triggers often happen subconsciously and the body reacts, but is not sure what it is that it reacts to. Acknowledging that we are often invited in without realising it places the focus on our responsibility to ethically reflect on our affective reactions and our continuous process of becoming.

The question then emerges of how we can be ethically responsive to all "other agents that emerge with our own agency in the inquiry, as well as to others affected by these emergent agencies" (Rosiek, Snyder & Pratt, 2019:6). Significant to Barad's (2007:185) argument is this interlinking of ethics, knowing and being as an undividable "ethico-onto-epistemological" practice. Barad (2007) argues that all intra-action matters and the processes of becoming are deeply ethical matters. The in-between or links between the body that is affected and the mind that interprets and rationalises become important. Watts (2013, cited in Rosiek et al., 2019:7) says that this implies that we live in a "moral universe in which everything is an agent or part of an agent and every action carries a moral dimension". This changes the relationship between the subject and other agents (human, non-human, objects) from a spectator and investigator to a participant in the "ethical relationship with other agents" (Rosiek et al., 2019:10). It is the relational entanglements that enhance transformation of the self in relation to the other. The aim is then to not only understand the other differently, or further the other, but also to transform one's own learning, knowing and being in the world through the relational engagement (Rosiek et al., 2019). The question is whether we ourselves become different and whether our relationship with other agents is also transformed (Rosiek et al., 2019:6). It is therefore not only the doing or final products of the visual redress projects, but also the relations with others that should become transformative.

My perspective on the visual redress projects is from a privileged white Western point of view. South Africa consists of different cultures with different indigenous, Asian and Eurocentric worldviews, and it is also a reality on SU's campus. What is to be done to address the embodied and material aspects in relation to the discursive in a space where different worldviews and ways of understanding knowledge exist? Indigenous theories developed ideas regarding agency of non-human things before it was highlighted in new materialist perspectives. Rosiek et al. (2019:6) argue that in indigenous theories, non-human agency is taken as a given. It is not as in the Eurocentric perspective, where objects of our research wait passively to be discovered and described (Rosiek et al., 2019:6). In indigenous theories, authors would not try to justify the non-human, as it is already part of the ontological understanding of the world. Binary oppositions in indigenous thinking were not established and need no correction, as in the Eurocentric traditions. For the indigenous thinker, the experience of the world is relational – nothing exists alone and there is no distinction between self and other, subject and object, rational and emotional, mental and physical. Watts (2013) argues that in the Eurocentric perspective, the focus is more on the abstract understanding of agency instead of a lived and practical experience of non-human agency. Watts (2013) suggests that it is often difficult to engage with or respect indigenous theories from a Eurocentric perspective because of different ways of viewing the world. According to Watts (2013), a person with an indigenous perspective also often struggles to assimilate in an environment where binaries are the norm. This aspect is important to take into consideration for the visual redress projects, but also how that could affect learning.

I am aiming to find different embodied/material/discursive ways to be affected by other social, racial and gendered humans and material objects in ways that could be transformative. However, it is crucial to not only be affected by others, but also to understand how my existence affects others. Reflecting on my own existence means that I have to acknowledge my own positionality. Positionality is the social and political context that creates my identity in terms of, for instance, class, race or gender, but also education, language, history or geographical location. Positionality refers to what we know or understand of the world. Positionality also describes how my identity influences, and potentially biases, my understanding of the world. I can be biased without realising it because of my understanding of the world. There are therefore many potential challenges regarding one's positionality, as it can have a huge effect on the type of person that I am, the visual redress projects and processes in which I engage and the research that is produced because of that.

Conclusion

In this chapter I described the projects and processes that I facilitated and were involved in during the last ten years. Many of the projects and processes did not culminate in actual artworks that still exist, but it is the embodied interaction process that, even though visually transparent, counts. The visual and the non-visual have an influence and leave a visible mark on both the body and the mind. It is very difficult to measure the invisible, because we cannot see it, but visual redress is not only about the visual, but also about the affective, mental changes or bodily learning that took place. The end result of visual redress is to create social cohesion, and social cohesion is learned not only cognitively, but very importantly also in a bodily way.

What became more prominent in my own learning processes in the last two years was the importance of embodied learning and the affective reaction of the body in relation to the mind or cognitive experiences of learning. These subtle but constant underlying forces that often control our behaviour should come to the fore and inform our understanding of ourselves and the relation with others – both human and non-human forces. It is often not the policies or the big actions that make a difference, but the constant, subtle, everyday experiences of our entangled existence that have an affective influence and direct our actions. The affective reaction to the Marais statue is a very real experience for different people (race, gender, class), because it represents the past, but also because of what it is made of and how it is put high on a pedestal. Haraway (1988, cited in Barad, 2007) sees matter as lively, processual and transformative, where the embodied/material/discursive forms assemblages that are fluid and exchangeable. We could walk past a statue and feel the sweat, feel the anger or guilt rise up in us, and we could then direct this emotion to the person we meet next without realising the relation/non-relation between the statue and the person in front of us. The entanglement of issues became more prominent in my own understanding of how they influence or direct my own actions and therefore my teaching and learning. The barriers and strategies that I identified earlier are in fact not separate entities – they are entangled. Even if we believe that dialogue is a crucial aspect in critical citizenship education, the dialogue depends on the power relations that underpin that. The complex relations in-between these aspects became more important and started to open new space for transformation.

Affect theory marked a significant turn to the interlinking of the social, cultural and political with the psychic and the unconscious (Zembylas, 2014). Art and art processes use sensational affects as a way to communicate and create knowledge. Knowledge is produced through engagement between self and material. Art could serve as a trigger for more critical inquiry (Golanska, 2020) and deeper engagement with social, political or gendered issues, such as the case of the Marais statue in relation to the eleven women sitting in a circle. The Marais statue is still the 'prominent' figure on the Rooiplein, but with the entanglement with dialogue, community interaction and reflection its prominence could became less prominent, as the socially constructed ideas of what a person on a pedestal means or represents become broken down when it is placed next to a symbol of a group of women in a circle. Repeating the hegemonic type of symbols of the past could be detrimental. In new materialistic thinking, the human becomes part of a more flattened ontology and not considered as the centre of existence. Decolonisation regarding visual redress is not a process of reacting to the past by following and repeating it. Instead of reacting and copying the old, colonised symbols, new symbols should be conceptualised within the immediate context. The emphasis should therefore be on a continuous building of the post-apartheid decolonised university. The collaborative, embodied/material/discursive way of being in the world could be a more conducive symbol used in public spaces. The Marais statue visually represents and reminds us of the past, to which we do not want to return, but the women in a circle represent a place and space of dialogue and collaborative reflection.

References

Barad, K. 2007. *Meeting the universe halfway: Quantum physics and the entanglement of matter and meaning.* Durham: Duke University Press. https://doi.org/10.1515/9780822388128

Barrett, E. & Bolt, B. 2007. *Practice as research: Approaches to creative arts enquiry.* London: I.B. Tauris. https://doi.org/10.5040/9780755604104

Clark, M. & Costandius, E. 2020. Redress at higher education institutions in South Africa: Mapping a way forward. *de arte,* 55(3):26-48. https://doi.org/10.1080/00043389.2020.1728874

Clough, P. 2007. *The affective turn: Theorising the social.* Durham: Duke University Press. https://doi.org/10.1215/9780822389606

Costandius, E. 2012. *Engaging the curriculum in visual communication design: A critical citizenship education perspective.* Published doctoral dissertation. Stellenbosch: Stellenbosch University.

Deleuze, G. & Guattari, F. 1997. *What is philosophy?* (Trans. G. Burchell & H. Tomlinson). New York, NY: Columbia University Press.

Deleuze, G. & Guattari, F. 2004. *A thousand plateaus: Capitalism and schizophrenia* (Trans. B. Massumi). London: Continuum.

Dolphijn, R. & Van der Tuin, I. 2012. *New materialism: Interviews and cartographies.* Ann Arbor, MI: Open Humanities. https://doi.org/10.3998/ohp.11515701.0001.001

Dope Saint Jude. 2018. *Dope Saint Jude Twitter page*. Retrieved from https://twitter.com/DopeSaintJude/status/1147049370325569536 [Accessed 2 October 2020].

Fataar, A. 2018. Decolonising education in South Africa: Perspectives and debates. *Educational Research for Social Change*, 7:vi-ix.

Golańska, D. 2020. Creative practice for sustainability: A new materialist perspective on artivist production of eco-sensitive knowledges. *International Journal of Education through Art,* 16(3):1-26. https://doi.org/10.1386/eta_00035_1

Johnson, L. & Morris, P. 2010. Towards a framework for critical citizenship education. *The Curriculum Journal,* 21(1):77-96. https://doi.org/10.1080/09585170903560444

Johnson, R. 2017. *Embodied social justice*. London: Routledge. https://doi.org/10.4324/9781315439648

Lefebvre, H. 1991. *The production of space*. Oxford: Blackwell.

Le Grange, L. 2016. Decolonising the university curriculum. *South African Journal of Higher Education,* 30(2):1-12. https://doi.org/10.20853/30-2-709

MacLure, M. 2013. Researching without representation? Language and materiality in post-qualitative methodology. *International Journal of Qualitative Studies in Education*, 26:658-667. https://doi.org/10.1080/09518398.2013.788755

Mauthner, N.S. 2018. A posthumanist ethics of mattering: New materialisms and the ethical practice of inquiry. In: R. Iphofen & M. Tolich (eds). *Foundational issues in qualitative research ethics*. Los Angeles, CA: Sage, 51-72. https://doi.org/10.4135/9781526435446.n4

Merleau-Ponty, M. 2002 [1945]. *Phenomenology of perception* (Trans. C. Smith). New York, NY: Routledge. https://doi.org/10.4324/9780203994610

Rosiek, J.L., Snyder, J. & Pratt, S.L. 2019. The new materialisms and indigenous theories of non-human agency: Making the case for respectful anti-colonial engagement. *Qualitative Inquiry,* 26(3/4):331-346. https://doi.org/10.1177/1077800419830135

Schmahmann, B. 2013. *Picturing change: Curating visual culture at post-apartheid universities*. Johannesburg: Wits University Press. https://doi.org/10.18772/12013045805

Smith, L.D. 2011. *An overview of signature learning with special reference to its future adoption at Stellenbosch University.* Stellenbosch University. Retrieved from http://blogs.sun.ac.za/teaching/files/2011/12/Final-report-22-September-20112.pdf [Accessed 2 October 2020].

SU (Stellenbosch University). N.d.(a). *100 years of learning, growing and moving together (Centenary commemoration).* Retrieved from http://www0.sun.ac.za/100/en/It [Accessed 2 October 2020].

SU (Stellenbosch University). N.d.(b). *Graduate attributes.* Retrieved from http://www.sun.ac.za/english/learning-teaching/student-affairs/Documents/Graduate_Attributes_ENG.pdf [Accessed 2 October 2020].

SU (Stellenbosch University). 2013a. *Report of the task team on the inquiry into unacceptable welcoming practices.* Retrieved from http://www.sun.ac.za/english/learning-teaching/student-affairs/Documents/ENG_Finale%20Verslag%20-%20Onaanvaarbare%20verwelkomingspraktyke%20(Eng)%20-%20IJR-weergawe.pdf [Accessed 2 October 2020].

SU (Stellenbosch University). 2013b. *SU HOPE Project.* Retrieved from http://www.sun.ac.za/english/faculty/arts/graduate-school/about-us/donors/su-hope-project [Accessed 2 October 2020].

SU (Stellenbosch University). 2013c. What makes you feel welcome at SU? Report. Own documentation.

SU (Stellenbosch University). 2017. *Recommendations of the task team for the decolonisation of the Stellenbosch University curriculum.* Retrieved from http://www.sun.ac.za/english/transformation/Documents/SU%20Decolonisation%20Task%20Team%20Final%20Report%20with%20Annexures.pdf [Accessed 2 October 2020].

Watts, V. 2013. Indigenous place-thought and agency amongst humans and non-humans (First Woman and Sky Woman go on a European world tour!). *Decolonization: Indigeneity, Education & Society,* 2:20-34.

Zembylas, M. 2014. Theorizing 'difficult knowledge' in the aftermath of the 'affective turn': Implications for curriculum and pedagogy in handling traumatic representations. *Curriculum Inquiry,* 44(3):390-412. https://doi.org/10.1111/curi.12051

Section B

Site-based visual redress initiatives at the university

Chapter 5

Preserving knowledge: The Stellenbosch University Library visual redress journey

Ellen Tise, Stephané Conradie and Mimi Seyffert-Wirth

Introduction

This chapter addresses the Stellenbosch University (SU) Library's visual redress journey within the context of the Library's mandate of preserving knowledge past and present. Libraries have the responsibility to preserve, conserve and provide access to information and all human knowledge, without barriers. The chapter discusses the SU Library visual redress activities within this context and the broader SU visual redress projects. A brief historical overview and context of the Library and its Special Collections division will be provided, followed by discussions of visual redress initiatives, such as the name change of the SU Library and the Visual Arts student project, and other activities such as the refurbishment of spaces to make the Library more inclusive, the centenary exhibition of the Library in 2018, signage and the relocation of artworks, historical artefacts and maps from public areas.

Two major visual redress projects coincided with the University's visual redress project initiatives after 2015, namely the name change of the Library and the Visual Arts student project. Other initiatives in the Library started earlier. These include changing the signage in the Library to three languages (Afrikaans, English and isiXhosa) which has been ongoing since 2005, the removal of artwork and staff photos of years ago from public places such as the staff room around mid-2006, including the removal of the bust of JS Gericke from the entrance of the Library and the DC Boonzaier collection of sepia sketches to Special Collections. With the exception of the renaming of the SU Library, which was a formal process, and the Visual Arts student project, which was an academic project, the other visual redress activities in the Library were informal. These were a result of SU's developments that flowed from its broader transformation agenda, the HOPE Project, changes in student demographics and engagement, changes in the staff profile of the Library and feedback/comments received from clients and alumni. In some cases, staff and other stakeholders were consulted, but final decisions were taken by Library management.

Historical overview and context of the Stellenbosch University Library

Just more than a century ago, when Victoria College officially became Stellenbosch University in 1918, the institution already had a well-developed library service, which was situated in the CL Marais Building. The Library started out as a reading room in 1895. It had a formal set of regulations, an officially appointed librarian and a library advisory committee that consisted of five distinguished professors (Library and Information Service, 2018:4).

In 1895, a notice appeared in the Calendar of Victoria College, which stated that "the College has a Reading and Reference Library for the use of students and during the past year an additional room has been set apart as a Reading Room" (Calendar of the Victoria College, Stellenbosch, session 1895-6, 1895:15). This reading room was situated in the Old Main Building and the material available there originated from the collections of the Stellenbosch Gymnasium, the Arts Department of the Gymnasium and the Stellenbosch College, later known as Victoria College.

As early as 1912, the Scots-American millionaire Andrew Carnegie donated the sum of £6 000 towards the extension and maintenance of the library of Victoria College. An additional donation of £1 500 from the Carnegie Corporation made to SU in 1938 as well as contributions from alumni enabled the University to build a new library. In 1938, the Carnegie Building was erected on the site of the Pavilion rugby grounds, adjacent to and north of the present Administration Building (Block B). This building would become the home of the University Library for the next 50 years.

The next phase of the University Library was the erection of the JS Gericke Library, named after Reverend JS (Kosie) Gericke, who served as vice-chancellor of the University from 1952 to 1981. The construction of the JS Gericke Library building commenced in 1981 and in 1983 the move to the new building took place. This building occupies the unique position of being built underneath the centrally situated Jan Marais Square. The reason for this unique position is that in planning a new library, it was found that, apart from the Jan Marais Square, no centrally situated building sites were available on campus. However, the historical importance of the Jan Marais Square and the architectural aesthetics of the historic buildings surrounding the square meant that this site could not be defaced with a multi-storeyed building. It was therefore decided to build underground (Library and Information Service, 2017).

As can be noted from the above, the history and visual images of the SU Library is intrinsically linked and part and parcel of the University's history and as such, it was not a surprise that during the 2015 #RhodesMustFall and #FeesMustFall protests the SU Library was identified as an 'untransformed' space and that visually prominent areas such as the Library's Special Collections reflect only white Afrikaner history. This situation inspired the Visual Arts student project in the Library, among other projects, which will be discussed later in this chapter. The next section provides an overview of the Special Collections division, followed by a discussion of some of the visual redress activities in the Library.

Special Collections

The Special Collections division in the SU Library consists of three sections, namely Africana, Manuscripts section and Rare Books. It is one of the spaces in the Library with a very distinctive historical visual appearance, primarily shaped by the material and collections housed there, as well as a few prominent pieces of furniture and artwork, each with its own historical significance and intrinsic value. This section will provide a short history of all three sections, address the current visual representation of the division as well as visual redress in the division and lastly focus on the role of digital technologies in terms of Special Collections and visual redress.

The well-known definition of 'Africana' by Douglas Varley (1949:5), former head of the South African National Library, reads as follows:

> When we speak of Africana we mean to imply all those objects large and small, natural and man-made, that relate to the history of Africa and of Southern Africa in particular … More specifically, we think of Africana in terms of human settlement in the sub-continent – but always in terms of history and the living past.

Varley's definition is still considered today, although the term 'Africana' in later years came to refer more specifically to books, illustrations, printed material and art (Bradlow, 1970:46). Most important, however, is that the items should have some connection with southern Africa. According to Kennedy (1965:1), for South Africans this specifically means old and rare books associated with their own country.

The Africana section of Special Collections is primarily built on the Hugh Solomon Collection, which was donated to the Library in 1958, a donation facilitated by the then rector of SU, Prof. HB Thom. This unique and valuable collection consists of 18th- and 19th-century travellers' journals and other early views of Africa, historical maps of Africa, as well as rare pamphlets and pictorial Africana. Through the years, the collection has been augmented with books on all aspects of sub-Saharan African history.

The Manuscripts section was founded in 1967 with the specific purpose of housing the DF Malan manuscript collection, which was donated to the Library as part of a bigger donation, which included furniture and artefacts, to the University. Soon more donations followed, especially from Afrikaans literary figures, which resulted in the section having a focus on Afrikaans literature, South African cultural history and South African political history. In recent years it has been a strategic objective of the Library to enrich and diversify Special Collections by sourcing new collections that are more representative of our country's history and people. Some recent additions include the Frederik Van Zyl Slabbert, the Institute for Democracy in South Africa (IDASA) and the Maguire San Ethnobotanical collections. Today, the section holds more than 450 manuscript collections that vary in size, type and focus.

The Rare Books section was established in the 1960s to provide for the safekeeping of valuable art books and other rare materials. The collection was enriched by a collection acquired in 1986 by the Library from Commander Michael Scott, a collector of rare bindings, antiquarian books on various subjects and rare first editions of English literature. Other niche subject areas, such as books in native South African languages and rare children's books, were added as the collection grew. Today the collection boasts books published from the 15th century right up to the present day on a variety of subjects.

The three sections with their various backgrounds contribute to the visual representation of the division as a whole. This visual representation is perceived by some as colonial, dated, exclusive and even offensive. Libraries have a role as custodians of knowledge and history and a responsibility to fulfil their contemporary custodian role with sensitivity. Libraries also have the dual role of preservation and providing access to all information contained in them. In Special Collections, the complicated nature of these dual roles is amplified when taking into account the age and type of material preserved there.

As mentioned earlier, the current visual representation of the division is shaped by some key pieces of art, furniture, core collections and other items, which give the space its unique look and feel. One of the most prominent is the Hugh Solomon historical maps that adorn the back walls in the Africana section. They form part of a collection of over 100 maps of Africa, printed before 1860, including two manuscript maps. These maps are fascinating visual timelines of African history as seen through European eyes. While the Eurocentrism of these maps may be experienced as problematic by some, they have significant research and historical value. The oldest map in the collection, Abraham Ortelius's "Africae Tabula Nova Edita Antverpia", dating from 1570, for example, is considered by RV Tooley (1969:88) as "one of the corner-stones of any African map collection".

Another prominent feature in the Africana section is the freestanding weight-driven pendulum grandfather clock by Johann Junck, dating from 1777. This clock is the only one of its type that was made in its entirety at the Cape in the 18th century (Pearce, 1960:97). The clock was the property of previous SU rector HB Thom, and donated to the University after his death. The clock was the first object to be declared a national heritage object by the former Monuments Commission in 1963.

In the Manuscripts section, the space is dominated by a number of busts representing primarily Afrikaans literary figures whose collections are kept in the section. These include NP van Wyk Louw by Moses Kottler, WEG Louw by Nell Kaye and DJ Opperman by Philip Terblanche. Paintings from artists whose collections are held in the section also feature, including works by Sheila Cussons, Marjorie Wallace and Erik Laubscher.

In the Rare Books section of the Library, the atmosphere and visual representation are mainly shaped by the wooden cabinets containing antiquarian books with leather bindings, giving the relatively small space the look and feel of a traditional library. Over the last few years, visual redress efforts have been undertaken in the division. Most notable was the replacement of some artworks with art from the IDASA collection, depicting, inter alia, the Dakar Conference of 1987, in which some SU students and academics controversially participated with the then banned African National Congress, and the 1994 South African elections. These striking mixed-media works now grace the walls proudly next to items such as the autographed photograph of delegates of the 1908 National Convention in South Africa, which was a forerunner for the establishment of the Union of South Africa founded on a white polity in 1910. As such, collections representing South Africa's move to democracy are juxtaposed with collections representing the country's segregationist past.

Lastly, in terms of a holistic view of Special Collections, it is prudent to also focus on how modern technology and the internet helped libraries fulfil their dual role in providing access to information for all, while preserving the information for posterity. In 2013, the Library launched SUNDigital Collections, an online digital heritage repository showcasing unique library collections and providing researchers and the public with unhindered access to these collections. In the context of visual redress, the repository is important, as it is a graphically driven platform designed to showcase collections and individual items from the Library within context.

The repository currently hosts over 13 000 items in 27 collections. These range between collections covering southern African history from the 16th century, in the form of antiquarian map and vernacular architecture collections, to the 19th century, in the form of *Die Zuid-Afrikaan* newspaper and the WJ Leyds South African War collections, to the 21st century. Some significant collections include the Maguire San Ethnobotanical Collection, which features extraordinary images of indigenous African food plants and information related to the plants, the Rudolf Marloth collection of botanical illustrations and the André Pretorius collection featuring many South African architectural treasures that have since been destroyed or demolished. Collections on South African political history, such as the *Vrye Weekblad*, the Beyers Naudé and the

Frederik van Zyl Slabbert collections, are also hosted, as well as South African music and literature collections. Importantly, digital technologies have also given the Library an additional virtual space to focus on visual redress.

The Documentation Centre for Music (DOMUS), located in the Music Library, is also considered an important special collection of the Library and Information Service. DOMUS was formally created in 2005 after receiving collections through donations and bequests for over 50 years. These more than 70 collections are mostly of South African importance, but in some cases also have international significance. The vision of DOMUS (2006) is to …

> … promote music in South Africa and Africa by collecting, preserving, ordering and cataloguing the music and documentary collections of composers, performing artists, musicologists and music institutions. As an archive with strong connections to music research DOMUS aims, through strategic projects of research, publication, performance and recordings, to maintain the expressive cultures represented in these collections as an important part of a broad South African heritage.

While DOMUS started out by hosting more classical South African music documentation collections, e.g. the Albert Coates and Arnold van Wyk collections, its focus has shifted to be a much more inclusive music archive, especially through cooperation with Africa Open Institute for Music, Research and Innovation. Some of the significant collections that have been acquired include the Hidden Years Music Archive Project, collections on South African jazz cultures and the collection of the EOAN Group, founded in 1933 as a social and educational centre and cultural association that offered music training for the community of District Six.

Renaming of the JS Gericke Library

In 2015, the University's Committee for the Naming of Buildings, Venues, Facilities and other Premises proposed that the then named JS Gericke Library undergo a process of possible renaming as part of a larger transformation process for the furtherance of a welcoming culture at SU. In accordance with the policy, a task team, consisting of academic experts, relevant administrative staff and representatives from the Students' Representative Council (SRC), was put together during an inclusive process in 2016. The members of the task team were Monica du Toit (Transformation Office), Prof. Albert Grundlingh (Department of History), Prof. Gerhard Lubbe (Faculty of Law), Ellen Tise (Senior Director: Library and Information Service), Dr Trevor van Louw (SUNCEP), Stefan Laing (Chairman: Students' Representative Council, September 2014 – August 2015) and Prof. Hendrik Bosman (Faculty of Theology – convenor). The task team's commission included the following aspects:

- Determine possible reasons to rename the JS Gericke Library.
- Follow an inclusive process while considering a new name for the Library.
- The inclusive process should proceed within the context of the existing Policy on the naming of buildings, venues and other facilities/premises (SU, 2010), and according to the approved operational procedures.

In terms of the reasons for the renaming of the JS Gericke Library, there was consensus that the Policy on the naming of buildings, venues and other facilities/premises gave the University the right to reconsider names. Wide consultation on campus indicated that the JS Gericke Library was in the top 10 buildings whose names should be reconsidered. The main reason for this was that Dr Gericke neither made a significant financial contribution to the University Library, nor did he have any specific connection with the University Library. Whereas the name was relevant in an earlier context of the University, the sentiment was that it was no longer relevant in terms of the SU's vision for the future (Stellenbosch University, 2017).

Who was JS Gericke and why was the naming of the Library after him deemed 'sensitive'?

As stated earlier, JS Gericke (1911–1981) was vice-chancellor of SU from 1953 until 1981, a period of almost 29 years (from 1918 to 1981 the office of vice-chancellor was separate from that of the rector). According to a death notice in the *Cape Times* of 18 August 1981, Gericke was a "man of many parts who wielded considerable influence in religious, academic, cultural, political and business spheres" (*Cape Times*, 1981:9). Gericke studied Theology at SU and served as a minister in the

Dutch Reformed Church. He was awarded an honorary doctorate by SU in 1966 (Thom, 1966). Gericke was a prominent member of the Afrikaner Broederbond and served as a member of its executive council from 1961, and as vice-chairman of the same body from 1963 to 1970 (Stals, 1998:760). According to Van der Wijden (2012:108), Gericke was a member of the Afrikaner Broederbond since around 1936.

Taking into consideration Gericke's background described above, it is clear that in the context and in pursuit of the larger transformation process at SU and the furtherance of a welcoming culture, having a building named after a person so closely linked to what some described as the University's 'racist' past was no longer acceptable and needed to be changed.

Further, in accordance with the policy (SU, 2010), the following guidelines were followed for the renaming of the JS Gericke Library:

- Renaming of buildings takes place after consultation with local communities.
- Renaming should, as far as possible, be timeless.
- Transformation initiatives may not be restricted.
- Buildings should preferably have descriptive or functional names.
- Naming after persons carries a risk and should be considered carefully. The person's life and work should emphasise the core values of SU.
- Names of buildings may only be changed if the appropriate operational procedures are followed.
- The history of a renamed building can be communicated to the public in the form of a plaque.
- The renaming of buildings is delegated to the Executive Committee of the University Council.

To give effect to an inclusive process of consultation regarding the possible renaming of the Library, the following interest groups were involved in the process of consultation by means of a questionnaire:

- SU personnel: faculty executive committees, with special attention to the senior staff of the University Library
- SU students: via the SRC and student committees within different faculties
- Local communities in Stellenbosch: the Council for Church Cooperation and the Stellenbosch Heritage Project (e'Bosch)
- Family of Dr JS Gericke: three daughters.

After the extensive consultation process, the majority of the respondents were in favour of the renaming of the JS Gericke Library. The majority of respondents preferred a descriptive name, as opposed to a name that depicts a symbol or the name of a well-known person. More than 80% of the senior library staff preferred the descriptive or functional renaming. It was recommended that the name be changed to include 'Stellenbosch University' and that it is presented in the three prominent languages of the regions: Universiteit Stellenbosch Biblioteek / Stellenbosch University Library / IThala leeNcwadi leYunivesithi yaseStellenbosch. The University's Executive Committee accepted the proposed name of the main library that was recommended by the Committee on the Naming of Buildings, Venues, Facilities and other Premises. The University Council endorsed the name change at its meeting of 19 June 2017.

Figure 5.1: Entrance Stellenbosch University Library (photo by Hennie Rudman, 2020)

Visual Arts student project

Visual redress has been an important part of the decolonialisation conversations happening after the student protests of 2015–2016 at South African universities. The rationale for looking at the current visual landscape of our universities is a pivotal part of addressing representation within South Africa's history of colonisation, apartheid and the turbulence of our new democracy where the vast majority of the people in our country's histories have either been taught through a colonial lens or have been erased completely. Some examples of how students have addressed these issues were seen in the #RhodesMustFall movement, with the removal of the statue of Cecil John Rhodes from the University of Cape Town's upper campus and the burning and removal of some of the artworks in the University of Cape Town's permanent art collection. Although some praised the students' actions, others argued that there should be a less contentious way of dealing with visual representation on university campuses that, instead of advocating for the removal of statues, would open a dialogue in which the different perspectives and histories are placed in conversation with one another.

In 2018, Stephané Conradie (co-author of this chapter), a lecturer in the Department of Visual Arts, was approached by Prof. Elmarie Costandius from the same department to revisit some of the locations on SU's campus that had been highlighted by black students as areas of discomfort during the student protests of 2015 and 2016 as well as before. The Library's Special Collections division was highlighted as one of these spaces because of the collection of books, busts and other artefacts it housed. During the protests, students identified the Special Collections division as still housing remnants of the University's apartheid and colonial past. Students felt that there was no contextualisation of the University's continued hosting of books and busts that were viewed as residual materials of its Afrikaner nationalist past. They also felt that the collection was not representative of the histories of the majority of the people living in South Africa. This collection was interpreted as the University upholding its legacy as the architects of apartheid, while paying insufficient attention to the ongoing marginalisation of black people on campus.

Elmarie Costandius and Stephané Conradie approached the Special Collections division of the Library to host a workshop with second-year Visual Communication Design students from the Department of Visual Arts in the Faculty of Arts and Social Sciences, in which they were required to interact with the collection. In groups, they were given a tour of the Special Collections division, after which they were allowed to interact with some of the artefacts and books housed in the collection. After a brief introduction to the space, the students were required to research or investigate a person or an event in South Africa's recent history that did not fall into the main canons of South Africa's history or people/events that had been erased or misrepresented. During the colonial and apartheid eras it was common practice to provide historical biases, which included reductionist and essentialist viewpoints on race, gender and culture. They were then required to envision who they would have liked to see represented in Stellenbosch's present institutional landscape, such as the Special Collections division. After their initial interaction, they were required to do a thorough historical investigation into the life of the person or the circumstances leading up the event they had chosen. The Special Collections division of the Library was available to them for research purposes for this project and they were also encouraged to make use of the entire library. After compiling their information, they were required to design an imaginative poster or illustration of the person or event that incorporated both image and text. The students were divided into groups of two or three for this project.

The outcome of the project was a fully designed, produced and hand-pulled screen-printed poster that could function as an informative poster/design of a historical figure. Such a poster would be placed inside the Special Collections division of the Library as a basis for a dialogue with some of the books, busts and artefacts that were viewed as representative of South Africa's colonial and racist past. Along with their editioned prints, they included a short summery or description of the historical investigation they did into the person or event illustrated in their posters. The aim of the project was to introduce the students to decolonial practice-based research that specifically problematises representation in visual landscapes within institutional settings.

In the posters that the students designed during the workshop, activism was the most prominent theme that emerged. Two groups chose to look at LGBTQQIAP activists,[56] namely Beverley Palesa Ditsie and Tseko Simon Nkoli. Five other groups looked at how artists such as musicians Mariam Makeba and Ralph Rabie and writers and poets such as Miriam Tlali, Breyten Breytenbach and Keorapetse Kgositsile all used their art as a form of activism. Another group focused on Nkosi Johnson, particularly on the role that his adoptive and birth mothers played in his HIV/AIDS activism. Another group concentrated on some of the more difficult aspects of activism during apartheid by highlighting the complexities surrounding James Seipei's death and Winnie Mandela's alleged involvement in Seipei's death. A final group focused on the deaths of activists Mlungisi Griffiths Mxenge and Victoria Nomyamezelo Mxenge at the hands of the apartheid state.

---

56 Lesbian, gay, bisexual, transgender, queer, questioning, intersex, asexual, pansexual

Within the theme of activism, most students positioned their chosen historical figure(s) in a prominent position of honour, while allowing specific and important aspects of the activists' life histories to unfold in the surrounding compositions on the posters they produced. This tactic was deployed by the students to make visible their chosen historical figures, whose information would normally be hidden in the pages of the books Special Collections housed. The posters were designed to sit alongside and form a dialogue with some of the older artefacts in the Special Collections division. The purpose of the workshop was to create an inviting atmosphere where depictions of more recent and important historical figures would be able to entice students and researchers to interact critically with Special Collections' expansive archive. While there are many books, artefacts and artworks in the Special Collections division that could still be read as preserving colonial and apartheid legacies, new additions are continually being added to the collection that place emphasis on South Africa's democracy and the resistance struggles that led South Africa into a democratic era. This also reflects the tensions that are present within our current democracy, where the old and new are continually being negotiated.

One group's poster in particular (see Figure 5.2) dealt with the theme of negotiating difficult tensions in a deliberate and thought-provoking way. Their poster stood out because instead of elevating the obvious hero, in this case Winnie Mandela, the group chose to question the events surrounding James Seipei's death. Winnie Mandela died in April 2018, which was the same year that the students participated in this visual redress project. During the project, which took place in October, the group reflected on a documentary that was released celebrating Winnie Mandela's life. The group felt that although most people were celebrating Winnie Mandela's life, there were some controversial aspects of her activism during apartheid that made it difficult to separate her activism from the death of James Seipei. This group's poster has the following description taken from Augustyn and Zandberg (2018):

> James Seipei was born in 1974. At age 10, he had already made a name for himself as one of South Africa's youngest political activists against the apartheid system. Known as Stompie Moeketsi or Stompie Seipei, James was also fondly referred to as the 'Young General' and frequently encouraged other young people to take part

in the struggle. At the age of 14, James, along with four other boys, was kidnapped from Bishop Paul Verryn's home and beaten by members of the Mandela United Football Club, Winnie Madikizela-Mandela's personal bodyguards. His body was discovered on 6 January 1989, dumped near her house. Following the murder, the three surviving boys accused Bishop Verryn of sexual misconduct, but have since retracted their claims, stating that they were forced by their abductors to make these accusations. Ms Madikizela-Mandela pleaded innocence to allegations of orchestrating the abduction and murder. This did not stop the National Party's use of the murder as propaganda, nor the rumours that James Seipei's murder was tied to the murder of his doctor, Dr Abu Baker Asvat. Layered with uncertainty and allegations that both James and his murderer, Jerry Richardson, were police informants, the case of Stompie Seipei serves as a horrible reminder of the complexities inherent in oppression and resistance.

From the group's description, James Seipei takes on the role of an anti-hero for being a suspected informant, as well as being a young political activist. This is directly contrasted with Winnie Mandela, who is painted as a hero in post-apartheid South Africa. Activists currently still gravitate towards Winnie Mandela for her contribution to the liberation struggle. During the #FeesMustFall protests at SU, an occupied administration building was temporarily named after her. Instead of the common activist icon of Winnie Mandela, the artwork of this group foregrounds James Seipei as an iconic figure. His eyes glare at the lens, which faces him from the initial photograph the drawing was derived from. Surrounding him in the top left-hand corner are the newspaper clippings detailing the events that led to his death and the controversy that surrounded it afterwards. The clippings are printed in a brown ink and are difficult to read, mirroring the muddied nature of his death. The map of the Sowetan neighbourhood, where he lived and was murdered, forms some of the details in his face and spreads out into the background of the poster, grounding the composition and foregrounding the location of his death as well as where his body was found. All of the people who were involved in Seipei's death are printed in a translucent pink ink in the bottom right-hand corner. The translucent nature of the images points towards the ghostly nature of the past that still haunts Winnie Mandela's legacy currently, even after her own death.

*Figure 5.2: The Stompie Seipei saga
(screenprint by David Augustyn and Jacobus S.W. Zandberg, SU, 2018)*

The second theme to emerge from the project was the celebration of women who had been overlooked by South African historical canons. One of the groups working with this theme firstly looked at women who are still not widely recognised for the contributions they made in their specific fields of research. Secondly, within this theme, the group highlighted the unjust ways in which black women were objectified by colonial quasi-scientific pursuits. Another group chose to celebrate early forms of resistance to patriarchal systems by celebrating an unnamed San woman who stood up to her community and husband in an attempt to better her life for herself and her children. This overarching theme overlapped with the dominant theme of activism, as many groups also chose now prominent black women artists and writers as their focus, such as Miriam Makeba and Miriam Tlali. The groups who solely worked with the second thematic approach derived their information specifically from books they had come across in the Special Collections division in the SU Library.

The first group that focused on the second theme discussed in the previous paragraph took on a comparative approach, where they contrasted the different experiences of black women, such as Sara Baartman, with that of white women, such as Margaret Levyns, during South Africa's colonial and apartheid periods. The group's poster design (see Figure 5.3) looked at women's experiences relatively, in the way that science elevated, to some extent, the one group and subjected/objectified the other. The first group's poster description was taken from Du Plessis and Robinson (2018):

> Originally inspired by the role of women in the South African scientific community, specifically in the realm of botany, the group looked at the work of female botanists. During the early years of science in South Africa, when women were not yet accepted and valued as scientists, there were an unexpectedly high number of female botanists. We came to understand that this was a result of botany being seen as a somewhat acceptable pursuit for women, somewhere in-between the practices of gardening, drawing and science. This belief allowed women to use botany as a foot in the door to academic pursuits, a way to gain recognition and respect from the wider academic community. In particular, [we] looked at the work of Margaret Levyns, the first woman to be awarded a doctorate in science from the University of Cape Town. Some of Levyns's most notable work was on the genus Muraltia, specifically the Muraltia spinosa, colloquially known as the skilpadbessie. While some white women were fortunate to find a way to use science to gain standing in the patriarchal establishment, others suffered under science as a tool of oppression. Such was the case of Sara Baartman, a Khoikhoi woman, who was displayed in circuses, freak shows and travelling zoos around Europe, all because of her anatomy. Baartman, like many Khoikhoi women, had large buttocks and elongated labia. European men made a profit by displaying Sara's body to the public, while anatomists, zoologists and physiologists studied her anatomy and concluded that the Khoi people were the link between humans and animals. The group used the imagery of the skilpadbessie, found in Levyns's work on the genus, and labelled the images anatomically, as a tribute to how Baartman herself

was reduced to a scientific specimen rather than a human being, and her anatomy labelled as such. The two figures in the centre represent both women and their experiences of being elevated or subjugated through science.

The central motif in this group's poster design depicts Margaret Levyns and Sara Baartman. Levyns is positioned in the centre on top of Baartman to show that she had some successes in her career as a woman botanist. Baartman is positioned at the bottom of the central motif to indicate that she had little autonomy. She was objectified and sexualised for her 'different' body parts, which were seen as 'abnormal' relative to European standards of beauty during South Africa's colonial period. The central motif displays hierarchy. Along with the composition's hierarchical depictions in which both women are placed, the colours used to depict each woman indicates yet another difference of race. The pink of Levyns's body illustrates how white women had access to academic careers in botany. This is contrasted by the brown ink used for Baartman's body, demonstrating how brown Khoikhoi woman were sexualised because of their 'strange' body parts. As the group discussed in their poster's description, white woman were allowed to practise science, while brown women became the subject of quasi-science. The rest of the composition is dominated by scientific illustrative discourses. The flowers have two symbolic meanings. Firstly, they honour Levyns's work on the genus Muraltia. Secondly, the reproductive parts of the flowers are used to point to Baartman's sexualisation and objectification because of her elongated genitalia and large buttocks. The colour palette stays consistent throughout, playing on the colours of different body parts and normative depictions of race, rather than using the actual scientific colours of the actual flowers. The words used to describe Baartman's genitalia are strategically placed within the composition to mimic scientific illustrative methods.

Figure 5.3: Muraltia spinosa (screenprint by Anja du Plessis and Alexa Robinson, SU, 2018)

It was interesting to note that the outcome of this project was in contrast to the initial views that were highlighted by the students, namely that Special Collections only houses remnants of SU's apartheid/colonial/Afrikaner nationalist past and that the collections are not representative enough. The historical figures based on the material in Special Collections highlight that the collections are indeed more representative of other groups and showcase the efforts that have been made in terms of visual address in the section, as mentioned earlier.

Other visual redress processes and outcomes in the Library

Signage

One of the first notable visual changes in the Library was related to signage in 2005. As with other University buildings, the signage in the Library was originally in Afrikaans only, then later in Afrikaans and English, and since 2005 it was decided to change all the main signage into the three official languages of the Western Cape, namely Afrikaans, English and isiXhosa. With the changes in the demographics of students and the staff profile in the Library, the aim was to make the Library more inclusive and user-friendly.

Other (artworks, maps, etc.)

Following the signage, around 2006 to 2008, some artwork and artefacts that were regarded as colonial and not representative of an inclusive culture, including the bust of JS Gericke, old staff photos when there were mainly white staff working in the Library and the framed DC Boonzaier collection of sepia sketches representing famous figures of the 19th century, were removed from public spaces and relocated to closed areas. Some library staff and users reacted negatively to these changes and did not see the need to make the Library more inclusive. These events led to the Library re-examining the visual presentation of some of its collections and looking at ways to effect more changes. During this time, the University's Transformation Office informed the acting senior director of the Library at the time that the office received complaints from students finding the maps hanging on the wall outside Special Collections very "offensive".

After the complaints were received and deliberations between Library management and the staff of Special Collections, it was decided to temporarily remove the maps for security reasons and to safeguard the maps. There was a concern with the notion of 'censuring' library collections, but being cognisant of the damage to artworks at other universities in South Africa during the #RhodesMustFall period, the Library's view was that it is better to take preventative measures and to use this as an opportunity to contribute to the transformation and reconciliation processes at SU. The maps are now safely preserved in the strong room in Special Collections. In its place is an exhibition that highlights the University's 2018 centenary in the form of a wallpaper leading to the entrance of Special Collections, discussed below.

Spaces

In 2010, the Learning Commons – a flagship initiative of the HOPE Project – opened its doors. Its interactive learning spaces, equipment and facilities have since been supporting information literacy skills training for undergraduates. This was an important step towards achieving the Library's strategic goal to develop it as a vibrant and inviting physical and virtual space.

Master's and doctoral students, academics and researchers also received a dedicated space of their own when the state-of-the-art Carnegie Research Commons was opened in 2011. The facility encourages scholarly dialogue, quiet personal study and research support. Linked to this was the naming of the Research Commons as the Carnegie Research Commons in November. The naming ceremony also celebrated the University's century-old relationship with the Carnegie Corporation based in New York.

Centenary exhibition

As part of the University's centenary commemorations in 2018, the Library took the opportunity to showcase the past and present of SU through its centenary exhibition and the strides it had made in its visual redress journey. In 2018, a centenary exhibition celebrating SU's 100-year existence was put up in the SU Library. The exhibition is titled *1918–2018: Past and present / Hede en verlede*, and includes the subsections *Stellenbosch University Library and Information Service – then and now ...*, *Student life – the spirit of the times* and *Maties Sport – champions then, champions now*.

The exhibition is in the form of a very large piece of printed wallpaper leading up to the entrance of the Special Collections division. The exhibition is based on items in the Library, including items from Special Collections and SUNDigital Collections, and designed to tell a story by means of a visual timeline. A website allowing the viewer to interact with the exhibition was also created.[57] The viewer is encouraged to click through on individual images featured in the exhibition in order to find detailed descriptions of the images. The exhibition celebrates a specific event that has passed, but has become a vibrant visual addition to the SU Library and is therefore retained.

Conclusion

As mentioned at the start of the chapter, the visual redress initiatives in the Library and Information Service at SU were not all undertaken as part of the formal or as a result of the broader University visual redress project. Some of the initiatives happened to coincide with the University's project after 2015. Nevertheless, the visual redress journey of the Library, including the name change of the SU Library, the Visual Arts student project and the visual changes in Special Collections, has come a long way to address and contribute to greater representational inclusivity and advancing the transformation agenda of SU.

This chapter discussed the interaction among history, process, participation and contestation. The outcomes of the Library's initiatives illustrate the different ways of moving towards visual redress in one environment. Three examples stood out. First was the name change from JS Gericke Library to the Stellenbosch University Library. This was a consultative and participative committee process that resulted in a significant break with the past that presented an ideology that was exclusionary.

Second was the Visual Arts student project, an educational engagement and dialogical process that also produced fruitful outcomes. At the start of the project, students felt that the collections in Special Collections were not representative of the histories of the majority of the people living in South Africa. They perceived

---

57 http://timeline.lib.sun.ac.za

the collections as the University upholding its legacy as the architects of apartheid. However, the most prominent theme that emerged from the subjects selected by the students was activism, representing well-known activists who used their art as a form of activism. The outcome of the project can now be used as a basis for a dialogue with the books, busts and artefacts that were viewed as representative of South Africa's colonial and racist past.

Third were the visual redress efforts in Special Collections, such as the replacement of artworks, the acquisition of collections such as those of IDASA, Maguire San Ethnobotanical, Beyers Naudé and Frederick van Zyl Slabbert, which show a positive change without the Library compromising its custodian role to preserve and make knowledge and information available. Having said this, the SU Library can still do more to expand its collections to make it more representative and embracing of South Africa's heritage. This should not ignore the fact that libraries have the dual role of preservation and providing access to all information contained in them. SU Library's visual redress journey continues.

References

Augustyn, D. & Zandberg, J.S.W. 2018. *The Stompie Seipei sage* [screenprint]. Sun Digital Collections, Stellenbosch University. Retrieved from http://hdl.handle.net/10019.2/15463 [Accessed 5 September 2020].

Bradlow, F.R. 1970. Africana. In: D.J. Potgieter (ed). *Standard Encyclopaedia of Southern Africa*. Cape Town: Nasou, 46.

Calendar of the Victoria College, Stellenbosch, session 1895-6. 1895. College library and museum. Stellenbosch: Victoria College, 15.

Cape Times. 1981. Tributes to Dr Kosie Gericke, 18 August.

DOMUS. 2006. *Background*. Retrieved from https://www.domus.ac.za/content/view/12/26/ [Accessed 11 September 2020].

Du Plessis, A. & Robinson, A. 2018. *Muraltia spinosa* [screenprint]. Sun Digital Collections, Stellenbosch University. Retrieved from http://hdl.handle.net/10019.2/15474 [Accessed 5 September 2020].

Kennedy, R.F. 1965. *Africana repository*. Cape Town: Juta.

Library and Information Service. 2017. *History of Stellenbosch University Library*. Retrieved from http://library.sun.ac.za/en-za/AboutUs/Pages/history-central.aspx [Accessed 11 September 2020].

Library and Information Service. 2018. *Library and Information Service annual report 2018*. Retrieved from https://library.sun.ac.za/SiteCollectionDocuments/pubs/Annual%20Report%202018%20ENG%20(3MB).pdf [Accessed 11 September 2020].

Pearce, G.E. 1960. *Eighteenth century furniture in South Africa*. Pretoria: Van Schaik.

Stals, E.L.P. 1998. G*eskiedenis van die Afrikaner-Broederbond,* 1918-1994. S.l.: S.n.

SU (Stellenbosch University). 2010. *Policy on the naming of buildings, venues and other facilities/premises.* Retrieved fromhttps://www.sun.ac.za/english/Finance/Documents/Policies/NAAMGEWING%20EN%20VERNOEMING%20VAN%20GEBOUE%20ENG.pdf [Accessed 11 September 2020].

SU (Stellenbosch University). 2017. *Report of the Task Team on the possible renaming of the JS Gericke Library.*

Thom, H.B. 1966. Dr J.S. Gericke - Honorary doctorate - Stellenbosch University. H.B. Thom Collection, MS 191.T.7(6/14). Manuscripts section, Stellenbosch University Library and Information Service.

Tooley, R.V. 1969. *Collectors' guide to maps of the African continent and Southern Africa*. London: Carta.

Van der Wijden, M. 2012. Broederbond op Matieland: case study van de relatie tussen de Universiteit van Stellenbosch en de Afrikaner Broederbond, 1932-1955. Unpublished MA thesis. Antwerp: University of Antwerpen.

Varley, D.H. 1949. *Adventures in Africana*. Cape Town: UCT Press.

Chapter 6

Reflections on visual transformation in a science context and future implications

Faadiel Essop
Centre for Cardio-metabolic Research in Africa (CARMA), Department of Physiological Sciences, Faculty of Science, Stellenbosch University

Introduction

This chapter focuses on the institutional culture in the Faculty of Science at Stellenbosch University (SU). Although SU has attempted to promote inclusivity and equity redress, the institutional culture still requires transformation, especially in the Faculty of Science. As the narrator, I position myself and my experiences as a black scientist as central to the chapter's unfolding. I initially refer to my scholastic background, whereafter my years at SU are considered. I subsequently elaborate on a visual redress project I initiated for the Mike de Vries Building entrance on the SU main campus, where my department is located. The visual redress project was done under the supervision of a senior colleague from the Department of Visual Arts. A representative working group was established, which included students and staff members working in the building. Several interactive sessions (e.g. painting, discussions, movement routines) with the working group occurred and culminated in the construction of a collective art representation to be installed. The project's completion has several implications. The process adopted allowed for difficult issues regarding identity, redress and transformation to be dealt with in a sensitive and harmonious way. Moreover, efforts to complete the project also revealed the power plays of institutional bureaucrats. I propose a push-back against this to ensure that academic freedom and institutional autonomy are not further eroded, and also that 'scientific elitism' should be tackled such that the training of scientists be more closely linked to socio-political and historical contexts. Together, such holistic transformation efforts should enhance the social legitimacy of the Faculty and SU.

SU is a historically white Afrikaans institution that played a key role in the design and promotion of the apartheid ideology. After the abolishment of apartheid in 1994, the transformation of higher education became a priority, as highlighted in several national policy documents, for example the *White Paper on Education and Training of 1995* (DoE, 1995) and *Education White Paper 3: A Programme for the Transformation of Higher Education of 1997* (DoE, 1997). Such national imperatives resulted in the adoption of numerous institutional transformation policy documents by South African higher educational institutions, including SU. There is an ongoing process with continuous revisions of strategic plans and/or the adoption of new ones, for example the establishment of an Institutional Transformation Committee at SU in 2017, which includes representatives from all faculties. This is a high-powered committee chaired by the Vice-Rector: Social Impact, Transformation and Personnel. This was followed by a revised University Statute being gazetted on 16 August 2019, with its preamble indicating that SU is especially driven by constitutional values relating to human dignity, equality and freedom. Moreover, it espouses unity in diversity, tolerance and respect for different perspectives and belief systems (SU, 2019a).

Despite such efforts, the current institutional cultures of most universities still need transformation in order to redress the past and to become more representative and inclusive of the broader South African population. Focusing on SU, the transformational shift from a more Eurocentric to an authentic, fully representative African tertiary institution requires further actions. Of note, such changes are especially lagging in the science, technology, engineering and mathematics (STEM) disciplines at SU, as reflected by the underrepresentation of black people (in the generic sense) in terms of faculty and student demographics. When focusing on the Faculty of Science at SU, this is quite evident for academic and senior managerial positions (chairpersons, vice-deans and deans). For example, black people constitute only 22% of current academic staff in the Faculty of Science (33/148), with black women comprising a meagre 9,5%. The relatively slow progress of changing a predominantly white staff profile is quite obvious when analysing data from five years ago. In 2015, black academic staff made up 19% and black women 8,3% of the total academic staff in the Faculty of Science.

At the more senior levels, the numbers become progressively worse, as currently, only 6 out of 23 associate professors (26%), 4 out of 49 full professors (8%) and none of the distinguished professors are black. This brings the overall number to about 13% (10/78) black staff in senior academic positions in the Faculty, with black women making up only 3,8% of these positions. This does not compare well with the rest of the University in terms of comparable percentages for black academic staff in senior faculty posts and managerial positions (SU, 2019b). Even more alarming is the fact that there has only been one black departmental chairperson and not a single black individual appointed as a vice-dean or dean since the establishment of the Faculty of Science in 1866. Such a lack of inclusivity and transformation also extends to undergraduate student demographics and intellectual and physical spaces within the Faculty; for example, there is a plethora of buildings and lecture halls named after colonial and Afrikaner figures, such as JC Smuts, Merensky, De Beers, Perold and Broom, which serve as a constant reminder of an oppressive past.

As the narrator, I position myself and my experiences as central to the chapter's unfolding. I draw attention to my personal background as a black scientist (of Indian descent) who was schooled during the student activism years and as part of a culture of resistance to the apartheid state. My journey from the University of Cape Town (UCT) to SU (during 2007) will be touched upon. For the SU period, my earlier and subsequent experiences and feelings will be explored, leading up to the present. Here, I also detail some of my experiences as a black academic in the Faculty of Science and share my thoughts regarding institutional culture, and also my frustration (at times) with the relatively slow pace of transformation and redress. This will include brief reflections during my six-year tenure as the chairperson of the Department of Physiological Sciences at SU. Towards the end of the chapter I will elaborate on a visual redress project I initiated for the entrance of the Mike de Vries Building, where my current department is located. The process followed will be considered, from my personal perspective, and I will also reflect on the eventual outcomes and the broader implications of this initiative.

Pre-Stellenbosch period

I completed my schooling during the apartheid years and received my 'doctrinal training' as a result of various political activities (at high school) until I matriculated. In fact, during my matric year, we missed almost the entire schooling year as a result of a major national boycott by black students to protest against racist policies, systemic inequality and the brutalities of the apartheid regime. Despite such obstacles (in terms of my *formal* educational training), I continued with my tertiary education at UCT as a BSc student with strong interests in the biomedical sciences. UCT is a historically white, liberal English institution and this was strongly reflected in the institutional culture and symbology on its various campuses. The racism and social exclusion experienced during my university student years were a touch more subtle, but certainly existed. My interest in biomedical sciences meant that after completion of my BSc degree, I migrated from the main campus to the medical school, where I completed a PhD degree. Overall, my UCT student years fell within the last decade of the apartheid system and I therefore continued to play an activist role by participating in student protests, community upliftment projects and intellectual discussion groups, and also by conscientising others about not only the apartheid system, but also the plight of oppressed peoples on a more global scale. I would describe myself as being further to the left at the time, with my political philosophy being more in line with organisations such as the Pan Africanist Congress and the New Unity Movement than the charterist ideals of the African National Congress.

During this time (late 1990s), UCT was rocked by the 'Mamdani affair', which highlighted the problems with transformation at liberal English South African universities. Prof. Mahmood Mamdani (an esteemed Ugandan academic) attempted to introduce significant reform in terms of the African Studies curriculum, but his efforts were met with strong institutional resistance that ultimately led to his resignation in 1999. Kamola (2011:157) refers to the underlying context as follows:

> At the root of this debate, therefore, was a fundamental disagreement about whether, within a historically white university undergoing transformation, teaching Africa constituted an 'arbitrary' topic around which professors could develop pedagogy for skills training or, in contrast, whether teaching Africa amounted to a politically necessary opportunity to submit post-apartheid South Africa to academic interrogation. This disagreement took place within the context of UCT admitting larger numbers of black students, many educated in apartheid's substandard primary schools. Mamdani not only staked out an argument that teaching Africa was important in its own right, but argued that doing so was necessary for incoming, black students to begin the process of reconceptualising themselves as living on the African continent, itself a world with its own intellectuals, academic debates, and worthwhile contributions. He argued that, especially within a post-apartheid context, this vital intellectual project cannot be reduced to an opportunity to teach reading, writing and comprehension skills.

Likewise in 2001, Prof. Robert Shell (from Princeton University and director of the Population Research Unit at Rhodes University) submitted a comprehensive report that detailed the non-transformative management style at the East London campus (Southall & Cobbing, 2001). He accused the administration of engaging in politically motivated course closures, nepotistic hiring practices, seemingly race-based decisions concerning lay-offs, and in general a culture of "inbred white privilege, maladministration and mediocrity" (Taylor & Taylor, 2010:907). Shell was subsequently dismissed by Rhodes University.

After completion of my PhD degree, I remained at the UCT medical campus and eventually settled at the Hatter Institute for Cardiovascular Research to focus on better understanding the nature of the onset of cardiovascular diseases, with the aim of devising improved therapeutic interventions. This period fell during the post-apartheid era and I now settled and strongly focused on building my research and academic career. I was fortunate enough to work under a world-class clinician-scientist (Prof. Lionel Opie) who also took a personal interest in my career development. This was significant, as I did not really have a supporter previously, and it opened my outlook to include bigger horizons than before in terms of my career development. I also managed to spend time in the United States of America (USA) as a Fulbright Fellow during this period, further expanding my horizons regarding future career possibilities. During this post-doctoral period, I remained true to my original political ideals, but now my actions to promote transformation were executed in a different and less 'confrontational' manner. For example, I reached out to help lecture (short, part-time stints) at historically disadvantaged institutions such as the University of the Western Cape and the Peninsula Technikon (now part of the Cape Peninsula University of Technology), as there was a limited critical mass (of academics) in the host departments at the time. Part of such initiatives included lecturing short one-week distance modules in far-flung places such as Mafikeng, Windhoek and Mthatha, where I observed the plight of disadvantaged students in terms of inadequate resources and also the lack of infrastructure and facilities. However, what struck me at the time was the eagerness of students to acquire knowledge and their commitment to advance their careers despite such hurdles. I also served on the Faculty of Medicine's Transformation and Equity Committee at UCT, and as a research supervisor took a pro-active stance to recruit and mentor several young black African students who successfully completed their doctoral degrees. I took this approach because transformation was still lagging at UCT despite the stated intentions to advance this cause, while I also on occasions encountered a 'white privilege' mindset, an issue also highlighted in Shell's report for Rhodes University (Southall & Cobbing, 2001). This left me frustrated at times regarding my attempts to enhance transformation more rapidly, and also in terms of advancing my own career development.

The Stellenbosch University years

The Department of Physiological Sciences at SU advertised an associate professor tenured post in 2007 and I applied, albeit reluctantly. Although I only had a contract position at UCT, I loved the research work that I was pursuing and saw no reason for leaving other than for a full-time position and also the possibility of academic promotion. I was indeed successful with my application, but was not overly elated, as I was unsure of the unknown nature of SU's institutional culture. I eventually accepted the offer, which, in hindsight was an excellent move, and started my career at SU early in 2007. The first few years were something of a culture shock, as I did not know anyone on campus and found it difficult to kindle meaningful relationships with colleagues outside of my host department. I later realised that it took longer to form such relationships at SU than at UCT, although I managed to succeed in establishing solid relationships in the long run. The language issue also cropped up and I found it more of a nuisance and a waste of time to ensure the translation of all documents and lectures into Afrikaans. Moreover, the *lingua franca* for communication and at meetings at the time was Afrikaans, with interpreting offered at times. I do enjoy speaking a creolised version of Afrikaans, but my formal literary skills are less optimal, as my post-matric tertiary education was exclusively in English. I also believed that the significant emphasis on the Afrikaans language represented a barrier to transformation, as it excluded black students and staff from studying or working at SU. However, I knew what I was signing up for and therefore tolerated this situation, while being mindful that a predominantly Afrikaans approach was not sustainable if the University wanted to attract more black students and staff in the long run.

Another issue that confronted me early on was the institutional culture and symbology, namely the Afrikaner and colonial names featuring as statues and on plaques, lecture halls and buildings that dotted the beautiful campus. The other aspect that also worried me deeply at the time was that the Faculty of Science management, staff and student demographic were still predominantly white, male and Afrikaans. However, I grew to love the campus with its scenic setting and also thoroughly enjoyed working with some special colleagues and students, although such concerns often left me wondering how the *status quo* could be changed and/or what role I could play in this process. As I was a relative newcomer, I did not really share my thoughts with others and mostly self-reflected on such matters.

After I was appointed as the chairperson of our department in 2009, I became more emboldened in terms of pursuing some of my views on transformation. A sad statistic to note is that I was the first person of colour to become a chairperson at the Faculty of Science at SU, and this is still the case at present. Moreover, the regular chairpersons' meetings (of eight departments) largely consisted of older white men, a throwback to the past indeed. However, such observations are certainly more nuanced and it was not simply a matter of being black or white. For example, Prof. Eugene Cloete, the then dean of the Faculty of Science, took a strong interest in my career by acting as a mentor in terms of career goals and future planning and building my leadership skills. He also encouraged me, and thereafter strongly backed my application, to be promoted to full professor in 2011. Prof. Cloete also urged me to apply for a vice-dean's position in our faculty, where I was one of the final three candidates selected for the position after the interview process. However, I unfortunately lost the popular vote at the Faculty Board meeting, and the same process repeated itself three years later. On the second occasion, several colleagues commented afterwards that I delivered an excellent presentation, but I sadly lost the Faculty Board vote again. I then decided to seriously consider not applying for similar positions again, as, in my opinion, a systemic flaw exists in terms of the Faculty Board's (still predominantly white) voting process that makes it much harder for black academics to succeed in such instances.

As chairperson, I more aggressively put transformation on the agenda and set out to increase the number of black students registering for our courses and also to conscientise my colleagues about the importance of such interventions. Here, we were more successful to enhance transformation at the postgraduate level and I am pleased that such efforts continued after my six-year tenure as chairperson, as this outlook is now firmly entrenched. I also attempted to accelerate the appointment of black staff, and although there was some progress, we still fell short. I discovered that one of the problems was that not enough black academics would consider applying to SU due to concerns regarding the institutional culture and the language policy. In addition, I felt that not enough efforts were made by some of the decision-makers to really try to recruit good black academics to fill positions.

The Mike de Vries Building

During this period, I also increasingly thought about ways to change the name of the Mike de Vries Building (where our department is located) and to create a more inclusive environment in terms of symbology used within the building's physical spaces. Of note, I learnt at the time that the building was originally named after Dr Daniel Francois Malan, one of the chief architects of apartheid and former prime minister of South Africa (1948–1954), but that it was renamed in 2004 after Prof. Mike de Vries, a former vice-chancellor of SU (1979–1993). However, this change still did not go far enough in my opinion, as it still represents the *status quo* of a strong Afrikaans culture at SU. This viewpoint should also be considered within the context of the physical spaces within the Faculty that are still dominated by buildings, lecture halls and statues named after Afrikaner and colonial figures. However, these remained only thoughts at the time, as I was quite occupied as the departmental chairperson and I was also not yet at the 'tipping point' for taking up such challenges.

During the last few years, I have observed far more impetus towards transformation initiatives at SU and also in a broader sense – both nationally and globally. This was the period of the nationwide #FeesMustFall student protest movement that also called for decolonisation of curricula and the establishment of more inclusive university campuses and institutional cultures. I was pleased to (finally) observe the name change of the graduation venue from the DF Malan Memorial to the Coetzenburg Sports Centre (2014), the removal of DF Malan's bust from the same location (2015), the removal of a plaque honouring former prime minister Hendrik Verwoerd (2015) (the chief architect of apartheid) and the adoption of a new language policy in 2016 (English as primary medium of instruction, but with good support for Afrikaans students). These were small, but important steps, while the emphasis on visual redress projects also excited me, as there were now tangible expressions on campus of some of my own thoughts, for example *The Circle*, which is a bronze art installation that depicts eleven women figures that captures a diverse range of leaders, past and present. This art installation is situated opposite the Perold Building, where the dean of the Faculty of Science's office is located. Upon reflection, the national and global shift towards inclusivity and redress together with such changes certainly bolstered me to push a more holistic transformation agenda (in terms of the role and purposes of a university). Within this context, an inclusive culture, according to Badat (2010:19) involves …

> … the questions of the opportunities for intellectual, social and citizenship development and for success. It extends to the issues of institutional and academic cultures, and largely ignored epistemological and ontological issues associated with learning and teaching, curriculum development and pedagogical practice. It further extends to the very ideas and conceptions of the purposes and roles of universities.

In line with this outlook, I was elected to serve on the University's Employment Equity Advisory Committee under Prof. Nico Koopman (Vice-Rector: Social Impact, Transformation and Personnel). My role here is ongoing, but with a robust intention to implement the required systemic changes within the University to accelerate transformation, promote redress projects and enhance the institutional culture. Some of the changes in the pipeline for which I am strongly advocating include adding transformation as a key performance indicator for staff and improving the advertising and selection process for new appointments to ensure increased transformation of SU's staff cohort. These are draft documents that still need to be formally adopted within the broader University, but it certainly does leave one with a sense of optimism going forward. In line with Badat's (2010) views, I expanded my transformation horizons by branching into the scholarship of teaching and learning, and increasingly intersected with colleagues from the humanities and arts disciplines. As a result, my research interests have broadened to now include areas such as the decolonisation of science curricula, exploring conjoint projects between the arts and the sciences, and tackling visual redress issues.

The visual redress project

The time was therefore ripe for action on my side and I zoned in on the Mike de Vries Building as part of the wave of visual redress projects sweeping the campus. This collaborative visual arts project was initiated in August 2019 following an address by Dr Leslie van Rooi, SU's senior director for Social Impact and Transformation, to our Faculty Board meeting on 1 August 2019. During this time, he discussed various visual redress projects on campus, triggering an idea to transform a blank wall located in the entrance lobby of the Mike de Vries Building into a meaningful, thought-provoking and inclusive space for all. The building is currently shared by three departments in the faculties of Science (the departments of Physiological Sciences and Chemistry) and AgriSciences (the Department of Animal Sciences). I emailed him the following day about the matter to discuss the possibility of renaming the building and having some form of artwork installed in the foyer. In my email I also requested him to send me details on the process and regulations pertaining to renaming buildings and new naming of, for instance, a lecture hall, and requested the details of contact persons in the arts departments for ideas and help with the artwork.

Dr van Rooi subsequently put me in touch with Prof. Elmarie Costandius (Department of Visual Arts at SU), who is one of the key figures, together with other staff members of the Transformation Office, in driving visual redress efforts at the University. She agreed to lead this process and we worked closely under her guidance for the duration of the project. She strongly advocated a bottom-up process and I therefore liaised with the respective departmental chairpersons to each put forward suitable names of staff and students. This resulted in the establishment of a representative working group of 11 people, consisting of postgraduate students and academic and non-academic staff members inclusive of race, gender and age differentiation. For the period August–December 2019, Prof. Costandius arranged numerous interactive sessions, which were done in English to allow for inclusivity, with the nominated staff and students. The sessions each lasted several hours and resulted in the creation of a visual artwork that would be representative and inclusive, and that would also resonate with the University's stated vision and mission.

All sessions occurred in the Mike de Vries Building, with some held in the Department of Animal Sciences and the rest in the relatively large Open Floor Laboratory located in the Department of Physiological Sciences. The first session commenced with introductions and I welcomed all the participants and explained the reason for the planned sessions. Prof. Costandius thereafter briefed the group regarding the meaning of visual redress and its underlying philosophy and also referred to previous projects completed at SU. The first session was initially characterised by some nervousness, as the participants were unsure of the processes to follow. This session took place in the boardroom of the Department of Animal Sciences and the participants sat around a very long table. Several glass cabinets with dusty, old scientific equipment on display created a unique old-world feel and reminded the participants of a long-past era at SU. The participants were instructed to tape together several pieces of large sheets of paper that stretched across the length of the table and then each had to freely express their feelings regarding themes such as inclusivity and redress, but only by using the medium of art. I noticed everyone being quite reserved and working in a constrained manner in terms of the art representations. However, the participants were continually encouraged to be 'free' and to just express themselves, and soon the relatively mute atmosphere morphed into a more vibrant one, with greater interactions as the participants started straying across each other's artworks, thereby in a sense 'breaking' personal barriers that may have existed among them. Now conversations and discussions occurred freely between professors and students, Afrikaans and isiXhosa speakers, white and non-white persons, etc. After several hours, each budding artist verbally shared and expressed the meaning of their respective representations. This was done in a safe and welcoming space and everyone felt at complete ease to share their feelings and thoughts, while others listened attentively at the same time. The artwork was thereafter carefully stored away and completed during a later session. The first session therefore served as an excellent ice-breaker and created a strong sense of camaraderie among the group, with the initial scepticism replaced by genuine collaboration and sharing, and also a sense of excitement to be part of this unique project.

Such sessions continued on a regular basis until the end of 2019, but with different materials and methods employed in order to ensure intragroup sharing and to also capture the group's broader feelings in terms of the artworks generated. For example, materials such as plants, twigs, wool and old books were used to create artistic renditions on various themes such as transformation, identity, inclusivity, SU as an institution and the experience of working in the Mike de Vries Building. Prof. Amelda Brand (Department of Drama) was co-opted for a few sessions that covered the same themes as before, but now allowing for active group movement and closer physical interaction at times. It would be best to sum up all such experiences as often being outside the comfort zone of the working group, which one could easily stereotype as 'straightjacketed' or 'socially inhibited' scientists. However, all participants fully embraced and participated in the range of activities and this resulted in excellent group dynamics and the free sharing by all participants of their identities, experiences, ideas and thoughts. Here, the specific artworks produced acted as a vehicle to allow for such sharing with the rest of the group members. A unique process thereby unfolded that allowed for different views and opinions to be freely and safely expressed, while at the same time permitting others to reflect on these. Several working group members later indicated that they actually looked forward to such sessions and found it "therapeutic" and "good for the soul". In fact, word quickly spread about the nature of such sessions and soon other staff members and students who were not part of the working group expressed their desire to participate. The nature of the sessions together with the sentiments expressed are consistent with the idea that the visual arts product is not a noun, but a verb. Therefore, the *process* itself becomes educational, as explained by Booth (2013:24):

> We believe that collaborative visual art projects hold great potential in facilitating critical citizenship and social transformation in South African higher education. In this regard, visual art does not refer to visual art products per se, in other words to art as a 'noun', but rather to the processes involved in artistic practice – to art as a 'verb'.

Perold and Costandius (2015:210) further state that a focus on artistic practice "allows space to think of art education not as mere education about art, in other words art education restricted to students enrolled in formal art courses, but as education through art".

The design and creation of such artworks were therefore employed within a broader context, in other words not to only produce them (as a final product), but also to employ the process to allow for various interpretative possibilities within a pluralistic context. It also created unique opportunities for meaningful dialogue on current realities and future possibilities – all steps towards the promotion of enhanced transformation, inclusivity and redress (Perold & Costandius, 2015). The processes we followed resulted in a significant degree of self-reflection (at individual and collective levels) and the discovering and embracing of different group member identities and background stories. Below are some examples of images of artworks produced during the sessions.[58]

---

58 All the photographs in this chapter were taken by Elmarie Costandius.

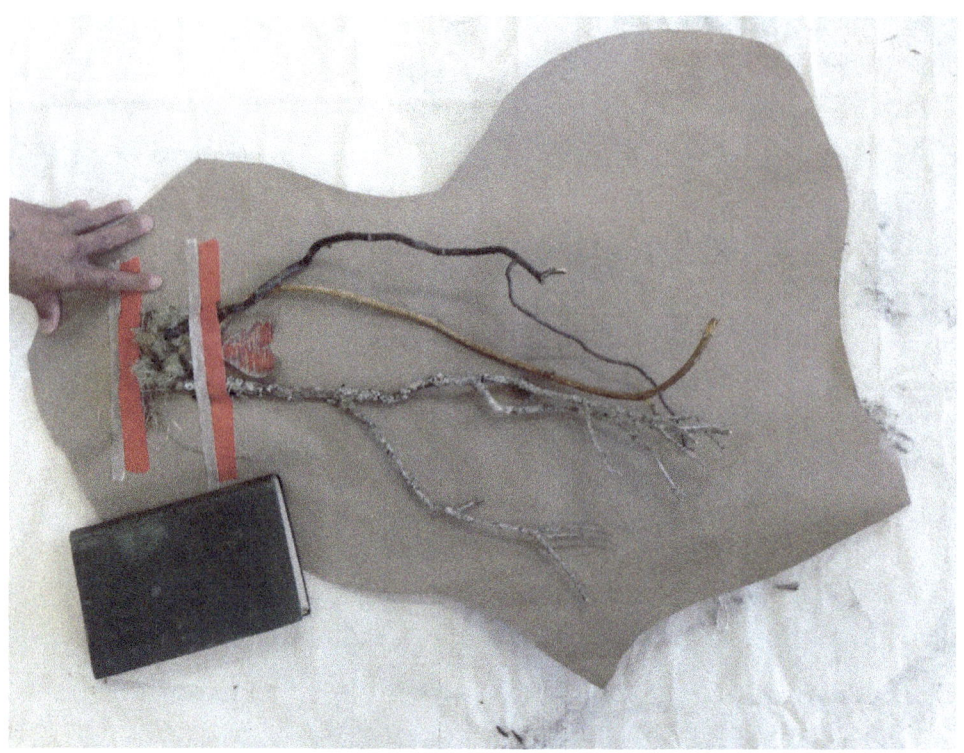

The sessions culminated in the construction of a single, collective art representation by the working group that consisted of 16 smaller art panels with the addition of some English phrases. The phrases selected were those that most frequently emerged from all the group sessions. The collage was put together by Prof. Costandius, who took high-image quality photographs of all artworks produced during this time and then selected 16 representative images for the final design. This collage was saved as a single printed copy, whereafter the various phrases were added to some of the panels. The image was subsequently shared with all the participants for feedback and it was unanimously approved (refer to the image on the next page). The next step was to generate a large, high-quality print of the image and to then install it onto the blank wall located in the entrance foyer of the Mike de Vries Building.

The attempts at the actual installation of the visual redress project revealed unique insights into Faculty management's perception of the process and also the nature of the artwork. The project budget amounted to either around R35 000 (single canvas with 16 fixed art representations) or R46 000 for a 'living' artwork (canvas with 16 moveable/replaceable art representations). For the latter, the idea would be to repeat the same process (different group sessions) at a later stage but with new participants, and to then add fresh images and phrases to the overall collage. This approach would ensure that the artwork remains innovative and contemporary. Dr van Rooi (Transformation Office) donated R30 000 towards the costs and I subsequently emailed the office of the dean (Faculty of Science) to lobby for the remainder of the funding. However, to my surprise, the Faculty manager questioned the process followed, indicating a lack of consultation on our part. The Faculty manager also expressed unhappiness with elements of the design (namely only English terms used and the work not being 'scientific' enough) and insisted that changes be made to the visual redress artwork generated. We were also informed that the decision regarding its installation would need to stand over until a later stage. This together with the Covid-19 pandemic has resulted in a delay in this process during 2020.

Challenges

In my opinion, this response reveals three aspects that deserve further reflection. Firstly, I perceived this type of mindset as a throwback to my past experiences, in other words of managerialism and authoritarianism once more attempting to suppress the collective and democratic 'voice'. Here, tools of managerialism seem to be employed to focus on various technicalities, for example the view that the correct procedures were not followed, or that there are potential problems regarding the windows and wall surfaces in the foyer of the Mike de Vries Building. This carries a risk that it can eventually result in the artwork being significantly altered or even that the project be terminated. I wish to argue that such a response should be viewed within the context of increased corporatisation of tertiary institutions, a global phenomenon that is firmly in line with neoliberal economic imperatives. Here, the focus is to ensure sustained economic growth by deregulation (the 'free market'), competition, fiscal austerity and reduced government spending. This economic philosophy also spilled over to the higher education sector and thereby the founding principles of earlier modern, tertiary institutions such as the University of Berlin (established in 1810) – for example academic freedom, unity of research and teaching, and providing moral and intellectual education – are increasingly abandoned, as the 'market' now dictates the agenda (Winkler, 2018). As a result, there has been a shift away from internal (within the University) deliberations and free decision-making to the increased appeasement of external demands (e.g. fiscal austerity, quality assurance, accountability) of various stakeholders, an ongoing process already pointed out almost two decades ago (Du Toit, 2000; Southall & Cobbing, 2001). Du Toit (2000) rightfully contends that this poses an existential threat to academic freedom and institutional autonomy with the erosion of traditional academic structures and the emergence of the 'managerial university'. Habib, Morrow and Bentley (2008) also alert us to the role of institutional bureaucrats in this regard and how the new managerialism actually undermines collegiality. They propose that several reforms should be implemented to address this problem, for example that external stakeholders should represent a "multiplicity of voices, including those of intellectual dissenters. This is necessary for the production of knowledge itself, since ideological pluralism promotes the critical engagement and reflective discourse necessary for testing ideas and sharpening conclusions" (Habib et al., 2008:148). Others also reason that institutional managers and bureaucrats should be made more accountable to the academic fraternity and the broader public as well (Du Toit, 2000; Southall & Cobbing, 2001).

Secondly, the concern that the visual artwork was not 'scientific' enough, as it would be housed in a building used by scientists and agricultural scientists, should also be carefully considered. I am of the opinion that this likely stems from the notion that many scientists view their discipline as 'neutral' and therefore devoid of any socio-political and historical contexts. This 'scientific elitism' can therefore absolve scientists from such contexts such as the past injustices committed during apartheid and also contemporary, pressing issues such as equity redress, decolonisation and inclusivity. One can easily visualise some colleagues claiming that "this is not Science and therefore not really any of our concern!" I believe that such an approach represents a threat to the long-term existence of the STEM disciplines, as it is essential to exhibit a willingness to critically engage with one's past in order to ensure the social legitimacy of the Faculty of Science and also SU itself. Habib et al. (2008:148) espouse this viewpoint by stating the following:

> … demographic and ideological pluralism is also institutionally strategic, giving social legitimacy to universities. This is essential, especially in a country with a history of exclusion, where material backlogs create numerous competing demands on the public purse. Legitimacy, an important source of power, occurs when citizens recognise the university as reflecting their concerns, hopes and aspirations.

However, such a holistic outlook is currently undervalued not only in the Faculty of Science, but also in more general terms for the STEM disciplines.

The neoliberal emphasis on the corporatisation of universities resulted in a strong push towards the STEM subjects, which is in itself not problematic. However, a noteworthy concern is that current STEM curricula are often completed in a 'silo'-typed fashion, thereby entrenching the notion of scientific elitism (Loudon, 2018). Therefore, although contemporary STEM graduates are well trained in a technological sense, they are often found lacking in skills such as creativity, interpersonal dynamics and an understanding of the nature of science, and a deeper appreciation and awareness regarding cultural and societal workings/legacies. This 'double whammy' of scientific elitism together with lingering white privilege certainly has an impact on the institutional climate (in the Faculty of Science) within its various intellectual and physical spaces. For example, the first question posed (by a senior professor) after a recent presentation on decolonisation of the curriculum to our Faculty Board was "How long is it before we decolonise ourselves out of business?" Therefore, I contend that it is essential to vigorously and honestly tackle such identified gaps within the Faculty of Science context, as the adoption of a holistic and inclusive philosophy should lead to numerous benefits for both students and staff. I am especially arguing for greater cross-collaboration between departments and faculties in order to ensure more well-rounded STEM graduates at SU. These thoughts are aligned with Reiter's (2017:10) views:

> By studying philosophy, literature, religion, art, music, history, and language, students begin to see the interconnectedness of all areas of knowledge and how the Humanities and STEM subjects all fit together and complement each other. The challenges that the students of tomorrow will have to face are far greater than those we face today.

The adoption of such an approach should better facilitate a more inclusive academic culture, authentic redress, improved social cohesion (among both staff and students), more dynamic curriculum offerings (e.g. greater intersection between Science, Art and Humanities faculties), and improved interaction by scientists with broader society to better enable the implementation of socially responsible scientific and technological advancements. I believe that the lack of such holistic-orientated curricula and training within the STEM disciplines can help explain the justifiable recent outcry against two research studies published by SU and UCT scientists. In the first study, SU researchers came to the conclusion that non-white women possessed a lower cognitive function that was influenced by their degree of education (Nieuwoudt, Dickie, Coetsee, Engelbrecht & Terblanche, 2020). This article has since been retracted by the publishing journal. This was followed by a UCT study published in 2020 where the author concluded that black students did not study the biological sciences as a result of their culture and materialistic outlook (Nattrass, 2020). It is crucial that future curriculum planning and/or revision within our Faculty and within the broader STEM context should incorporate a greater understanding of human complexities. Nussbaum (2006) indeed calls for the cultivation of humanity in our students, stating that three capacities are essential to achieve this goal, namely a critical examination of the self and traditions, for students to recognise themselves as human beings bound to others (by concern and recognition) and the adoption of an empathetic approach to others in addition to merely acquiring factual knowledge.

Finally, there is the issue of language usage. As the sessions were all conducted in English, it was a natural consequence to add phrases using this language. The only exception was *ubuntu*, a Nguni Bantu term meaning 'humanity', or in a wider sense, 'I am because we are'. After some deliberation between Prof. Costandius and me, we agreed that some of the terms should indeed be translated into Afrikaans and isiXhosa, as this would help promote greater diversity and inclusivity, as was our original intention. This resulted in minor alterations to the visual artwork, namely the addition of four English, three isiXhosa and two Afrikaans phrases (refer to the image on the next page). It is our strong opinion that this should be the final version of the artwork for installation in the foyer of the Mike de Vries Building, with no further changes.

Implications

The completion of this visual redress project in the Faculty of Science at SU has several implications. At a personal level, its accomplishment generates a sense of achievement and fulfilment, and it also signifies an important symbolic step in a faculty that still requires transformation to create more inclusive intellectual and physical spaces. Of note, my personal efforts to help transform the campus should be viewed through a caring lens, as my emotional attachment to SU means that I only wish to ensure that *all* students and staff can feel that they *truly* belong at this excellent institution. This project also broadened my own research interests, with increased collaboration and interactions with colleagues located within the arts and humanities disciplines. I am now committed to help break down subject-specific 'silos' and view the current visual redress project as the start of a wider research portfolio that will increasingly intersect with such disciplines. I also wish to argue that the broader acceptance of such a shift is crucial within the STEM disciplines, as it provides an important and necessary context to successfully tackle, complete, implement and disseminate science-based research work and findings.

The result of this process, namely the generation of a physical artwork, which should hopefully be installed during 2021, signifies another step towards greater inclusivity and belonging. My perception is that many students and staff would appreciate this effort and that it will also inspire others to follow and to thereby accelerate transformation at SU. The process followed did indeed allow for the negotiation of the "Third Space" (Bhabha, 1995), in other words "to function as part of the collective institutional culture while simultaneously facilitating interaction and dialogue free from dominant institutional protocols and expectations" (Perold & Costandius, 2015:221). It allowed for difficult issues regarding identity, apartheid, redress and transformation to be dealt with in a sensitive and harmonious way. Moreover, it also created the necessary safe spaces to facilitate free sharing, attentive listening and self-reflection, and helped to unite participants in terms of common goals and themes. I would therefore advocate for this process to be rolled out to other departments and faculties at SU and also other tertiary institutions (nationally and globally).

Our efforts to complete the project also revealed the power plays of institutional managerialism and bureaucrats. I believe that it is crucial that university staff members begin to resist the accepted norm to ensure that academic freedom and institutional autonomy are not further eroded in servitude of external stakeholders and neo-liberal economic imperatives. This means that university staff should better organise themselves to claim this space more robustly within tertiary institutions. Such efforts should also include calls for increased accountability of institutional bureaucrats and managers, together with the establishment of greater diversity in terms of external stakeholders.

Lastly, the notion of 'scientific elitism' should also be tackled with increased vigour, as scientists and their research endeavours need to be more closely linked to socio-political and historical contexts. I contend that Nussbaum's (2006) "cultivation of humanity" within the STEM disciplines may be achieved by the revision of curricula, the breakdown of discipline-based intellectual silos and increased adoption of visual redress projects. Here, it would be useful for SU to consider the approach taken by the prestigious Massachusetts Institute of Technology (MIT) in the USA, where dynamic curricula such as a BSc in Humanities and Science are offered. However, this may be a longer-term goal and therefore alternative, more feasible options should be considered in the interim. For example, compulsory first-year humanities-arts-science modules could be offered to all first-year BSc students, with a similar three-week theory module presented to all BSc (Hons) students. In this regard, Fitzgerald (2014:n.p.) explains in a still relevant newspaper article:

> MIT's curriculum has evolved significantly over the past 50 years to require all undergraduates to spend substantial time on subjects like literature, languages, economics, music, and history. In fact, every MIT undergraduate takes a minimum of eight such classes – nearly 25 percent of their total class time.

This should ensure that STEM graduates become creative and nimble thinkers who are able to conduct innovative scientific research that is deeply rooted in a more humanistic outlook. This approach should be strongly lobbied for within the Faculty of Science at SU (and beyond) to ensure its *actual* implementation. Together, such imperatives should help speed up transformation, but now also tackled in a more holistic and relationally engaging manner and not only as a 'numbers game'. Such holistic transformation efforts should in turn enhance the social legitimacy of the Faculty and SU and help to strengthen public trust in our institution.

Conclusion

Transformation and equity redress are still lagging at historically white Afrikaans tertiary institutions such as SU. This chapter explored this phenomenon by focusing on a visual redress initiative conducted in the Faculty of Science at SU. I argue that the visual redress process discussed in this chapter offered significant benefits, as it presented unique opportunities to participants to freely and safely share their views, and also allowed for deeper self-reflection. I therefore propose that such initiatives be rolled out to the broader SU community (and beyond), as they provide a unique mechanism to honestly and openly deal with difficult issues such as the damaging legacy of apartheid, equity redress, and how to create truly inclusive physical and intellectual spaces. I also argue that this process revealed the growing influence of managerialism in tertiary institutions and then discussed how this, if left unchecked, may have a negative impact on institutional and academic freedom. A recent example at UCT perfectly illustrates this threat, as its council suspended the university's ombud for alleged 'misconduct' (Seekings, 2020). This followed the ombud reporting several serious allegations to council regarding the conduct of UCT's vice-chancellor. Seekings (2020:n.p.) warns that "[t]his saga reveals how creeping managerialism within the university risks sliding into 'executive authoritarianism', fuelled by the current hyper-racialised climate, and culminating in the persecution of whistle-blowers".

Moreover, during this process, the notion of 'scientific elitism' emerged as an important factor that may explain (in part) the relatively slow progress regarding transformation, equity redress and institutional culture in STEM environments particularly. I propose that the latter should be tackled by curriculum renewal that includes a greater intersection between the natural/biomedical sciences, arts and humanities. Together, such efforts should help accelerate both qualitative and quantitative transformation in the Faculty of Science at SU, and thereby help advance current attempts by management in this regard. A more diverse student and staff cohort together with a robust inclusive ethos should in turn be a strong catalyst to further propel research endeavours, innovation and excellence in the Faculty.

References

Badat, S. 2010. *The challenges of transformation in higher education and training institutions in South Africa.* Development Bank of Southern Africa. Retrieved from https://www.dbsa.org/EN/About-Us/Publications/Documents/The%20challenges%20of%20transformation%20in%20higher%20education%20and%20training%20institutions%20in%20South%20Africa%20by%20Saleem%20Badat.pdf [Accessed 28 September 2020].

Bhabha, H. 1995. Cultural diversity and cultural differences. In: B. Ashcroft, G. Griffiths & H. Tiffin (eds). *The post-colonial studies reader.* London: Routledge, 206-209.

Booth, E. 2013. A recipe for artful schooling. *Educational Leadership: Creativity Now!,* 70(5):22-27.

DoE (Department of Education). 1995. White Paper on *Education and Training.* Notice 196 of 1995. Retrieved from https://www.education.gov.za/Portals/0/Documents/Legislation/White%20paper/White%20paper%20on%20Education%20and%20Training%201995.pdf?ver=2008-03-05-111656-000 [Accessed 28 September 2020].

DoE (Department of Education). 1997. *Education White Paper 3: A Programme for the Transformation of Higher Education.* Notice 1196 of 1997. Retrieved from https://www.gov.za/sites/default/files/gcis_document/201409/18207gen11960.pdf [Accessed 28 September 2020].

Du Toit, A. 2000. From autonomy to accountability: Academic freedom under threat in South Africa? *Social Dynamics,* 26(1):76-133. https://doi.org/10.1080/02533950008458687

Fitzgerald, D.K. 2014. At MIT, the humanities are just as important as STEM. The Boston Globe, 30 April. Retrieved from https://www.bostonglobe.com/opinion/2014/04/30/mit-humanities-are-just-important-stem/ZOArg1PgEFy2wm4ptue56I/story.html [Accessed 27 August 2020].

Habib, A., Morrow, S. & Bentley, K. 2008. Academic freedom, institutional autonomy and the corporatised university in contemporary South Africa. *Social Dynamics,* 34(2):140-155. https://doi.org/10.1080/02533950802280022

Kamola, A.I. 2011. Pursuing excellence in a 'world-class African university': The Mamdani affair and the politics of global higher education. *Journal of Higher Education in Africa*, 9(1/2):147-168.

Loudon, G. 2018. Creativity can be the bridge between science and humanities education. *The Conversation*, 16 October. Retrieved from https://theconversation.com/creativity-can-be-the-bridge-between-science-and-humanities-education-99610 [Accessed 2 September 2020].

Nattrass, N. 2020. Why are black South African students less likely to consider studying biological sciences? *South African Journal of Science*, 116(5/6):12-13. https://doi.org/10.17159/sajs.2020/7864

Nieuwoudt, S., Dickie, K.E., Coetsee, C., Engelbrecht, L. & Terblanche, E. 2020. Age- and education-related effects on cognitive functioning in colored South African women. *Aging, Neuropsychology, and Cognition*, 27(3):321-337. [Retracted article] https://doi.org/10.1080/13825585.2019.1598538

Nussbaum, M. 2006. *Education for democratic citizenship*. Public Lecture Series 2006, No. 1. The Hague: Institute of Social Studies.

Perold, K. & Costandius, E. 2015. Exploring the transformative potential of collaborative art projects in South African higher education. *South African Journal of Higher Education*, 29(6):206-225.

Reiter, C.M. 2017. *21st century education: The importance of the humanities in primary education in the age of STEM*. BA thesis, Dominican University of California. https://doi.org/10.33015/dominican.edu/2017.HCS.ST.09

Seekings, J. 2020. Defend the whistle-blower: UCT shoots the messenger, ignoring the message. Daily Maverick, 30 September. Retrieved from https://www.dailymaverick.co.za/opinionista/2020-09-30-defend-the-whistle-blower-uct-shoots-the-messenger-ignores-the-message [Accessed 30 September 2020].

Southall, R. & Cobbing, J. 2001. From racial liberalism to corporate authoritarianism: The Shell affair and the assault on academic freedom in South Africa. *Social Dynamics*, 27(2):1-42. https://doi.org/10.1080/02533950108458711

SU (Stellenbosch University). 2019a. *Statute.* Retrieved from https://www.sun.ac.za/english/Documents/Strategic_docs/statute2010.pdf [Accessed 27 August 2020].

SU (Stellenbosch University). 2019b. *Transformation at Stellenbosch University 2019.* Report prepared for the Department of Higher Education and Training. Retrieved from https://www.sun.ac.za/english/transformation/Documents/Transformation%20at%20SU%202019%20Report%20to%20the%20DHET.pdf [Accessed 27 August 2020].

Taylor, Y. & Taylor, R. 2010. Academic freedom and racial injustice: South Africa's former "open universities". *South African Journal of Higher Education,* 24(6):897-913.

Winkler, R. 2018. Universities in the neoliberal age. *Mail & Guardian,* 14 September. Retrieved from https://mg.co.za/article/2018-09-14-00-universities-in-the-neoliberal-age [Accessed 2 September 2020].

Chapter 7

Committed to Transformation: The journey of the Faculty of Medicine and Health Sciences' Charter

Khairoonisa Foflonker

Introduction

> Stellenbosch University's Faculty of Medicine and Health Sciences acknowledges, regrets and sincerely apologises for our complicity in the historical injustices of South Africa's past and we furthermore recognise how these injustices continue to perpetuate inequities today. We abhor all forms of unfair discrimination, exploitation, oppression, intimidation and bullying. (Faculty of Medicine & Health Sciences Charter, 2019).[59]

This chapter explores the development of the Charter of the Faculty of Medicine and Health Sciences at Stellenbosch University (SU) and demonstrates how both the development of the Charter and the accompanying visual redress process have made a significant contribution to transformation and decolonisation. The Faculty Charter is "a pledge to create inclusive, fair and friendly environments in every aspect of our daily interactions. It is intended to serve as a guide for our behaviour and an instrument to assist in holding us accountable for our actions" (FMHS, 2019:n.p.). Moreover, the Charter recognises the pain and injustices of the past, while simultaneously offering an aspirational guideline for the future. Visual representations of the Faculty Charter include Perspex panels, brochures, slogans and symbolic stickers as reminders of our individual and collective commitment to the processes of transformation and decolonisation, which foster inclusivity and nurture a sense of belonging for all.

The Faculty Charter in context

The Faculty of Medicine and Health Sciences (FMHS) was established at SU) 64 years ago in 1956, in a period marked by gross socio-political and economic inequality characterised by personal indignities enforced by apartheid laws. Below is a timeline indicating pivotal moments in the history of the Faculty:

---

59 FMHS Charter (2019) available at http://www.sun.ac.za/english/faculty/healthsciences/Documents/FMHS_Charter_2019.pdf

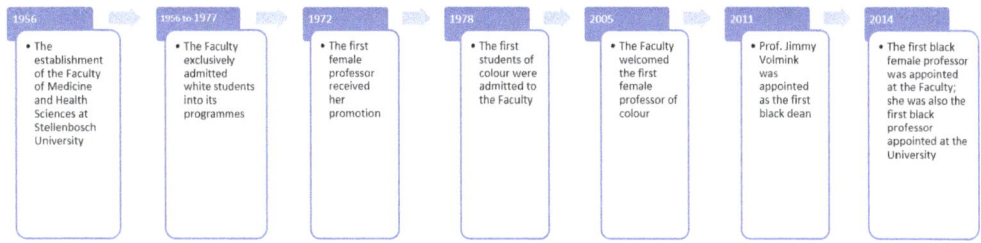

Gender discrimination was evident, as womxn[60] did not enjoy equal status to men in the Faculty, despite improvements in recent years (SU, 2018). SU is the place where the intellectual architecture of apartheid, including eugenics projects that justified scientific racism, thrived (Lee, 2013; Mbali, 2013; Walters, 2019). The senior leadership of SU acknowledges and regrets its history and has subsequently embarked on a process of transformation as well as visual redress (SU, n.d.; SU, 2018). Visual redress involves reviewing and, where necessary, renaming buildings and reconfiguring the visual symbols that evoke a sense of belonging or alienation to those who live in, work at and visit affected institutions. Processes related to transformation and decolonisation rupture the ideologies and practices of the past by rendering exclusion, inequality and oppression visible. Developing new symbols, renaming buildings and reclaiming spaces that previously excluded and alienated the marginalised groups are ways in which visual redress projects significantly contribute to shifting the institutional culture. Therefore, the aim of visual redress is to construct the University as a space where all people, especially those hitherto excluded, should find a sense of belonging and acceptance.

A sense of belonging is also impacted by location. The FMHS forms a single, enclosed campus at Tygerberg that stands adjacent to Tygerberg Hospital. Many of our SU staff and students traverse a dimly lit passage that connects the campus and Hospital for work and the clinical training components of their studies. Here they interact with patients and staff from various communities. In contrast, the Stellenbosch campus is spread across the picturesque town of Stellenbosch, located 31 km away from the Tygerberg campus. Whilst lively in character, Tygerberg

---

60 The x in womxn recognises that gender identity is non-binary and independent of assigned sex at birth. This spelling is intersectional, as it is cognisant of the complexities of the coloniality of gender, and incorporates transgender womxn, womxn of colour, womxn from developing countries, as well as other marginalised identities (Matandela, 2017).

campus is largely 'clinical' and austere in appearance. According to students, the location of the campus has a negative impact on their well-being. This is particularly the case for students who have left their homes from other provinces and countries to join one of the most prestigious universities on the continent.

In this chapter, I will demonstrate how the development of the Faculty Charter, as well as the accompanying visual redress processes, has made a significant contribution to the process of transforming the culture and spaces within the Tygerberg campus.

Methodology

This chapter is based on a grounded theory approach, which involves the collection of data without any preconceived theoretical notions or categories (see Strauss & Corbin, 1990). The research was driven by a single conceptual question with no imposition of a hypothesis, demonstrating that the development of the Faculty Charter and the accompanying visual redress processes have made a significant contribution to transforming the culture and spaces at the Tygerberg campus. Qualitative data was collected from three student engagements in three residences with approximately 60 commuter and residence students on 26 September 2018, a World Café held on 16 October 2018 with 60 staff and student participants, and a number of emails related to the content of the draft Charter. In addition, eight in-depth qualitative interviews were conducted with former and current staff as well as current students and alumni in August 2020 to gain a longitudinal perspective of the transformative changes or lack thereof within the Faculty. The data was coded for themes, after which the categories that emerged were analysed. A retrospective literature review was conducted based on the grounded theory approach to unpack codes and themes that emerged from the data to avoid making assumptions regarding what the data might reveal.

This chapter is written from my personal perspective as the chairperson of the Faculty Charter task team. I reflect on my positionality in relation to this visual redress process throughout this chapter. The story of the Charter's development is therefore informed by my personal reflections regarding my involvement in the process of visual redress. While the chapter is not presented from a position of neutrality or objectivity, my intent is to offer a balanced account of the processes of institutional change.

Codes and themes that emerged from the data demonstrated transformative learning, a sense of belonging or alienation and the presence of visual redress, transformation and decolonisation or lack thereof. The goal of facilitating transformative learning is underpinned by perspective transformation, which is defined as ...

> ... the process of becoming critically aware of how and why our assumptions have come to constrain the way we perceive, understand, and feel about the world; changing these structures of habitual expectation to make possible a more inclusive perspective, and finally, making choices or otherwise acting upon these new understandings (Mezirow, 1991:167).

I argue that in the process of developing the Faculty Charter, safe spaces for reflection were created, thereby enabling transformative learning by including students and staff who participated in the dialogues in which the Charter was deconstructed and co-constructed.

Contextualising the Faculty and institutional culture

The Faculty and institutional climate contributed to fatigue and frustration on the part of both staff and students with the slow rate of the processes of decolonisation and transformation. The sentiment among many task team members, mostly womxn, was that a handful of people were *doing* the work of change. Visual redress involves confronting the silences and screams within the Faculty's institutional culture. The absence of art is utterly stark at the Tygerberg campus, creating a sense that it is an extension of Tygerberg Hospital. The effect of silent walls is that it appears to hold secrets of the intersecting manifestations of oppression and marginalisation.

The winds of change

Reflecting back on his arrival in the Faculty in 1989, Prof. Moosa explained: "If you went into the Dean's area, you would find almost exclusively white faces and you will find almost exclusively males in senior positions." Subsequently, the images depicted in the Dean's corridor have diversified to include women, people of colour and students.

Prof. Volmink became the first black[61] Dean at the Faculty of Medicine and Health Sciences in 2011. His introduction to the Faculty was marred by the response to his application to study Epidemiology in the 1980s, at the height of apartheid. When Prof. Volmink called the University to enquire about the status of his application, he was informed that the University was not admitting people of colour into the programme, and was advised to "apply next year because the situation might have changed". Prof. Volmink explained his situation at that time: "I want to further my education and you know colour is still a barrier".

Prof. Volmink was recruited for the position of Deputy-Dean of Research under the leadership of Prof. Wynand van der Merwe, a progressive white Afrikaner Dean, and joined SU as a staff member for the first time in 2006. Prof. Volmink was surprised to encounter a warm welcome from the Dean and staff. However, Prof. Volmink soon discovered that he was often the only person of colour in the room and that some senior colleagues believed that he had only been appointed because he was not white.

Early in his term as Dean, Prof. Volmink appointed a diversity expert to speak to staff and students in the Faculty and investigate "what doesn't work for them [and] how things can be improved". Among 62 recommendations ranging from race to issues regarding disability, one of them "made the sky fall down". The rapporteur's findings revealed that …

---

61 I intentionally removed the term 'African' to reflect the Africanness of other racial groups within South Africa. For example, indigenous ethnic groups such as the San, Griqua, Baster and KhoiKhoi were racially classified as 'coloured' under apartheid laws, which referred to both 'mixed-race' and indigenous people, thereby rendering their African identity invisible.

> ... the students were saying that in the hospital sometimes the doctors write the notes only in Afrikaans, and because they don't speak Afrikaans, they can't understand what's in the notes... there are doctors from other countries ... and so they can't read the notes either. So that's clearly a patient safety issue that they feel needs to be addressed. So, in the report there was this one line that said that it is recommended that in the hospital environment a decision is taken to use a language of communication that everyone can understand.

Consequently, there was a 'concerted call' by staff members, alumni and Council members, who had resisted his leadership as person of colour, to have him removed from his role as Dean, as they deemed him unfit. When Prof. Volmink made the report available online in an effort to be 'held accountable', a media frenzy ensued, but ultimately, the battle to oust Prof. Volmink was lost. This pivotal moment set the stage for further transformation in the Faculty.

Examples of visual redress that were highlighted by both staff and students interviewed included renaming residences, which they viewed as key markers of transformation, diversity and inclusivity. In 2014, the Ubuntu House residence was renamed to reflect the spirit of *ubuntu*, as the students were striving towards unity and humility. In 2018, another residence was renamed Nkosi Johnson House after the South African child activist with HIV and AIDS who had a profound impact on public perceptions of the pandemic and its effects before his death at the age of twelve. In 2019, a third residence was renamed eNkanyini House to reflect the students' commitment to unity and relationship building. *Nkanyi* is the Xitsonga word for Marula and *eNkanyini* is translated as "by the Marula tree". Traditionally, marula trees have been the favoured meeting place for many village communities and are seen as a central gathering point.

One of the transformative changes that Cindy, a former student leader, highlighted was the Undergraduate Commitment Reading at the Dean's Welcoming Programme in all eleven official languages and South African Sign Language. This pledge is made by the first-year students in which they commit themselves to the ethical responsibilities associated with becoming medical and health sciences practitioners. After the Dean's welcoming for first-year students, parents and students explained that having the reading in multiple languages, including their home languages, made them feel welcome and included at SU. Similarly, another important symbol of transformation is the Preamble to the South African Constitution that is featured prominently in the Clinical building. Yonela, a senior black academic staff member, explained: "There's a sentence of a statement that is done in the different languages … that's a powerful thing … I could also see my own mother tongue there. So it gives you a sense of belonging."

A space that features a uniquely South African theme is the foyer of the Department of Medicine, which includes a black and white painting of Steve Biko, African sculptures and the iconic photograph of the 1956 Women's March in Pretoria. Two rooms were renamed in this department: one was named after Cecilia Makiwane, the first black registered professional nurse in South Africa and an early activist in the struggle for womxn's rights, and the other was named after Dr William A. Soga, the first black medical doctor in South Africa. Personally, having our Faculty Charter task team meetings in the Cecilia Makiwane room, a site of contestation, made the process even more meaningful in light of the transformative work that the task team was undertaking.

In the last decade, the demographic profile of students within the Faculty has shifted from being predominantly white to having people of colour in the majority. Female students constitute the majority in the Faculty. Students, being the lifeblood of universities, have catapulted universities into progressive change. During the 2015–2016 #FeesMustFall protests, students demanded the decolonisation of the University through discarding Afrikaans as the medium of instruction, free education and a re-imagining of curricula, spaces and institutional culture. According to Xaba (2017:99), the national collective #FeesMustFall movement consisted of "various black radical feminist, pro-black movements and student organisations across the different universities, which had been challenging White supremacy at universities and the exclusion of black students who are poor". In 2019, the SU Anti-Gender-Based Violence (GBV) movement engaged in protests that culminated in the Anti-GBV memorandum served to the Rectorate. These movements have set the stage for change within the University in rapid and unprecedented ways, culminating in changes to SU's language policy and the establishment of six institutional

Anti-GBV working groups comprising of staff and students who worked together to map the manifestations of rape culture and GBV on campus.

Same shoe, different foot

Despite efforts to transform and decolonise the Faculty, several sites of contestation remain largely unchanged. Prof. Volmink explained that it was difficult to recruit diverse staff into the Faculty "because the University is seen to be associated with racism and conservatism, [hence] people of colour don't even bother to apply".

Students who do not speak Afrikaans view the language as a barrier. Kabelo identifies as a black bisexual male student who joined the Faculty in 2015. Despite having "heard stories that Stellenbosch is racist", Kabelo joined SU, as he was offered the SU Recruitment Bursary. He overlooked the fact that Afrikaans was the language of instruction because he had no other funding opportunities. Kabelo explained:

> So I got here and … the lecturer is speaking Afrikaans and then you have to get earphones. And then you have to listen to what the lecturer, the translator is saying, and sometimes you miss the whole thing because the translator is just toning it down … you become like a stranger … you become like invisible … that also starts affecting your self-esteem … you can't get to your full capacity, because now you have all these limitations.

Kabelo described his personal experiences as a junior undergraduate student within the Faculty:

> I am a bisexual man … [and] there was no one fighting or advocating for people of a different sexuality. People in the entire sexuality spectrum … You'd feel whenever you tell people about your sexuality, they step back. They don't want to talk to you anymore.

Kabelo highlighted that there has been an increase in representativity within the student leadership structures – including those advocating for LGBTQIA rights – at the Faculty over the last four years. These changes motivated Kabelo to apply for leadership positions and offered him a sense of belonging: "I deserve to be here … 'Oh, they're black, I'm also black'. I can also do it".

Ascentia Seboko is a black female PhD candidate who obtained an undergraduate degree and lived in a residence at the Stellenbosch campus prior to joining the FMHS for her postgraduate studies. She described her experience as an honours student within one division (different from the division in which she is pursuing her PhD) at the Faculty as a "welcoming environment", but simultaneously not "very inclusive". Furthermore, she explained: "You don't feel represented. You don't feel like you have a voice" as "one of very few people of colour" in the field of science. Despite being surrounded by staff who are "always willing to help", she explained that there are "certain things they don't understand. Being a person of colour … [and] a first-generation student coming into an environment, science, the academic world. You don't really know a lot and you know you don't have all the resources". The lack of representativity in the division was alienating: "So it's a sense of do I belong? Or you know like 'am I just here for the numbers?' Is there really a place for me here?" Ascentia's experience of the lack of inclusivity motivated her to take up leadership positions and join the Faculty Charter task team to create "a more inclusive environment".

The power of representation is often severely underestimated. The lack of representation of womxn and people of colour in senior positions within academia and student leadership has a negative impact on students. Feelings of isolation are indicative of the need to create more welcoming and inclusive environments in which a sense of belonging is felt by *all*. In addition to increased representation, I would argue that visual redress projects play an important role in shifting the institutional culture with diverse languages, signs and symbols that are indicative of a commitment to transforming the institutional culture and spaces.

The *beitel*[62] sculpture has been a site of contestation at the Tygerberg campus. The sculpture is accompanied by an excerpt from an Afrikaans poem by NP van Wyk Louw: *"'n beitel moet kan klip breek as hy 'n beitel is"*.[63] Some staff and students are vehemently opposed to the presence of the *beitel* due to the association with a monolithic Afrikaans culture upheld by Stellenbosch University during apartheid

---

62 Beitel is the Afrikaans word for 'chisel'

63 Translated from Afrikaans: A chisel must be able to break stone if it is a chisel.

and beyond. Consequently, staff and students want the harsh metaphor embodied in the sculpture removed. There is a difference in opinion between Afrikaners who view the *beitel* and the accompanying quote in a different way. In contrast, some view it as purely problematic due to the historical context, while others resonate with it. One Afrikaner alumnus interviewed explained his understanding of the sculpture and poem as a motivation to work hard:

> In Afrikaans circles … If someone was doing something and they were not up to standard with something… It speaks to a very specific group of people, and that could make people feel alienated. I can clearly see that because they don't have an idea of why this thing is here … it was put there … because it was trying to inspire the young doctors to become good doctors. (Roos)

Another perspective he offered is that the *beitel* should remain in its place of prominence and that a contemporary artwork or sculpture should be placed adjacent to it, so that past and present are in conversation with each other. Roos explained:

> We should not necessarily have to erase history, that won't be good. But the question is whether they are still relevant, all of them? Maybe keep the few relevant ones. But add new relevant pictures as well, that speak more to the context you are in.

Prof. Nulda Beyers was one of the first female professors in the FMHS and has recently retired. According to Prof. Beyers, if the removal of statues and building names is deemed the most inclusive way forward, it would be important to consider "what are we putting in place of those statues? What are we going to name the buildings so that the next generation doesn't want to smash it down?". These are crucial considerations as the processes of decolonisation of spaces unfold in the form of visual redress at SU. We must take cognisance of the fact that our actions and inactions will be judged by future generations, and the latter may be deemed as complicity in the face of decolonisation.

The controversial Sports Science article (Nieuwoudt, Dickie, Coetsee, Engelbrecht & Terblanche, 2019) on the cognition of coloured womxn was retracted because it contained assertions about coloured womxn that were not supported by the data presented in the article (Soudien, 2020:103). Many students and staff were deeply offended by this article. Task team members engaged rigorously with the content of the article, as it included gross stereotyping and an inaccurate representation of coloured womxn that was deeply offensive. The Dean of the FMHS responded by hosting a symposium that was attended by an unprecedented number of staff and students. This was a crucial moment, as it ruptured the status quo and forced staff and students to reconsider the ethics of research. It compelled us to see how people of colour and womxn have been categorised and undermined, not only as research subjects, but also as members of the Faculty.

The Faculty Charter development process

In November 2017, Prof. Volmink, the Dean and chairperson of the Dean's Advisory Committee for Transformation (DACT), presented the need for a task team to develop a Transformation Charter for the FMHS. The Dean nominated Prof. Rafique Moosa, head of the Department of Medicine, with substantive institutional memory, to lead the process. Prof. Moosa has a record of successfully transforming spaces and practices within both the Faculty and Tygerberg Hospital. Prof. Moosa described the staff as "almost exclusively white and predominantly male with very few women" upon his arrival in the Faculty in 1989. He added that the Faculty management at the time was very "conservative" with an "apartheid style" of management.

Prof. Moosa declined the Dean's nomination and nominated me to lead the Faculty Charter task team. He agreed to participate in the process as an advisor instead. Prof. Moosa explained the reasons for nominating me as chairperson: "Firstly, your newness to the Faculty. So you didn't actually have any baggage." Not having preconceived notions of the culture within the Faculty was helpful in this process, as I was able to ask difficult questions without holding strong assumptions about people and their institutional roles. He added, "Secondly, you actually had experience in terms of transformation at UCT … Thirdly, I thought your gender was important … [and] you weren't afraid to speak up about things you felt weren't right". Prof. Volmink asserted that my nomination was due to being a woman of colour with facilitation expertise and experience, which he thought would assist the process to navigate potentially difficult conversations.

Members of the Faculty Charter task team were recruited by an open appeal to *all* staff and students in the Faculty to join the DACT sub-committee that was sent via an email from the Dean and social media. All the members – except for two who were nominated by their heads of department – participated in their personal capacities. I asked the members to nominate a chairperson among anyone in the room and was nominated by task team members. It was important for me to do so in the interest of transparency and fairness. Having arrived at the University and Faculty just four months earlier in July 2017, I realised that by accepting the nomination, I could be a part of a process that would drive inclusive change.

The process of developing the Faculty Charter was based on immersive collaboration with staff and students from various backgrounds. Members were encouraged to join us as often as they were available, and this led to the group spanning in numbers from seventeen to forty. A core group of committed members attended most of the meetings, which provided continuity of process. We began the process by co-constructing the ground rules and saw the importance of equality of voice of all members – staff and students from all backgrounds and positions. Members felt strongly that we should learn from one another and respectfully challenge any member whose utterances were deemed offensive, whether wittingly or unwittingly. Two of the ground rules included learning to sit with our discomfort and to refrain from interrupting one another – especially when personal narratives that challenged our own worldviews were presented. These ground rules enabled a safe space for reflection as well as engagement with concepts that created ambivalence, anger or pain. One of the white male student members observed a generational difference in the struggles of some of the fellow task team members:

> A lot of people [were] speaking about their past experiences … I'm a post- and would not say I'm a pre-democracy baby. Even though I was born in 1991, my entire life I know is post-apartheid. I could see some of the older people in the group who were going through … trauma [and] memories … There were a few people I think that were in discomfort and pain, but I appreciated their willingness to persevere through that. Because without that, you will not have the voice that you needed to put down into the Charter. (Roos)

The majority of our members were womxn, which is no surprise, given the demographic composition of the Faculty. Regrettably, we did not have the participation of as many undergraduate students as we would have liked; however, we had several postgraduate students join the task team. Members engaged in robust dialogue and in spite of having many disagreements, we left every task team meeting with a working consensus on the way forward.

In the first few months, it became apparent that we needed to develop a safe space before discussing the content of the Charter. Members realised that developing the Charter would not be possible if we tried to rush the process with a focus on the outcome:

> [W]hat stands out for me in the whole process was the catharsis … we actually didn't get anything going for the first six months because people just wanted to talk. And what touched me was the honesty of the women, especially the black women, women of colour. The pain they actually had gone through … I know what racism is about and I've been subject to it. … somebody called it being doubly black … So as a person of colour I feel … that …being a woman of colour obviously adds another dimension which I as a male would never have been aware of. (Prof. Moosa)

An appreciation of the experiences and life struggles of task team members emerged. The distinction between empathy versus lived experience was made by a student who recalled observing a moment of conflict between two of our members who had a difference of opinion along racial lines:

> A lot of the time people mistake empathy for actually knowing what you are going through. You can't know what another person is going through until you have actually experienced it … all you can do is listen and understand. That's it. You can't say you know and you … decide for them like this is how they should have felt … You can't tell me how I should feel about a certain situation. You have never been black. You've never had people … just look at you like you shouldn't be here. It's hard to explain to somebody who's never experienced it. (Seboko)

As a diverse group of students and staff, we discussed concepts such as transformation, decolonisation, diversity, inclusivity, sexuality, privilege, white fragility, xenophobia, sexism, GBV and allyship. We shared reading material from across the continent and globe. Critical diversity literacy formed an important part of the initial work of the task team, as it enabled the participants to engage in respectful discussion on the aforementioned concepts. Members were encouraged to watch and read material in their own time. Reading was not simply an academic exercise, but an educational empowerment experience, as the material was a point of departure for discussion. This approach was particularly helpful in educating those who were privileged as well as the international students and born-free generation who did not live under apartheid and had little understanding of how its draconian laws affected the South African population.

It is not sufficient to encounter the other in the work environment or classroom and expect that change will manifest. Truly inclusive processes of social change require *meaningful* interventions underpinned by transformative learning. Mezirow's (1978) transformative learning theory draws attention to dilemmas that occur when individuals have experiences that do not fit within the realm of their expectations. Hence, these experiences do not make sense to them and they cannot resolve situations without some change in their worldview. Mezirow (1995:50) refers to these as "disorienting dilemmas" that could be triggered by a life crisis or major life transition, but may also result from an accumulation of transformations in meaning schemes over a period of time.

In May 2018, task team members boarded a bus to the Worcester campus, where Prof. Julian Sonn, a seasoned diversity and inclusivity practitioner, facilitated a process that resulted in the core themes and substance of the Charter. I could have facilitated this workshop, but realised that we would benefit from Prof. Sonn's expertise, as he had been working closely with the SU Transformation Office in facilitating numerous workshops at the University and had a greater understanding of the institutional context. During this workshop, we engaged in heated discussions in which members gave voice to their pain and frustration and offered ideas regarding the history of apartheid and the future of decolonisation. Some task team members did not have direct experience of apartheid, as they had either not been born yet, or hailed from other countries. The dialogical space enabled them to learn deeply about the lived experiences of others.

As a facilitator, I have witnessed "disorienting dilemmas" that occur when there is a rupture in the worldview of a person who is presented with new perspectives that are alien to them. An example was a heartening conversation I had with a fellow task team member, a white man, who had misunderstood the concept of decolonisation. He erroneously believed that decolonisation involved discarding Western thought by replacing it with African and Southern theories and practices. He was surprised when I explained that decolonisation involved complementing, enhancing and leading with African thought, culture and curricula, as well as presenting an opportunity to rethink Western canons. Contextualising the curriculum, being "all-inclusive" (Fataar, 2020:4) and offering greater recognition and dignity to those holding African perspectives are the key pillars of decolonisation (De Sousa Santos, 2014). In failing to recognise how power is articulated within knowledge hegemonies and support structures, universities create a veil between themselves and students as well as staff who appreciate the context and importance of indigenous knowledge production. Consequently, people of colour are alienated and some are labelled as 'troublemakers' within the institution. For this colleague, being presented with new information on the definition and process of decolonisation challenged his worldview and therefore his "disorienting dilemma" gave rise to space for a fresh perspective. In witnessing his disorienting dilemma, I realised that this moment was made possible by creating a safe space for individuals to raise uncomfortable topics without 'losing face' or fearing reprisal.

Over the 18 months that the Charter was developed, it became evident that the interventions we facilitated, including the task team meetings, the World Café and student engagement discussions, had opened up spaces for staff and students to engage in critical reflection on the institutional culture as well as their own roles and complicity in upholding asymmetrical power relations. Mezirow (1978) argues that transformative learning takes place by integrating new knowledge within existing knowledge, beliefs and lived experiences. I would argue that the dialogues in which we engaged ignited the process of social change.

We spent several months redrafting the Charter to include ideas and terms that were meaningful and aspirational. Members decided that the Faculty Charter should omit the terms 'transformation' and 'decolonisation', as we felt that these processes should be *embedded* in the Faculty's ethos, culture and structures. We also kept in mind the fact that concepts such as decolonisation are contentious and even alienating to some, but did not omit them for this reason. There was a strong view that we should avoid using terms that could be dated or would diminish in meaning by the passage of time.

Members engaged in debates on the use of specific terminology that paid recognition to the diverse groups and a painful history. Roos stated: "I think I grew a lot as an individual getting people's perspectives and understanding where they come from. Why, for example, the use of certain words is important and why not others."

The opening lines of the Charter framed it within a history of injustices and acknowledged that some injustices continue to exist in the present.[64] Terms that were the subject of much debate within the task team included 'regrets', 'complicity', 'injustices' and 'abhor', as they were deemed too severe by some. Eventually, the majority agreed, as they could see that these words held deep meaning for those who were oppressed under apartheid and for those who continue to be marginalised.

Furthermore, action words were utilised to describe the commitment made by those taking the pledge. These words appear in bold below:

- **Celebrating** all forms of diversity on our campuses, including, but not limited to: ability, sexuality, gender, origin, language, race, culture and belief system.
- **Ensuring** that all individuals on our campuses enjoy a sense of belonging.
- **Cultivating** empowering environments in which individuals are able to express themselves freely, while considering and respecting the rights and freedoms of others.
- **Fostering** an environment in which everyone can learn, work and thrive; thereby enabling individuals to reach their full potential and become active citizens.

---

64 See footnote 58

- **Nurturing** learning, teaching, working and research environments in which we engage with all our stakeholders with dignity, respect, fairness and transparency.

- **Protecting** the human rights of all our stakeholders and striving to ensure a positive impact on the communities we serve. (FMHS, 2019:n.p.)

A section of the Charter focusing on 'communities' was included. We understood that the communities the Faculty served extended beyond the patients treated and research subjects studied by our staff and students. The communities also represented the places from which our students and staff hail – locally, nationally and internationally. Hence, our contributions to the University and broader communities stem from multiple geographic locations and diverse cultures.

In 2018, multiple engagements with staff and students were aimed at gaining broader feedback regarding the draft Faculty Charter while simultaneously creating more inclusive spaces for dialogue. The invitation to these dialogues included the tagline: "All voices welcome! All voices heard!" On 26 September 2018, three dialogues were facilitated by student and staff facilitators with approximately 60 commuter and residence students. Some student attendees described the dialogues as meaningful, heated, uncomfortable and exciting. Dialogue topics included access, language, toxic masculinity and mental health.

On 16 October 2018, 60 staff and students participated in a World Café, in which task team members facilitated discussions on various dimensions of the draft Faculty Charter. The World Café approach emphasises equality of voice and the participants were appreciative of the depth of engagement. Having members of the Dean's Management Team in attendance as participants gave credence to their commitment to creating a more inclusive Faculty.

In November 2018, feedback from staff and students who attended the dialogues and the feedback received via email were collated. Themes that emerged from this data were used to amend the draft Faculty Charter. In addition, task team members made a commitment to take the draft Charter back to their respective environments and use it to engage in dialogues on transformation and decolonisation in their meetings with staff and students.

Once the Charter was completed, it became abundantly clear that the Charter launch was relegated to 'women's work', much to the deep collective disappointment of the womxn in the task team. Prof. Moosa shared his sentiments on the lack of male participation towards the end of the process: "What also stood out for me was the complete lack of involvement of males. Men just didn't get involved. That was so striking. And … there were too few white people as well." He elaborated: "I was often the only male in the meeting. And it was from that point of view that I felt that women were yet again … being let down by the men."

The first Transformation Charter was developed by the Department of Medicine 14 years ago in 2006. Prof. Moosa led the committee that developed the Department's Charter in the face of considerable resistance. The directive to develop the Department's Charter was given by his predecessor head of department, Prof. Stephen Hough, whom Prof. Moosa described as a "very progressive" Afrikaner man. The Department of Medicine's Charter served as the forerunner and framework for the Faculty Charter task team, as we reviewed it at the beginning of our process. The idea was to see what was possible, and not to use it as a template. There are several common concepts shared between the two Charters, including a memorandum to accompany the Charter. The memorandum forms the next phase of the process and is aimed at offering practical solutions that can be implemented within a specific timeframe.

I provided regular feedback regarding the Charter development and visual redress processes directly to the Dean via emails and at the DACT meetings, where suggestions regarding these processes were offered. I also presented the Charter at the Faculty Board meeting, which was attended by the Rector, Prof. Wim de Villiers, and it received positive feedback from him and colleagues present at the meeting. In addition, the Charter was presented at the Institutional Visual Redress Committee, where it was also well received. The Charter was completed at the end of the first quarter of 2019, and the Dean advised us to plan the launch along with the visual redress elements thereof.

Launching the Faculty Charter

Most of the task team members had no expertise with visual redress, and hence, the chairperson of the Faculty Visual Redress Sub-committee of DACT recommended that we approach Prof. Elmarie Costandius of the Department of Visual Arts to guide us with her expertise. She played a pivotal role in advising how to depict the Charter visually. Task team members concluded that the visual representations of the Charter would play a crucial role in reminding one another of the process of transforming. Subsequently, we created a slogan representing our commitment to transformation and decolonisation: "Committed to transforming" – an action word that has no end. This slogan was translated into isiXhosa as *Siyazibophelela kutshintsho* and Afrikaans as *Verbind tot transformering*. Presenting the slogan in three languages is a reflection of diversity and inclusivity within the Faculty. We agreed that these three languages had to be represented because they constitute the dominant languages spoken in the Western Cape.

In the same vein, we developed a symbol of intersecting hands in three colours: the SU maroon and mustard, as well as the Faculty teal colour. These three colours also represent the three dominant languages spoken in the Western Cape, as well as a multitude of cultures, 'races', belief systems, dis/abilities, genders and the socio-economic backgrounds of the staff and students. The hand symbol is also carried through the borders of the Perspex installations of the Charter located in the Education building as well as within the brochure. The brochure[65] is available in digital format on the Faculty website and was printed in the form of an A5 booklet. When folded, the cover page of the booklet features the hand symbol and slogan in all three languages. The second page (on the left-hand side) features the Afrikaans version of the Charter, which we agreed was important, but would be decentred. The third page has the isiXhosa version of the Charter, as we agreed that it should have a high degree of prominence. The final page in the brochure includes the English version of the Charter as an international and common language to all at the Faculty.

---

65 http://www.sun.ac.za/english/faculty/healthsciences/Documents/FMHS_Charter_2019.pdf

The Faculty Charter was launched in the form of three Perspex panels in Afrikaans, English and isiXhosa in the Education building on 14 October 2019. The task team members debated the order of these panels and decided that Afrikaans would be placed on the left in recognition of its standing – both in the past and present, English in the middle with greatest prominence, followed by isiXhosa on the right as one of the dominant African languages spoken in the Western Cape. This language order was different to the brochures that were handed out to those who attended the launch.

Figure 7.1: Faculty Charter launch, 14 October 2019, including the dean, members of the Dean's management team, the Deputy Registrar, Prof. Julian Sonn, Dr Claire Kelly, the Faculty Charter chairperson and core members of the task team.
(Source: Marketing and Communications Division, Tygerberg Campus, SU)

Originally, the launch was planned for 5 September 2019, but we postponed it in light of the Anti-GBV protests that erupted on our campus. Both Faculty executive management and the Faculty Charter task team members did not wish to detract from the scourge of GBV in South Africa. Instead, we wanted to offer recognition to the womxn who suffered various forms of violence – both those who have survived and others, such as Uyinene Mrwetyana, who suffered tragic deaths.

The Perspex Charter installations in the Education building and hand symbol stickers were part of Phase 1 of the Faculty Charter visual redress initiative. The Faculty's Visual Redress Sub-committee will decide on how to integrate the Charter in different buildings. Furthermore, the Charter forms part of the Human Resources induction programme presented to new staff at the Faculty. In this way, staff will see the Faculty's commitment to equity, transformation and decolonisation.

Conclusion

The Faculty Charter is a pledge to create an inclusive, fair and welcoming environment for all. Seboko, a task team member, shared her sentiments on the importance of the Charter: "What it means for me is that we are actively striving towards a more welcoming environment. A more inclusive environment. A more aware environment … I think that's [a] very present reminder that this is what we want to move towards". Another member felt that there is "some scope for holding people accountable to the Charter" in so far as the staff's commitment to transformation should be taken into consideration when promotions are being applied for: "I think the faculty should take a firm stance and say no … No matter how much money you bring in, [if] you are not promoting the Charter, you are not promoting the ethos that we are standing for" (Roos). Similarly, the Dean and several members of the task team would also like to see the ethos of the Charter reflected in the key performance agreements of staff members.

The aim of the Charter and its visual representations is to enable all who walk and wheel through the campus – visitors, students, staff, parents and prospective students – to feel they belong. Visual representations of transformation and decolonisation are a means to overcome alienation and to create spaces for reflection, dialogue and safety for marginalised groups.

Transformation is an appeal to our common humanity, not simply a process of demographic changes. Engaging with this Charter development process has been a humbling and transformative experience for me as the chair of the Faculty Charter task team. For me, the process reached full circle at the Dean's Lunch in July 2019.

That afternoon, I sat at a table with fellow members, and we realised that the most incredible by-product of participating in the task team was that colleagues and students from divisions and programmes who normally would not have met had had an opportunity to collaborate on a transformative project.

In conclusion, I have demonstrated throughout this chapter the crucial role that meaningful dialogues had a transformative impact on the Faculty culture. I hope that the Faculty Charter will galvanise other faculties to follow suit. In July 2019, I was asked to lead the process of developing the Transformation Charter for the Division Student Affairs, and we have recently embarked on this process. Moreover, given the successes of previous dialogues, the Charter is intended to be the catalyst for future engagements concerned with transformation and decolonisation within the Faculty and the University more broadly.

References

De Sousa Santos, B. 2014. *Epistemologies of the South: Justice against epistemicide.* Boulder, CO: Paradigm. https://doi.org/10.4324/9781315634876

Fataar, A. 2020. *Pursuing decolonial knowledge building in South African higher education.* (Forthcoming book chapter).

FMHS (Faculty of Medicine and Health Sciences). 2019. *Faculty Charter.* Retrieved from http://www.sun.ac.za/english/faculty/healthsciences/Documents/FMHS_Charter_2019.pdf [Accessed 3 June 2020].

Lee, P. 2013. Dead woman's skull leads to racism-in-science project. *University World News,* 26 April. Retrieved from https://www.universityworldnews.com/post.php?story=20130426100245191 [Accessed 28 September 2020].

Matandela, M. 2017. Redefining Black Consciousness and resistance: The intersection of Black Consciousness and black feminist thought. *Agenda: Empowering women for gender equity,* 31(3/4):10-28. https://doi.org/10.1080/10130950.2017.1402410

Mbali, M. 2013. Rethinking Maties' apartheid past. *Mail & Guardian,* 7 June. Retrieved from https://mg.co.za/article/2013-06-07-rethinking-maties-apartheid-past/ [Accessed 28 September 2020].

Mezirow, J. 1978. *Education for perspective transformation: Women's re-entry programs in community colleges.* New York, NY: Teachers College, Columbia University.

Mezirow, J. 1991. *Transformative dimensions of adult learning.* San Francisco, CA: Jossey-Bass.

Mezirow, J. 1995. Transformation theory of adult learning. In M.R. Welton (ed). *In defense of the lifeworld.* New York, NY: SUNY, 39-70.

Nieuwoudt, S., Dickie, K.E., Coetsee, C., Engelbrecht, L. & Terblanche, E. 2019. Retracted article: Age- and education-related effects on cognitive functioning in colored South African women. *Neuropsychology, Development, and Cognition. Section B: Aging, Neuropsychology and Cognition*, 27(3):321-337. https://doi.org/10.1080/13825585.2019.1598538

Soudien, C. 2020. Difficult knowledge: The state of the discussion around 'race' in the social sciences. In J. Jansen & C. Walters (eds). *Fault Lines: A Primer on Race, Science and Society.* Stellenbosch: African Sun Media, 103-118. https://doi.org/10.18820/9781928480495/06

Strauss, A. & Corbin J. 1990. *Basics of qualitative research: Grounded theory procedures and techniques.* London: Sage.

SU (Stellenbosch University). N.d. *Visual redress.* Retrieved from http://www.sun.ac.za/english/transformation/visual-redress [Accessed 3 June 2020].

SU (Stellenbosch University). 2018. *Centenary address by Prof. Wim de Villiers, Rector and Vice-Chancellor.* Retrieved from http://www.sun.ac.za/english/management/wim-de-villiers/Documents/20180323%20Wim%20de%20Villiers%20-%20Eeufees%20Centenary%20(FIN).pdf [Accessed 7 October 2020].

Walters, H. 2019. Racial classification and the spectre that haunts. In G. Mare (ed). *Race in Education.* Stellenbosch: African Sun Media, 111-136. https://doi.org/10.18820/9781928480150/04

Xaba, W. 2017. Challenging Fanon: A black radical feminist perspective on violence and the Fees Must Fall movement. *Agenda*, 31(3/4):96-104. https://doi.org/10.1080/10130950.2017.1392786

Interviews:

Interview with Ascentia Seboko via Microsoft Teams, 13 August 2020.

Interview with Cindy (pseudonym) via Microsoft Teams, 18 August 2020.

Interview with Dr Eduard Roos via Microsoft Teams, 11 August 2020.

Interview with Kabelo (pseudonym) via Microsoft Teams, 18 August 2020.

Interview with Prof. Jimmy Volmink via Microsoft Teams, 12 August 2020.

Interview with Prof. Nulda Beyers via Skype, 12 August 2020.

Interview with Prof. Rafique Moosa via Microsoft Teams, 14 August 2020.

Interview with Yonela (pseudonym) via Microsoft Teams, 14 August 2020.

Chapter 8

Law and visual redress: The space between insider and outsider

Bradley Slade

Introduction

I can identify with the statement that Stellenbosch University (SU) was "historically not designed with my body in mind" (Carolissen, 2018:467).[66] The same holds true for the former Model C schools that I attended from the young age of seven. The majority of the people looked different. They also acted differently from what I was used to. The cultural and religious practices at these schools were foreign to me. There was, however, little choice but to adapt once I crossed the big road separating the 'coloured' neighbourhood where I grew up, Idas Valley, from white Stellenbosch. I also crossed that road to attend SU. I still cross that big road when I drop my daughter off at my alma mater before I drive further into the centre of town, where I park my car and proceed to my office in the Old Main Building. I am a lecturer in the Faculty of Law at SU; a faculty that is situated in the Old Main Building. However, SU in my hometown of Stellenbosch still feels like a foreign place, and at times I feel like a visitor or a guest. At the worst of times, I feel like an intruder or an ungrateful guest because of my resistance to the dominant forces and to conform to the dominant institutional culture. At times, I feel that I am not welcome, that I do not belong.

The combined visuals on campus play a huge part in provoking the feeling that I am not welcome, of feeling that I do not belong (see Clark & Costandius, 2020:4–5). With visuals, I include statues, names of buildings and lecture halls, and pictures of people on the walls in various spaces. The impact of the visuals creates a feeling of otherness, as the visuals mostly give recognition and honour to a particular group of society to the exclusion of others. The powerful feelings invoked by visuals cannot be discounted (*Nelson Mandela Foundation Trust v Afriforum NPC*, 2019). SU has acknowledged the importance of visual redress, and defines it as follows:

> An attempt to right the wrongs of former and current powers by removing hurtful symbols (e.g. of apartheid), social injustice and misrecognition; and by remedying

---

66 More broadly, the belief that the "academy was not made for blacks (or women)" has gained prominence (Khunou, Canha, Khoza-Shangase & Phaswana, 2019:5).

the harm that has been caused by these visual symbols by compensation through new visual symbols that should have African centrality as an outcome and that should allow for the inclusion of a variety of expressions, stories, identities and histories (SU, n.d.:3).

Redress, therefore, requires setting things right, compensating, and removing the cause of the hurt (SU, n.d.:3).

As the visual symbols on the SU campus have an impact on notions of social injustice and misrecognition, and by extension, also belonging, I am starkly reminded of the words in the Preamble to the Constitution of the Republic of South Africa 1996 (Republic of SA, 1996), which states that "South Africa belongs to all who live in it, united in our diversity". The constitutional vision of belonging is therefore an important concept in a democratic South Africa, as the question of who belonged in South Africa was previously racially determined. As such, the Preamble can be direction-giving in reflecting on visual redress and visual redress processes that may ultimately impact on notions of belonging. Various redress processes in the Faculty of Law indeed opened conversations about what it means to be an insider or an outsider, and what it means to belong. As such, this chapter provides a personal reflection on these visual redress processes, and how I experienced them in relation to my sense of belonging.

The chapter is structured as follows: it starts by considering the role of law in establishing the prevailing visuals in institutions of higher learning, such as SU. It proceeds to unpack the impact that the prevailing visuals have on black staff and students, like myself, who traverse these spaces. I then reflect on visual redress processes in and around the Old Main Building. As the law played an instrumental role in the type of visuals at SU, the chapter also considers what role the law, particularly the Preamble to the Constitution, which was also the subject of a contested visual redress project on the SU campus, can play in guiding visual redress processes and broader transformation in general.

The role of law in establishing the prevailing visuals

The Union Constitution of 1909 created a divided state: democratic government for the minority white population and autocratic administrative rule of the majority black population. The segregation policy later became the official state policy named apartheid when the National Party came to power in 1948. The policy of apartheid was implemented by a variety of laws that regulated aspects of public and private life. Chief among these were the Population Registration Act (1950),[67] the Group Areas Act (1950),[68] the Reservation of Separate Amenities Act (1953)[69] and the Immorality Amendment Act (1957).[70]

The system of apartheid was therefore a deliberate policy to give effect to white supremacy and racial segregation (*Nelson Mandela Foundation Trust v Afriforum NPC*, 2019: para 44).[71] It was based on the belief that black people "were intellectually inferior, lazy and lesser beings in every respect of consequence" (*City of Tshwane Metropolitan Municipality v Afriforum*, 2016: para 2). As a result of the policy of apartheid and the reservation of institutions for the white population, the visuals in and around these institutions by and large only represent white men. The same is true for historically white universities (Schmahmann, 2013)[72] such as SU.

On the SU campus, many buildings were named after white men who either played an important role in the apartheid government or were esteemed academics and academic leaders at the institution. While some of the more problematic names,

---

67   This Act categorised all people into different racial groupings.

68   This Act ensured residential separation. It was under this Act that many black people were forcibly removed from places such as Die Vlakte in Stellenbosch and District 6 in Cape Town.

69   This Act made the creation of separate amenities such as parks, beaches and toilets for different racial groups compulsory. These facilities were not required to be of the same standard, which meant that the white amenities were vastly superior.

70   This Act criminalised sexual intercourse between black and white people.

71   HF Verwoerd, a professor at SU from 1928 to 1937, was also prime minister of South Africa from 1958 to 1966, a time during which black suppression intensified.

72   It was typical for the Afrikaans-speaking universities to celebrate the heroes of the Afrikaner volk (e.g. the statue of T Steyn at the University of the Free State) and the English-speaking universities those of imperialists (e.g. the statues/busts of Rhodes at the University of Cape Town and Rhodes University).

such as DF Malan, have been removed (Brink, 2006:1)[73] and others, such as RW Wilcocks,[74] are in the process of removal, a host of academic buildings were named after former deans or rectors who were white and male.[75]

Similarly, various plaques in buildings mostly gave recognition to white men only. In May 2015, 21 years after formal apartheid ended, a plaque with the inscription "In grateful memory of the Honourable HF Verwoerd, Prime Minister of the Republic of South Africa, after whom this building was named on 3 April 1963 and who on 6 September 1966 died in Parliament in the service of his people" was removed from an academic building on the SU campus. In the Old Main Building there is still a plaque (see Figure 8.1) listing the professors of the Old Main Building and the Faculty of Law, which contains the names of white men only, among others HF Verwoerd, who was professor in Sociology and Social Work from 1928 to 1937.[76]

---

73 DF Malan was prime minister of South Africa from 1948 to 1954. During his tenure, the foundation for apartheid was firmly established. He was also the chancellor of SU from 1941 to 1959. For this reason, Brink speaks of the close link between the University and the 'power structures of Afrikanerdom'. The DF Malan Gedenksentrum, a building erected close to the Danie Craven Stadium to honour Malan's memory, was renamed the Coetzenburg Centre.

74 RW Wilcocks chaired the Wilcocks Commission (Commission of Inquiry regarding the Cape Coloured population in the Union, 1938), which, among other things, expressed certain stereotypes about 'coloured' people that would later inform policy decisions of the apartheid government.

75 Examples include the GG Cillié Building (which houses the Faculty of Education) and the CGW Schuman Building (which houses a large component of the Faculty of Economic and Management Sciences). GG Cillié was the institution's first professor of Education in 1911, as well as the first dean of the Faculty of Education when the Victoria College officially became Stellenbosch University in 1918. The following year, Cillié also became the University's very first rector, a position he held until 1925. CGW Schuman was a founding member and dean of the Faculty of Economic and Management Sciences and also served as acting rector.

76 HF Verwoerd played an instrumental role in the establishment of the apartheid state. The introduction of the Population Registration Act, the Reservation of Separate Amenities Act and the Bantu Education Act came at the time when Verwoerd was the minister of Native Affairs. In the education context, a plaque honouring HF Verwoerd that is still visible at a public university after 1994 is lamentable given his ideology regarding the education of black people.

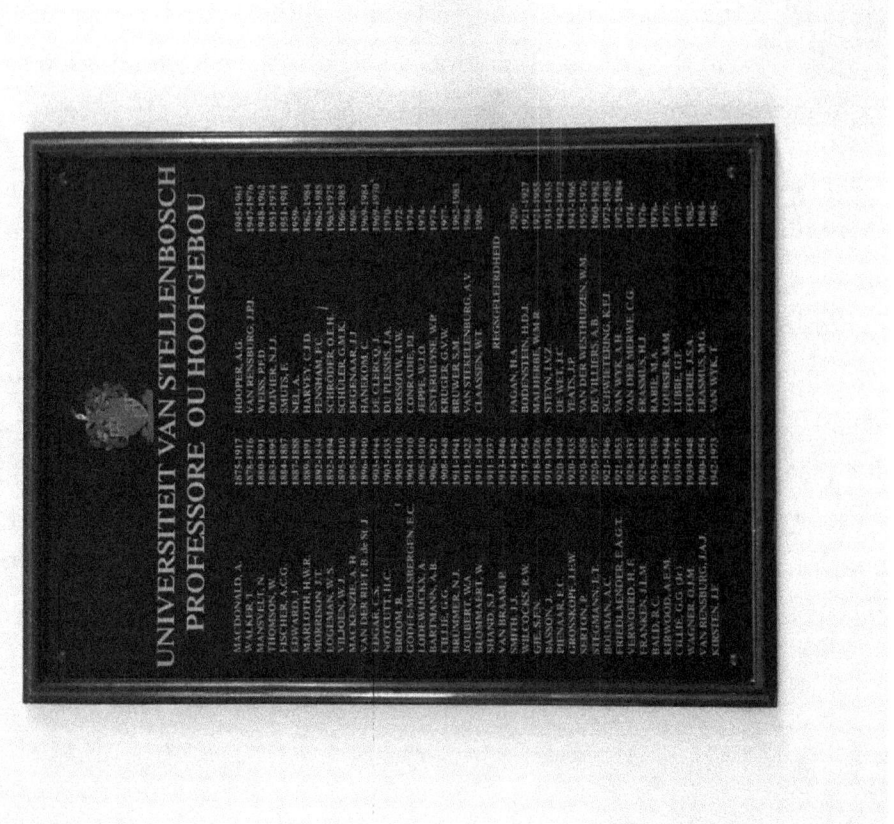

Figure 8.1: Plague in Old Main Building (reproduced with permission)

In numerous rooms, including lecture halls across campus, the photos of previous professors adorn the walls. These photos again are mostly of white male professors. An example is the photos that were in lecture room 2027 of the Old Main Building up until the end of 2019 (Photo 8.2). These were large black and white photos of some of the retired professors of Law. I remember attending lectures in room 2027 as a final-year LLB student in 2008 and feeling uncomfortable with these men staring down at me. Part of the reason for the unease, apart from the imposing nature of these photos, was the fact that they did not represent anyone with whom I could identify.

Figure 8.2: Photos in lecture room 2027 (reproduced with permission)

The names of buildings, the names on the plaques and the faces on the pictures portray those who occupied important positions in the institution and serve to show a history of racial domination. It vividly shows the exclusion of those who are black and female. Apart from showcasing the exclusion of black bodies from the space, the visuals do not reflect the 'hidden histories'. By hidden histories I mean the story of those who were allowed in the space, but for entirely different reasons and purposes, and whose contribution is not given recognition. In the case of SU, coloured[77] men like my maternal grandfather (who grew up in Die Vlakte, but moved to Idas Valley before the Group Areas Act effected the removal of the coloured people from that area) worked as a carpenter on various University buildings, including the GG Cillié Building, directly next to the area of Die Vlakte. These buildings were physically built by black men, yet the University allowed, or tolerated (Madlanga, 2018:359) these men here only for certain purposes. The University also did not actively object to the policy of the state that effectively excluded my grandparents and parents' generations from studying at SU. Although my sister and I were allowed to study at SU and both now work at the institution, we still navigate an institution with an institutional culture that negatively affects those bodies for whom the University was not built (Fikeni, Gobodo-Madikizela, Nhlapo & Walaza, 2020).

---

77 My grandfather was classified as 'coloured' by the apartheid government in terms of the Population Registration Act.

The impact of the prevailing visuals on black people

White men, such as DF Malan and HF Verwoerd, who were honoured by SU in various ways publicly and openly regarded black people as inferior. In democratic South Africa, these individuals should no longer be honoured or revered, and their statues and pictures and names should be removed (Mbembe, 2016:29–30).[78] Such an approach would be in line with the interpretation of the Preamble to the Constitution as given by the Constitutional Court in *City of Tshwane Metropolitan Municipality v Afriforum* (2016) (discussed later in the chapter). However, many other white men whose names appear on buildings or whose faces are in various rooms were not necessarily public figures who openly supported the policies of apartheid or considered black people as inferior. It may therefore be appropriate to engage more deeply with these visuals in undertaking visual redress (Jansen, 2020:132).[79]

Regardless, when the names, pictures and statues of white men are viewed as a whole, or as a collective, they invoke certain negative feelings among those who are not represented in the imagery or names (Mbembe, 2016:29–30).[80] Schmahmann (2013:189) argues that pictures of predominantly white men "seemed, at least to some, to be imbued with evidence of the policies and practices that prevented people of colour from accessing the university's hallowed halls as students or staff members, let alone becoming members of its senior management". Therefore, taken as a whole,

---

78 In this regard I align myself with Mbembe. He states that the "Rhodes' statue has nothing to do on a public university campus", as it is representative of "people who have tormented and violated all that which the name 'Black' stands for while they were alive" (Mbembe, 2016: 29). To the contrary, Schmahmann (2020:142) argues that "removal is not necessarily the most productive or transformative way of negotiating such object". In relation to the Rhodes statue at the University of Cape Town, Schmahmann (2013) relays that the sculptor of the Rhodes statue was Marion Walgate, a female sculptor, and that it is important to note that this sculpture was one of the first major works being commissioned to a woman.

79 See, for instance, Jansen (2020), who speaks about the statues of CR Swart and MT Steyn on the campus of the University of the Free State and the vastly different roles they played in South Africa's history. Jansen makes the point that failing to make a distinction between different historical figures in deciding what is the appropriate course of action regarding the preservation or removal of a statue would be to fail in the educational aspirations of a university. While I don't disagree with Jansen, it is important to have regard to the combined effect that visuals that only, or mostly, represent white men may have on black staff and students.

80 On writing about decolonising the university, Mbembe (2016:29) speaks of pictures, icons and symbols "that mentally harass Black students [and staff] on an everyday basis because these students [and staff] know whom these images represent … figures of people who truly believed that to be Black was a liability".

the visuals on a campus such as that of SU serve as a reminder of the exclusionary practices that it adhered to since its inception and the negative long-term effect such exclusion has on black people (Roithmayr, 2014).[81] The perpetuating "sea of whiteness" further keeps a certain history alive (Ahmed, 2012:38).

The visuals on campuses more generally are also interwoven with the institutional culture of an institution. Schmahmann (2013:16), for instance, states as follows:

> Images and objects which form part of the traditions and visual rhetoric of the institution – its coats of arms or portraits, or the sculptures outside its buildings … are sometimes interpreted as examples of exclusivity and bias within a university's institutional culture.

The "Report by the Ministerial Task Team on the recruitment, retention and progression of black South African academics" further links the dominant institutional culture and the negative effect that it has on black academic staff (DHET, 2019:31). At institutions such as SU, the "deeply imbedded culture of whiteness, that has yet to yield to substantive respect for and affirmation of difference and creation of inclusive cultures, has been a major further impediment to change" (Badat, 2016:7). The slowness by which the visuals and the predominantly white teaching staff change at historically white institutions, such as SU, is testament to this. The fact that it takes so long to remove some of the problematic visuals, or contextualise others, serves as a potent reminder of the history of exclusion and the continued resistance to transform institutions of higher learning (Nell, 2018:1–2).[82]

It is therefore necessary to embark on a visual redress process that aligns with the overall aim of transforming the institutional culture. Institutional culture is pervasive, subconscious and subtle, but in historically white institutions it grants privileges to those who are "white, male, heterosexual and middle class while marginalising those who are not" (Schmahmann, 2013:16). Although strides have been made, the visual

---

81 See Roithmayr (2014) for an account of how racial inequality, which disadvantages black people, is reproduced.

82 See, for instance, Nell (2018) for an account of how class photos, which created a sense of exclusion (socially, economically and physically), misrepresentation, misrecognition and of not belonging among black students were ultimately taken down by black students in the Faculty of Theology at SU.

rhetoric at SU shows this institutional culture. White male names on buildings and plaques, statues of white men in open spaces and white faces on walls are still in a dominant position, similar to the dominance of white men in the (senior) academic staff component and management positions.[83]

Ultimately, it must be accepted that visual redress, the removal of hurtful symbols and engagement on how to redress those seemingly innocuous symbols are central to the rupturing of an institution's colonial and apartheid past (Fikeni et al., 2020:51). Visual redress, as part of the broader process of transformation of the institution, must therefore be seen as part of a process of deep change in the institutional culture, a culture that negatively affects black academic staff and students.

Visual redress projects at the Faculty of Law: Reflections on two visual redress projects from different vantage points

I pointed out above that visuals representing a particular segment of society while excluding others lead to feelings of alienation and marginalisation. Various visual redress processes in the Faculty of Law hinted at who has a voice, who has power, who is an insider and who is an outsider; in other words, who belongs. I now turn to reflect on two of these processes from two different vantage points. In the first, I was an observer of a visual redress process that was undertaken in my working environment and in which I, as an academic staff member, was consulted. In the second, I was the custodian of a visual redress project that sought to elicit conversations about being an insider or an outsider, about who belongs and who does not belong.

Observing the installation of the Preamble in front of the Old Main Building

The first process relates to the installation of three steel plates with the words of the Preamble in three languages (isiXhosa, English and Afrikaans) in front of the Old Main Building. Prof. Geo Quinot from the Department of Public Law spearheaded the project. I was very much in favour of installing the Preamble directly in front

---

83 The Ministerial Task Team reported that 77% of the instructional/research staff at SU are white.

of the Old Main Building and supported it in my capacity as chair of the Faculty of Law's Transformation Committee. Teaching constitutional law, I found the idea of installing the Preamble to the Constitution, which speaks to "recognising the injustices of the past", of honouring those who fought for justice and freedom, the belief that South Africa belongs to all who live in it, healing the divisions of the past and improving the quality of life for all people, directly in front of the Old Main Building, which houses the Faculty of Law, appropriate. I was elated when the model of the installation was presented, as the planned depiction of the Preamble would break the very clear lines of the colonial Old Main Building, and thereby visually break or disrupt the power that colonialism may still hold in this space. Such a gesture would be analogous to the Constitution's ideological disruption of the ideology of colonialism and apartheid. Furthermore, positioning the plates with the Preamble directly in front of the building would emphasise the central role that the Preamble and the Constitution play in establishing a new society that is based on an egalitarian vision of society compared to the racial exclusivism for which the Old Main Building was originally built. I was also excited that the Preamble would be positioned in such a manner that it would serve as a guide to enter the Faculty of Law. The Preamble serves as the statement that sets out the Constitution's "purpose and underlying philosophy" (*City of Tshwane Metropolitan Municipality v Afriforum*, 2016: para 5). It is therefore appropriate for the Preamble to herald entry into the Faculty of Law, where strides are being made to give effect to the purpose and philosophy of the Constitution and specifically the Bill of Rights.

Although the process was launched in 2017, the installation was only completed towards the end of 2020 (see Photo 8.3). A major factor that delayed the installation was the objections of a group outside of the University, namely the Stellenbosch Interest Group (SIG).[84] According to reports, the SIG objected to the imposing

---

[84] The purpose of the SIG, as stated on its Facebook page post of 6 December 2017, is as follows:
The protection of our common heritage, inclusive of both the built and the natural environment; The preservation of the unique character of Stellenbosch and surroundings; Insistence on Town and Regional Planning of the highest order to promote controlled development which respects the historical fabric and which enhances and adds quality to the environment in and around Stellenbosch; To ensure, as far as possible, that development is based on sound architectural principles and design in harmony with the natural and historic character of Stellenbosch.
I have many questions about what is meant by "common heritage".

height of the installation, as it would block an unobstructed view of the Old Main Building (Keet, 2019). Furthermore, the argument was that because the words of the Preamble would not be legible from a distance, the three plates would simply be "onnodig en wanordelik"[85] (unnecessary and disorderly) (Keet, 2019). Although I have opinions on the merits of the objections raised by the SIG, my reflection goes beyond the merits of the objections. It was sobering to observe that an organisation such as the SIG has the capacity and agency to mobilise formal objections against the installation, all the way to the provincial Member of the Executive Committee for Arts and Culture.[86] I wondered why other groups or individuals, such as those who were evicted from Die Vlakte further down the road, were not joining the conversation either for or against the installation. I was astounded about the manner in which legal procedures were being used by outsiders in a manner that contradicts the wishes of those inside the University context.[87] For me, this process elicited questions such as: what grants a certain group the power or voice that can in effect be more powerful than others?, who belongs to the place (both Stellenbosch and SU) so as to have a voice with power?, and to whom does an unobstructed view of the Old Main Building belong?

---

85 As per Patricia Botha, chairperson of SIG.

86 This is comparable to the manner in which Afriforum and the Federasie van Afrikaanse Kultuurvereniginge (FAK) would organise and rally against banning the gratuitous display of the old flag; see Nelson Mandela Foundation Trust v Afriforum, discussed further on in this chapter.

87 Here I include staff and students, the latter requesting some form of visual redress to break the dominance of the Old Main Building.

Figure 8.3: Preamble in front of the Old Main Building (photos by Strijdom van der Merwe)

In a challenge to the change of street names in Pretoria, the Constitutional Court in *City of Tshwane Metropolitan Municipality v Afriforum* relied on the Preamble to contextualise the issue. Although this decision dealt with street names that honour only a certain group of society, the Constitutional Court's statements concerning belonging are important for the transformation of the broader society. The Constitutional Court emphasised the underlying philosophy of the constitutional dispensation as expressed in the Preamble, namely that South Africa belongs to all who live in it. The installation of the Preamble in a prominent place, directly in front of the Old Main Building, can therefore serve as a reminder that unlike in the past, when the University only belonged to a certain group of people, the University and, more broadly, the entire country, belong to all who live in it. In this regard, the importance of the symbolism of the installed Preamble in three languages directly in front of the Old Main Building cannot be underestimated.

Furthermore, I am hopeful that the conversations by those walking through or past the Preamble may be directed to topics that include injustices of the past, healing of wounds and belonging, which is necessary if the constitutional vision of establishing a more just and equal society is to be embraced. The Preamble installation contributes to altering a dominant institutional culture. It serves to decentre the visual symbolism of an imposing colonially inscribed building, which is alienating to black academic staff and students. The installation centres an inclusive and welcoming symbolism in such a way that people, including me, who have up to now been inscribed with outsider status, would begin to develop a sense of belonging in our institutional workspaces.

Curating the insider/outsider installation

The conversation on insiders and outsiders forms part of another visual redress process that I oversaw in my capacity as chair of the Faculty of Law's Transformation Committee. This idea emerged at a Faculty workshop facilitated by Prof. Elmarie Costandius in a process of concept mapping (Jackson & Trochim, 2002:312).[88] Participants were encouraged to map or draw different concepts and then link these various concepts to discover a general theme or idea. It was during this process that the idea of the Old Main Building as a fort was presented. As a fort, it included and protected some within, while excluding others. The most striking points raised during the workshop were those related to the Old Main Building and the exclusion of black bodies, most notably those of the forcibly removed community of Die Vlakte

---

88 Jackson and Trochim (2002:312) explain concept mapping as "an informal process whereby an individual draws a picture of all the ideas related to some general theme or question and shows how these are related".

who lived in close proximity to the building. Naturally, the conversation was also much broader, as the meanings of inclusion and exclusion are complex and varied, and dependent on a variety of factors, including, but not limited to, gender, sexuality and religion. Universities are by nature exclusionary spaces due to admission and appointment requirements. Although exclusion is no longer determined by race or gender, there remain factors that determine who is included and who is excluded.

After the workshop, the Transformation Committee, with the assistance of Prof. Costandius, embarked on a temporary insider/outsider installation. The purpose of the insider/outsider installation would be to start a conversation about who is an outsider, who is an insider, on what basis are these determined and what are the effects of such characterisations. For this purpose, we acquired several life-size cardboard people, or 'standees'. We placed a standee with a description 'outsider' outside the building, but in such a manner that the 'outsider' can 'see' a standee with the description 'insider' through the glass doors or windows. Students and staff were encouraged to converse with the standees by writing on them. The installation was to run for two weeks and the standees would be in different locations each day and could be rearranged. As we intended, many of the staff, students and even some learners from a nearby school engaged in conversation with the standees. On one standee, carrying the description 'outsider', the following was written: "If you black in this space, you automatically outside. This place is toxic", and "They look at my skin colour before I do or say anything". This captured a perspective of what it means to be black inside the Old Main Building and speaks to its existing institutional culture. There were also some neutral messages without institutional judgement posted on some of the other standees. On the standee with the inscription 'excluded', the quote by Alfin Toffler, "The illiterate of the 21st century will not be those who cannot read and write, but those who cannot learn, unlearn and relearn", was posted.

A specific incident that occurred during the installation caused me to reflect on my own status as a hesitant and uncomfortable insider. During the installation, one of the standees was removed, censored and returned to the installation by two female colleagues, without engaging me as the project custodian. Someone drew a male genital on a particular standee, which represented a female body. The standee was removed and only returned after an A4 piece of paper with the word 'censored' was placed over the male genital. The censoring of the male genital evoked the following response by a female graduate student:

> Despite this being a cardboard person it represents a person – a female person. The penis was most likely intended to be funny. Instead of engaging in the violation of the female body in an act of entertainment, our faculty is hiding it. Is this speaking to the mindset of the university? Of refusing to engage in anything that makes us uncomfortable?

One can probably interpret the drawing of the picture differently, but the questions that were raised are valid and would gain prominence when the gender-based violence protests erupted on campuses soon after the standees project was launched. It is interesting to note how quickly the actions of individuals were attributed to the Faculty, and ultimately to the University. This may be how the behaviour of individuals shape a certain institutional culture.

The action of removing the standee and the censoring of the picture that elicited the response of the student sort of left me out in the cold. Initially, I wondered why I, as custodian of the project, was not approached by my colleagues before they decided to remove, censor and replace the standee. Was the picture of such a nature that engagement was unnecessary, so the question about removal and censoring was a given? I for one did not think so. But I also did not have an immediate answer. For that reason, I was still consulting with people on how to deal with the standee and the drawing that was added. Some views offered during consultation expressed the need for providing room for engagement in light of the #EndRapeCulture campaign that has been ongoing on campus. The censoring of the drawing via its removal, however, killed that idea for me for the time being. I do, however, acknowledge that my female colleagues may have been affronted by the image in a way that I could not imagine. However, it was striking how easy it was for them to remove this standee from the installation and then return it (without the part that is affronting to them being exposed), while other pictures and symbols that affront me on a daily basis still adorn the walls and the plains.

One way to see what happened during this temporary installation is to regard myself as someone without power or agency, but that the power and agency rest elsewhere. In this regard, although I am meant to be an insider, the incident illustrated why I am actually an outsider. Although I am included in formal work-related tasks and processes, I am in fact excluded from informal conversations about what processes should be adopted to deal with a contentious issue in which I actually have a stake. Does this mean that I have no power, that I do not belong, or that I am still really an outsider – "an outsider within"? (Collins, 1986:S14–S32; Fikeni et al., 2020).[89]

Opening up important questions, this specific visual redress process gave me a reason to pause for reflection. And the mere fact that I had these questions probably meant that I was able to put my finger on an institutional culture that alienated me as a black student and continues to alienate me as a black staff member. The upshot is that the visual redress process opened a conversation that would allow me and my colleagues to work towards a position where we are forced to think about how our actions, sometimes unconsciously inspired, affect others not similarly situated. This should enable a critical conversation on the prevailing institutional culture.

The Preamble as guiding visual redress process and unpacking institutional culture

The feeling of not belonging in a public institution of higher learning contrasts with the Preamble's notion of belonging. What may therefore be required is a change in the visuals so that feelings of alienation can be transformed into feeling a sense of belonging.[90] As Mbembe (2015:5) indicates, it is not a matter of charity or hospitality or a liberal notion of tolerance or requiring assimilation. It is about "ownership of a space that is a public, common good" (Mbembe, 2015:5), which requires also addressing the institutional culture that gives rise to feeling neither at home, nor belonging. Addressing the institutional culture can take place through the process of

---

89 Black academic staff often express feeling invisible in historically white institutions.

90 Creating a space where black students and staff would choose to spend time to, in the context of the academic environment, be co-creators of knowledge.

engaging with the visuals and imagining and re-imagining what they can look like. The lessons learnt from these processes are also important in unpacking institutional culture that leads to exclusionary practices and behaviours.

Schmahmann (2014:1) states that the removal of offensive images and names on buildings can create a feeling of loss of culture or heritage, as it "eradicate[s] signs of each and every contribution made by white men". On the other hand, it is argued that certain images must be removed, as they lead to "self-humiliation and self-debasement" (Mbembe, 2016:32), and therefore alienation. The Constitutional Court's decision in *City of Tshwane Metropolitan Municipality v Afriforum* presents the Preamble as a medium through which these challenges can be mediated. According to the Court,

> … colonialism or apartheid is a system so stubborn that its divisive and harmful effects continue to plague us and retard our progress as a nation more than two decades into our hard-earned constitutional democracy … Almost all cities, towns and street names continue to reverberate with great sounds of veneration for the architects of apartheid, heroes and heroines of our oppressive and shameful colonial past. (*City of Tshwane Metropolitan Municipality v Afriforum*, 2016: para 4)

The cultural monopoly by one race can no longer be condoned. There is therefore a need to undo the effects of a system of racial, ethnic and tribal stratification of the past. This, according to the Court, is achieved *partly* by the removal of names (and one can include statues, pictures and symbols) that exalt elements of our past that cause grief to other racial groups or reopen supposedly healing wounds. It also means removing innocuous names that only honour or recognise people or history of one group (defined culturally or racially). In this regard, the Court stated that …

> … [n]o measure of sophistry, contortion, or strategy ought to be allowed to entrench any form of racial domination or exclusivity to privilege, honour and opportunities … White South Africans must enjoy a sense of belonging. But unlike before that cannot and should never be allowed to override all other people's interest … Any indirect or even inadvertent display of an attitude of racial intolerance, racial marginalisation and insensitivity, by white or black people must be resoundingly rejected by all South Africans in line with the Preamble and

our values, if our constitutional aspirations are to be realised. (*City of Tshwane Metropolitan Municipality v Afriforum*, 2016: para 9)

This approach was subsequently also adopted by the High Court in *Nelson Mandela Foundation Trust v Afriforum NPC* (2019). In this decision, the Court had to consider whether the gratuitous display of the old national flag constitutes hate speech. The Court reiterated that the foundational values of the democratic society, as stated in the Preamble of the Constitution, should bind South Africans and guide our actions when considering aspects that involve visuals, such as the gratuitous display of the old flag, which is divisive and has the potential to cause harm. The Court considered the meaning attributed to the old flag by the Nelson Mandela Foundation as articulated through its CEO, Sello Hatang. Sello Hatang spoke to the memories brought to the fore upon seeing the old flag. These include feelings of shame when white children would call his grandmother (and by extension himself) a baboon and the remembrance of a system that saw black people as the 'other' and denied them the opportunity to be human (*Nelson Mandela Foundation Trust v Afriforum NPC*, 2019: para 23). The flag is therefore regarded as a symbol of "racism, white supremacy and the subjugation of the black population" (*Nelson Mandela Foundation Trust v Afriforum NPC*, 2019: para 78). Even though the FAK claimed that the gratuitous display of the flag is important, as it is "a symbol of reconciliation and unity between the English- and Afrikaans-speaking population",[91] the Court reasoned that the unified white population oppressed the black population and therefore concluded that such an interpretation cannot be accepted in an inclusive democratic society. What this decision therefore illustrates is that visuals cannot be used in a manner that causes people to feel that they are the other, that they are not recognised as human and that they do not belong to or in South Africa.

It is arguable that these considerations, as informed by the Preamble, are important in visual redress processes and in the development of visual redress policies. Symbols, images and names, whether seen as individualistic or as a collective, that cause South Africans to feel that they do not belong, or that cause harm and suffering, should be subjected to a visual redress process. This process can take various forms, and

---

91 FAK affidavit as quoted in para 79 of the judgement.

the end result may be different in each unique context. What would be required, however, is that the process in itself (whether it results in a quick process of removal or a longer process of contextualisation or deconstruction) must be transformative in nature. The process should speak to individuals at a personal level in order to change behaviours, mindsets and world outlooks that keep a particular institutional culture in place and ultimately delay our progress as a nation.

Concluding remarks

In terms of the Constitutional Court's judgement in *City of Tshwane Metropolitan Municipality v Afriforum* (2016), there seems to be some constitutional parameters when it comes to the presence and/or removal of visuals in public spaces. Although it is relatively clear that there is no space for visuals that cause South Africans to feel that they do not belong, it must be recognised that the changing or removal of iconography alone is not sufficient to heal the deeps wounds left in the wake of colonialism and apartheid. What is therefore required is not simply installing new art or removing hurtful symbols, but instilling the constitutional values within the hearts of people. It therefore seems clear that visual redress alone cannot effect transformation (Clark & Costandius, 2020:1–2). As former Chief Justice Pius Langa said in relation to moving from a society characterised by strife and untold suffering to a society based on fundamental rights and freedoms: "This is a magnificent goal for a Constitution: to heal the wounds of the past and guide us to a better future. For me, this is the core idea of transformative constitutionalism: that *we must change*" (Langa, 2006:352, own emphasis). I take Langa's plea to mean that we must be open to listen to the pain and fears of others and have honest, and sometimes difficult, conversations about what it means to live in a democratic South Africa where each one is mindful of visuals, processes and behaviours that may alienate or marginalise others. We must therefore all be mindful of the ideal that South Africa belongs to all who live in it, and not just to those who hold social, economic, political or cultural power.

To this end, visual redress processes go a long way to start conversations on belonging, about who is an insider and who is excluded. South Africans who want to be part of a democratic South Africa must show up to the conversations and do some deep personal work reflecting on themselves in relation to others. Only by doing that would we be able to achieve a society where all may be able to claim to belong.

References

Ahmed, S. 2012. *On being included: Racism and diversity in institutional life*. Durham: Duke University Press. https://doi.org/10.1515/9780822395324

Badat, S. 2016. *Deciphering the meanings, and explaining the South African higher education student protests of 2015-16*. WISER. Retrieved from https://wiser.wits.ac.za/system/files/documents/Saleem%20Badat%20-%20Deciphering%20the%20Meanings%2C%20and%20Explaining%20the%20South%20African%20Higher%20Education%20Student%20Protests.pdf [Accessed 23 September 2020].

Brink, C. 2006. *No lesser place: The Taaldebat at Stellenbosch*. Stellenbosch: African Sun Media. https://doi.org/10.18820/9781919980966

Carolissen, R. 2018. Negotiating belonging through language, place and education: An auto-ethnography. In: R. Pattman & R. Carolissen (eds). *Transforming transformation in research and teaching at South African universities*. Stellenbosch: African Sun Media, 467-483.

City of Tshwane Metropolitan Municipality v Afriforum 2016 (6) SA 279 (CC).

Clark, M. & Costandius, E. 2020. Redress at higher education institutions in South Africa: Mapping a way forward. *de arte,* 55:1-22. https://doi.org/10.1080/00043389.2020.1728874

Collins, P.H. 1986. Learning from the outsider within: The sociological significance of black feminist thought. *Social Problems*, 33:S14-S32. https://doi.org/10.1525/sp.1986.33.6.03a00020

DHET (Department of Higher Education and Training). 2019. *Report of the Ministerial Task Team on the recruitment, retention and progression of black South African academics*. Retrieved from https://www.dst.gov.za/images/2020/02/Report_MTT_RRP_of_Black_Academics_web_final1.pdf [Accessed 23 September 2020].

Fikeni, S., Gobodo-Madikizela, P., Nhlapo, T. & Walaza, N. 2020. *Enquiry into the circumstances surrounding Professor Bongani Mayosi's tenure: Crucible for senior black academic staff?* Retrieved from https://www.news.uct.ac.za/article/-2020-06-22-report-of-the-professor-mayosi-panel [Accessed 30 November 2020].

Jackson, K.M. & Trochim, W.M.K. 2002. Concept mapping as an alternative approach for the analysis of open-ended survey responses. *Organizational Research Methods,* 5:307-336. https://doi.org/10.1177/109442802237114

Jansen, J. 2020. 'It's not even past': Dealing with monuments and memorials on divided campuses. In: F. Freschi, B. Schmahmann & L. van Robbroeck (eds). *Troubling images: Visual culture and the politics of Afrikaner nationalism.* Johannesburg: Wits University Press, 119-139. https://doi.org/10.18772/22020024716.10

Keet, D. 2019. SBG gekant teen struktuur voor historiese Ou Hoofgebou. *Eikestadnuus*, 21 January. Retrieved from https://www.netwerk24.com/ZA/Eikestadnuus/Nuus/sbg-gekant-teen-struktuur-voor-historiese-ou-hoofgebou-20190116-2 [Accessed 23 September 2020].

Khunou, G., Canha, H., Khoza-Shangase, K. & Phaswana, E. 2019. Black in the academy: Reframing knowledge, the knower, and knowing. In: G. Khunou, H. Canha, K. Khoza-Shangase & E. Phaswana (eds). *Black academic voices: The South African experience.* Cape Town: HSRC Press, 1-10.

Langa, P. 2006. Transformative constitutionalism. *Stellenbosch Law Review*, 18:351-360.

Madlanga, M. 2018. The human rights duties of companies and other private actors in South Africa. *Stellenbosch Law Review,* 29:359-378.

Mbembe, A. 2015. Decolonizing knowledge and the question of the archive. Public lecture presented at WISER, University of the Witwatersrand.

Mbembe, A. 2016. Decolonizing the university: New directions. *Arts and Humanities in Higher Education,* 15:29-45. https://doi.org/10.1177/1474022215618513

Nell, I. 2018. We know to whom we belong? The drama of ministerial practice in a postcolonial African context. *Verbum et Ecclesia,* 39:1-8. https://doi.org/10.4102/ve.v39i1.1822

Nelson Mandela Foundation Trust v Afriforum NPC 2019 (6) SA 327 (GJ).

Roithmayr, D. 2014. *Reproducing racism: How everyday choices lock in white advantage.* New York, NY: New York University Press.

RSA (Republic of South Africa). 1996. *Constitution of the Republic of South Africa.* Pretoria: Government Printing Works.

Schmahmann, B. 2013. *Picturing change: Curating visual culture at post-apartheid universities.* Johannesburg: Wits University Press. https://doi.org/10.18772/12013045805

Schmahmann, B. 2014. *Toppled statues and fallen icons: Negotiating monuments to British imperialism and Afrikaner nationalism at post-apartheid universities.* Inaugural lecture presented on 5 November 2015 at the University of Johannesburg.

Schmahmann, B. 2020. Knocking Jannie of his pedestal: Two creative interventions to the sculpture of JH Marais at Stellenbosch University. In: F. Freschi, B. Schmahmann & L. van Robbroeck (eds). *Troubling images: Visual culture and the politics of Afrikaner nationalism.* Johannesburg: Wits University Press, 140-165. https://doi.org/10.18772/22020024716.11

SU (Stellenbosch University). N.d. *Stellenbosch University Visual Redress Policy (Draft).* Retrieved from http://www.sun.ac.za/english/Documents/Visual%20Redress%20Policy%20draft_eng.pdf [Accessed 30 November 2020].

Chapter 9

Visual redress: Decolonising the Faculty of Theology at Stellenbosch University?

Reggie Nel

Introduction

Redress is not an easy term in South Africa. While it is complex and nuanced, always eluding the grasp, like all words, this particular term also carries with it the emotive baggage of a history of injustice. In the most recent context, Stellenbosch University (SU) now also speaks of *visual* redress. The current (draft) Visual Redress Policy formally defines it as …

> … [a]n attempt to right the wrongs of former and current powers by removing hurtful symbols (e.g. of apartheid), social injustice and misrecognition; and by remedying the harm that has been caused by these visual symbols by compensation through new visual symbols that should have African centrality as an outcome and that should allow for the inclusion of a variety of expressions, stories, identities and histories … (SU, 2019:3)

SU and its Faculty of Theology have embarked on this journey. We must not despise the day of small things! Therefore, in my short presentation in the process of my appointment as dean in 2017, I made a point of affirming how this university, over the last decade or so, has made an effort to restore dignity to those who suffered under forced removals because of apartheid legislation here in Stellenbosch. This is redress. I indicated that as an alumnus of SU, I will remain proud to be associated with these efforts. Also, as someone who lived in Idas Valley and attended Lückhoff High School, I was immersed in the narratives of members from the community – close family and friends – in relation to the perceptions of the *varsity in die dorp* (university in the town). These were bitter narratives of dispossession and alienation, even though many prominent members of our community, my role models in educational, religious, sports and cultural institutions, worked at the institution (see Biscombe, 2006:179–190). In my presentation, therefore, I argued that, flowing out of what was at the time SU's Institutional Intent and Strategy, we should appreciate these efforts, also as an institution, but we must also be challenged to treasure the riches of our local communities and serve their needs. This, I argued, in line with the language of intent and strategy, is transformation (or social impact) *through* the University.[92] Transformation is a systemic process that is directly linked to redress.

What, then, is this (SU's notion of) transformation as a systemic process and, more specifically for this contribution, its relation to the term 'visual redress'? More importantly, how would this look for a Faculty of Theology on a journey of decolonisation if it were to remain true to its intent and my commitments? In this chapter, I firstly recount this process within this Faculty. Through this, I will also grapple with some of the contestations and questions raised. Secondly, as a theologian influenced largely by the tradition of South African Black Theology (SABT) of Liberation, I will use what I consider a key postcolonial text, called the Confession of Belhar (NGSK, 1986:722-726) as the conceptual lens to re-read the history of what seems to be (also) a tragic narrative of land dispossession and cultural alienation. The key question is: How would this text frame the issues concerned in order to overcome this legacy – to decolonise? I chose Belhar, neither superficially because of the township Belhar's close geographical proximity to Stellenbosch here in the Western Cape, nor because of the symbolic resonance of the forced removals between these townships (Belhar) and the ones in Stellenbosch (which remain critical), but because as a religious text, inspired among others by SABT, the Belhar Confession inspired and formed generations of leaders in higher education, such as the former vice-chancellor and rector of SU, the late Prof. Russel Botman, who, I would argue, spearheaded a process of transformation (before #FeesMustFall) at SU. Prof. Botman's contributions were not merely confined myopically within theology or religious spaces, even though his public role was influenced from this deep (sacred) space, i.e. shaped by this Belhar tradition (Smit, 2017:79–81). It inspired what is now often referred to as Public Theology (Agang, 2020; Smit, 2017:87–88). Moreover, this tradition continues to inspire new waves of communities to ignite processes towards redress, and therefore also visual redress – dispossessed communities that face the brunt of colonial injustice and therefore call for redress. These are communities that owe it to the coming generations to reclaim their heritage, and from these sources, their 'own wells', so to speak, insist on redress as part of social (cultural, economic

---

92 See SU's Visual Redress Policy (SU, 2019) and Transformation Plan (SU, 2017).

and religious) justice. This, in my view, would be the basis for a university such as SU to pursue not merely symbolic redress, or worse, superficial cultural appropriation, but concrete social justice as the basis for deep and meaningful significance.

Lastly then, I will make some proposals that, I would argue, need to be central in the quest of the Faculty, but also the University, as they still seek to give credence to the notion of transformation *in*, but more so *through*, the University, for local communities, but also impacting similar calls in other parts of our continent and global South. I start by retelling the story, so far, within this faculty.

A (contested) narrative maintained in statues and pictures

It is traditionally accepted that the *Teologiese Kweekskool* (Theological Seminary), which was established in 1859 by the Dutch Reformed Church (DRC) in South Africa, became the stimulus for the establishment of Victoria College, later Stellenbosch University, in 1918. The *Kweekskool* is considered the predecessor of the current Faculty of Theology (Brown, 1994:85). This narrative is portrayed in the visual symbols on campus and the scholarship on its history. However, when the University was established, there was no distinct faculty of Theology. Two years later, in 1920, a faculty of *Godsgeleerdheid* (Divinity) was incorporated into the University. The Theological Seminary, often referred to simply as the *Kweekskool,* existed parallel but in close relationship to the University. This meant that the lecturers called at the *Kweekskool* also taught their subjects at the University Faculty, but that the control in terms of the appointment and discipline of the professors as well as the content of the curriculum remained with the DRC. It was only late in 1962 that a formal agreement was reached between the University and the DRC, for the first time incorporating the *Kweekskool* into the University and renaming the Faculty of Divinity the Faculty of Theology in January 1963 (Brown, 1994:89; Combrink, Muller & Hartney, 2009:35). This chapter is not simply another history of this *Kweekskool,* although it briefly raises some of these aspects that are critical to understand the current narrative and visual representation at the Faculty. I would, however, argue that what is often underplayed is how this stream (from the

Kweekskool) flowed into the University structure and initially stood in the tradition of a public call to practise theology from and for Africa, forming leaders for the realities of the time. The notion of a public theology from and for Africa was not known at the time, as it only emerged over the last few decades. One can, however, sense some early currents, but also some tension from other quarters to keep it an institution only serving self-interests. Let me then outline this argument in brief.

In 1824, Abraham Faure was tasked by the synod of the DRC to chair a commission to explore the formation of the *Kweekskool* (Coertzen, 2009:6–7). In the DRC history, many reasons were given for the formation the *Kweekskool*. At its first centenary celebrations, in the context of the rise of Afrikaner nationalism, it was described in *Die Kerkbode* of 28 October 1959 as *"'n inrigting uit die kerk en vir die kerk"* (an institution from the church and for the church) (Op sy mylpaal lees ons 100!, 1959:658). Indeed. Up to the establishment and inauguration of the *Kweekskool*, the *dominees* (ministers) of the DRC were trained mainly in the Netherlands, because initially the church resorted under a *classus* (presbytery) of the Reformed church in the Netherlands. But the supply of educated ministers was low (Coertzen, 2009:3). Therefore, the proposed theological formation centre to be established by Faure was to be indigenous and contextual – from the *Kaap*. Hence, one could also argue for a formation tradition from Africa, in Africa and for this church in Africa. Brown (1994:73–75) uses the notions of *"Kaapse Kweekskool"* (Cape Seminary), a theological seminary *"aan die Kaap"* (at the Cape) and a *"Kaapse Teologiese Kweekskool"* (Cape Theological Seminary) interchangeably. When theology professor BB Keet (1959b:686) reflects back in 1959 on the type of streams that flowed into the theology of the *Kweekskool*, he makes reference to a Scottish, Dutch and Swiss-Reformed stamp, but, importantly, challenges his readers towards what he calls a *"kragtige stoot"* (powerful push) towards an own *"Afrikaanse inslag"* (African stamp). A key question in retrospect is whether by this reference, Keet meant this African stamp in a narrow Afrikaner-nationalist sense, or broader (inclusive) African sense. What is known about Keet, though, is that he was one of the few professors at the Faculty (and perhaps University) who vehemently opposed the ideological (for him theological) justification of apartheid. One of his students at the time, Beyers

Naudé, would later play a key role in establishing the foundations of public theology, playing no small role in the liberation struggle in South Africa. However, this was not the only reason for the establishment of the *Kweekskool* and later the Faculty.

At the time, concerns were raised about the so-called liberal (modern) theology or rationalism (Coertzen, 2009:3) in European universities, and there was a call for formation in what was called 'evangelical' theology. It is therefore no surprise that the first professors, John Murray (1959) and Nicolaas Jacobus Hofmeyr (1859), whose statues stand in the front garden of the campus, were deeply passionate and conscious of the spiritual needs of the indigenous communities – albeit that they remained children of their time. In all of this, one needs to recognise the influence of a missionary-minded stream of theology in a tradition of Van Lier and Vos, but also propagated and taught widely, particular by the Murray brothers, Andrew and John (Keet, 1959b:658). Van der Merwe (1959:674) refers to John Murray's inaugural lecture, where he refers to the highest honour – *"de hoogste eer voor onze school om kweekelinge te sien"* – being graduands who offer themselves to take the name of Christ to the heathen in the farthest most parts of Africa.

When the University started in 1918 from Victoria College, as indicated earlier, it did not make provision for a theological faculty. Although preparatory studies for theological formation were the impetus for the formation of the Stellenbosch Gymnasium (1866) and "Arts Department" (1874), which became Victoria College (1886),[93] it was only in 1920 that a request was made to government to include a faculty of Divinity in the University. So, in 1920, this faculty was established in the University, with Prof. A Moorrees as the first dean. As indicated earlier, there were good relationships between the *Kweekskool* and the Faculty of Divinity of SU in terms of the status of the professors, the curriculum and the status of the qualifications. It was during the period before this incorporation that professors such as GBA Gerdener promoted the ideas of apartheid theologically, while, on the other hand, Keet resisted the theological (ideological) justification of a racist public policy. I come back to this tradition.

---

93 JS Gericke (1959:673) makes the statement that, in fact, the Kweekskool "gave" South Africa Stellenbosch University. See also the argument by Heese (2018:3) on how the establishment of the Kweekskool contributed to the development of the academic character of the town and the establishment of SU.

When it came to the choice for the specific location of the *Kweekskool*, which relates directly to the current buildings where the Faculty is hosted, it needs to be noted that before this space housed the *Kweekskool* and now the Faculty, the building was a *drosdy hof* (magistrate's court). The *drosdy hof* was initially built and inaugurated in 1687, intended as the official residence of the first magistrate of Stellenbosch, Johannes Mulder (Coertzen, 2009:77). Coertzen (2009:76) states that this is the most historic terrain in Stellenbosch. This is perhaps an overstatement. The building was, however, the first double-storey building in South Africa as a seat of local government for the interior region, but then, also, the first prison (!). However, it was destroyed in a fire in December 1710 and again in 1762 (Heese, 2018:4). The fourth *drosdy* was inaugurated in 1768 with the motto on a gable from Utrecht Rijksuniversity, *Sol iustitiae illustra nos* (May the sun of righteousness enlighten us).

The question is whether one can rightly maintain the traditional consensus that the Faculty of Theology originated in 1859 by a decision of and for the DRC, or whether we should conclude that it started in 1920 according to a decision of government to establish a faculty of Divinity at a state university, or even in 1963, when the *Kweekskool* became the Faculty of Theology. If the last argument is accepted, then indeed it has to be accepted that, while the *Kweekskool* initially influenced the establishment of the Faculty of Divinity, there were also tensions and deep contestations. Here, I would introduce a metaphor of a river with many streams. One cannot reduce the history of the Faculty to one narrative or source. Its flow is also shaped by the terrain and the various streams. It would seem that it can be confirmed that the first church (stream) that signed a formal agreement with this university and its faculty was the DRC in 1963, followed in 1999/2000 by the Uniting Reformed Church in Southern Africa (URCSA), the United Presbyterian Church of Southern Africa (2002), the Anglican Church of Southern Africa (2012) and the Volkskerk van Afrika (2016). It must be asked how the trajectories of all these partners influenced and reflect in the narrative and visual representation at the Faculty today. The traditional narrative of the history, as indicated briefly above, however, remains present in the statues, artefacts in the church archives and the official history books, but also in the stories told by these statues, pictures and plaques on the walls. It is the traditional narrative of only the *Kweekskool* – not the Faculty of Divinity, nor the call for an inclusive public theology of sorts, based at a public university, with various partners. These questions raised, also in the introductory narratives, are intimately tied to current local contestations and research dilemmas by students and Faculty members, and as suggested earlier, communities beyond the University.

More questions than answers: Process of visual redress emerging

Over the last three years, since the start of my term as dean at the Faculty of Theology at SU, I have been haunted by questions of how to continue and ensure an inclusive culture through the process of systemic transformation, and therefore visual redress, which would engender deep identification, not only from the current students and members of staff (and alumni), but also from the broader community within which we find ourselves. Here I will introduce three streams that flow into the visual redress river. The river received strong impetus – streams flowing into it – a few years before my arrival. I narrow this particular narrative down to the official processes within the Faculty.

When one reads the minutes of Faculty Board meetings, but also the reports from the Faculty to its various partners, especially since 2000, it seems that 2016 was a key year. Already in the first Faculty Board meeting of 2016, under the chairpersonship of the acting dean, Prof. H. Bosman, there is a pointed reference to "transformation" within the Faculty, which, it was decided, must remain an agenda point of all mass meetings (Faculty of Theology, 2016a). Further plans for the opening of an artefact exhibition on 23 February 2016 were also noted. It was, however, in the next board meeting in May (Faculty of Theology, 2016b) when the event that gave a sharper impulse to the call for visual redress was reported. On 4 April 2016, an unknown group, referring to themselves as the Black Theological Collective, apparently one evening removed the photographs and pictures of the various year groups from the walls. In response to this action, the Faculty decided upon a Faculty Indaba, which was scheduled for 29 July 2016, on what was identified at the time as "transformation (especially on language and photographs)" and a series of lunchtime conversations and workshops in liaison with the Theological Student Committee (TSC) (Faculty of Theology, 2016b). It was also decided to include the Black Theological Collective in this process. The level of their engagement in these processes is not clear from the minutes.

Subsequently, two task teams were called into being out of this Transformation Indaba, consisting of members of staff and students, which would address the *"herinrigting van die fakulteitsgebou om dit vir alle studente 'n verwelkomende en insluitende ruimte te maak"*[94] and the question of the sustainability of the parallel-medium language plan (Faculty of Theology, 2016c:n.p.). The Programme Committee was also charged with investigating the contextualisation of the BTh programme. This could perhaps be seen as the formal birth of visual redress in the Faculty. One has to concede, though, that it was not called thus, but rather that this decision was a direct response to the challenge from the Black Theological Collective within the context of systemic transformation. At the next board meeting it was reported that a "task team is appointed by the Faculty Executive to consider the next step in our transformation process in consultation with the TSC and Rev. Rene August (facilitator)" (Faculty of Theology, 2016d:n.p.). It is interesting that in both the board meetings of November 2016 and February 2017 one finds some nuance differences with regard to the Transformation Task Team, which was now also to include representation from the Transformation Office as well as staff and students. In the February 2017 meeting, this task team's mandate is stated to include matters such as "decolonising" and "Africanising theology" (Faculty of Theology, 2017b:n.p.). It was also communicated at this meeting that the "appropriation of the Transformation Plan of SU adopted in January 2017 will receive priority within the [Faculty of Theology]" (Faculty of Theology, 2017b:n.p.). It is therefore not surprising that at the next meeting (in May 2017) (Faculty of Theology, 2017c), more concrete plans with regard to the refashioning of the buildings were tabled. These plans are reported under the heading "Visual representation of theological training in FT building" (Faculty of Theology, 2017c:n.p.). The focus is on the history of theological training of all five partner churches, and Profs P. Coertzen and M. Burden were charged with the responsibility. They were to present a proposal

---

94 At the time, all the minutes of the Faculty Board were initially in Afrikaans. This phrase can be translated as the "redesigning of the Faculty building to make it a welcoming and inclusive space for all students".

by 18 July 2017 to be submitted to all key stakeholders. It was envisioned that the date of completion would be 2 April 2018. This process, however, ran into trouble when the five partners unanimously rejected the proposals and approach, suggesting a more inclusive process and outcome through a visual representation of theological training and the history of the Faculty. In terms of process, it is also reported that "in future" the Transformation Task Team will report "alongside" the Social Impact Committee at the Faculty Committee meeting (Faculty of Theology, 2017c:n.p.). This could mean different things. On the one hand, it could mean that up to this point the task team was seen as part of the Social Impact Committee and was now removed to stand on its own or, on the other hand, it could mean that the task team became a separate and autonomous core committee alongside the other committees of the Faculty. In the November 2017 board meeting, this task team reported for the first time as the "Transformation Committee" and one of its focus areas related directly to the matter of visual redress. At this meeting, proposals were invited to be presented to the committee. It was also proposed that Monica du Toit, head of the Transformation Office, be invited to assist the Faculty in this regard (Faculty of Theology, 2017d). How does one reflect on these developments?

It could be argued that this is part of a wider influence, as the University was also challenged during this period by its own students during the waves of student protests of 2015/6 – in essence, to decolonise itself (Chikane, 2018; Habib, 2019). Perhaps this is where the Black Theological Collective emerged. This was a key moment, and one of the responses was to remove the pictures and pursue the programme of visual redress. Therefore, when I joined the Faculty at the end of 2017, visual redress was already a standing item on the agenda of the Faculty. In its annual report for 2017 it is explained as follows:

> This faculty sees transformation as a process central to our core business strategy. It enhances sustainability but is key to how we affect societies. Therefore a faculty committee for transformation was established, in 2017. Transformation will affect curriculum content, staff composition and play a key role in creating a welcoming interior in the faculty. At least two task teams have started their work on this namely one for BTh Renewal and one for Visual Redress. The Theological Student Committee (TSC) also convened quarterly Courageous Conversations sessions

– a platform for discussing issues relevant to the faculty and environment, which contributes to transformation. (Faculty of Theology, 2017a:n.p.)

Prof. Nadine Bowers-Du Toit was the chair of the Transformation Committee in the Faculty and therefore led the visual redress process. However, she then went on research leave and the late Prof. Mary-Anne Plaatjies-Van Huffel acted as chair of both the Transformation Committee and the Social Impact Committee during the first semester of 2018. This meant that at the next meeting, processes were put in place to understand the policy environment and structures. However, in the meetings, the sentiment was raised under the title "Reclaim the spaces at the Faculty of Theology" that an initiative be developed to (re)claim the spaces of the Faculty, with specific reference to the statues, "in an innovative and creative way" (Faculty of Theology, 2018c:n.p.). This commitment and its interrelatedness with the newly emerging key performance areas of the University were then also stated in the Environment Plan (2019–2023) under the heading of transformation: "… inevitably impacts on the curriculum content, staff composition and a welcoming interior within the faculty building – within the broad parameters of contextual relevance and global excellence" (Faculty of Theology, 2018a:n.p.).

Parallel to this process within the Faculty, the institutional Visual Redress Committee was up and running, working on the policy for visual redress. Therefore, when Prof. Bowers-Du Toit returned from research leave in July 2018, she took the reins to lead visual redress in terms of the following guidelines, and in line with the institutional processes. It was affirmed that, strategically, the University wants to redress some of its spaces, in line with the emerging policy and definitions as stated earlier. This included the fact that signage would also be multilingual and that there would be a focus on addressing the issue of statues. Prof. Plaatjies-Van Huffel, who attended the institutional Visual Redress Committee meeting, reported the viewpoint that the University's way forward was not to remove statues per se, but rather to contextualise them historically and create more inclusive spaces within the buildings (Faculty of Theology, 2018b). At this meeting it was confirmed that Profs Plaatjies-Van Huffel and Retief Muller, the experts in church history, were to continue their work on the project to develop an inclusive timeline of the history of the Faculty. Based on this research, they were also requested by the Committee to propose how the current statues, including those referred to earlier, could be contextualised. Again, the commitment to gain advice from other environments was aired and it was resolved that Prof. Elmarie Costandius of the Faculty of Arts and Social Sciences would be approached to advise with regard to visual redress. Subsequently, the chairperson contacted Prof. Costandius for advice and guidance. The process with Prof. Costandius is published in another article by her and, in a sense, concludes the status of the process up to the present (Costandius & Brand, 2020).

Visual redress: Decolonising the Faculty of Theology?

This visual redress imperative emerged over a longer historical timeframe. While the current process flows from the challenge of the Black Theological Collective and gives urgency to the call for decolonising the Faculty, a second stream, it could be argued, flowed in the year 2000, when a group of 38 black undergraduate students and three lecturers, namely Profs Russel Botman, Dirkie Smit and Hannes Adonis, joined the Faculty of Theology (Plaatjies-Van Huffel & Taljaard, 2017:106). The three professors were members of the predominantly Black Uniting Reformed Church in Southern Africa – and at least for Botman and Adonis, key proponents of SABT. Before this, a very small number of black students completed programmes at the Faculty – me being the first in 1992.[95] Up to this time, the overwhelming majority of students in the Faculty were members from the white DRC. This shift in 2000 had a background.

Separate and parallel to the evolving of theological training in Stellenbosch, black ministers from a Reformed background were officially trained in apartheid institutions. These denominations forged partnership agreements with these institutions, among others the University of the Western Cape (UWC) (Kritzinger, Mokoena & Maponya, 2019:8–9). During the period between 1995 and 1999, the Faculty of Religion and Theology at UWC experienced some painful and

---

95 Bosman (2018:342–344) explains that in 1867, the Theological Seminary already accepted black students. That was, of course, before the founding of SU in 1918 and the Faculty of Divinity in 1920, as the official predecessor of the current Faculty of Theology.

far-reaching internal shifts. This led to URCSA deciding to shift its ministerial formation in the Cape Regional Synod to SU.[96] The partnership agreement with UWC came under pressure and a new partnership agreement was concluded with SU during the late 1990s. Subsequently, in 2000, URCSA students and academic staff joined the Faculty of Theology at SU. Before this initial merger and period, negotiations started with other denominations, such as the Moravian Church, and subsequently the Presbyterian Church, which started to raise questions about the history and visual representation within the Faculty buildings. This process, conversations and contestation remain. They touch on questions of language and, again, transformation. For some, this would be termed 'decolonising history' – the call for concrete justice as the basis for deep transformation and social impact. There is, however, a third stream and call for decolonisation, which flows into the river of visual redress at the Faculty.

Early in my term, Mr Karl King walked into my office. King introduced himself as a leader ('chief') and representative from the local Khoi community. Subsequently, he made a concerted effort to schedule regular appointments, and respectfully asked me – on many of these occasions – how the Faculty will address the cry from Khoi communities, the first peoples of this region of our continent. He made it clear that, among others, the land on which the current buildings housing the Faculty stand, and which are largely a visual representation of the identity of the Faculty, belongs to these communities. He argued that when the Dutch colonists landed in what eventually became known as the Cape of Good Hope, and therefore also the land on which the Faculty buildings stand, was inhabited and owned by the Khoi. Irrespective of whether King's claim can be sustained, or whether he actually represents the descendants of these communities, Gilliomee (2007:1) concedes that, while the first peoples of this southern tip of our continent were indeed the San people and later the Khoi, the Faculty buildings today indeed stand on the most eastern (southern) point of what was an island that was inhabited by these communities. And so, King argued that what he called the three *broeders* (brethren), meaning the DRC, the Theological Seminary and the SU, dispossessed their land.

---

96 See Cloete (2018:246–258) for an extensive account of these shifts, but also the contestations.

For King, this is a call for redress. As my interlocutor,[97] King remained friendly and patient, yet incessant. There is a deeper reason for redress, he argues. In terms of his religious tradition, he argued that moral regeneration in and among the descendants of the Khoi will only come through a spiritual revival, where the rights and call for justice by first peoples of the land, such as the Khoi, are foregrounded and restored. The redress is about (restorative) justice.

Many questions emerge from this dialogue. There are cultural-historical questions intersecting with theological questions. These have implications for public policy, in particular policies such as that of visual redress at SU. Does land belong to someone or a group, or should we also ask the theological question, is it God's land and what is land for? But of course, this also points to policy questions and the Faculty's internal processes of transformation, which directly relate to redress and specifically spatial and visual redress. Within the Faculty, a process of grappling with these questions is underway. Suffice to say, it calls for visual redress.

A Belhar perspective: Decolonising theology

Apart from the aforementioned contested history and three streams flowing into the quest for visual redress, the fundamental question is: why it is necessary for a dean of a Faculty of Theology – a theologian at SU – to ask these questions? In this regard, I will tap into the kind of theoretical frameworks that shape our subject matter, especially as they relate to the decolonising of theology.

Theoretically, I would position and root this quest for decolonising theology within the earlier call and challenge from proponents of SABT. Kritzinger (1988), in his engagement with SABT, calls for 'decolonising minds' in a section on "Theology for white liberation" (see also Kritzinger, 1990:57–59). I already alluded to the influence of SABT on the emergence of the Belhar Confession and its continued framing of a public theology. This has implications for public policy making today. The actions of the Black Theological Collective, but also the heritage of the cohort

---

97 As theologian, I would hold with others (e.g. Kritzinger) that the interlocutor plays a key role in refining one's questions, but also in disrupting hegemonic thought patterns.

of students and professors from UWC – a Belhar tradition – relates directly to the challenge from King. All these, I would argue, stand within a longer and richer theological tradition. Let me explain Kritzinger's call.

The traditional account of the history of the Faculty is a narrative of white agency and heroism within the framework of coloniality. In aiming to overcome coloniality within the white community, Kritzinger (1988:315–316) explains the function of SABT as follows:

> One of the most important functions of Black Theology is that it forces white theologians to come to terms with their own history and identity ... The only way in which white people in South Africa can shed their colonial mentality is by rereading their history with their eyes wide open to the voices of the victims, digging out from the past a human and liberating heritage which they can carry with them into a shared future with the black majority.

This is the call to white people today still. In addressing this, he then refers firstly to the rereading of history, the role of language and challenging white theologians to reject the 'vocabulary of oppression'. This resonates with the challenge from the Black Theological Collective and the current work of the Transformation Committee within the Faculty, but also the challenge from the class of 2000 and Karl King. But Kritzinger's call goes further. For him, the most important element in a white rereading of history is what he calls the "critical reappropriation of white historical figures and symbols" (Kritzinger, 1988:317). I referred above to the tradition of Keet and Naudé. Perhaps this is a tradition that can form the basis for the Faculty's public calling to form a new type of university and society. In line then with the proposal from Kritzinger, now writing with a younger cohort of proponents of SABT, theologians such as those of the Black Theological Collective, Katlego Mokoena and Moshe Maponya, I also hold that the Belhar Confession can function as a "normative guide ... that shapes our way of seeing", "an epistemological choice ... that shapes the nature of our attentiveness and observing" (Kritzinger et al., 2019:3). They explain that Belhar "envisages a praxis (seeing-thinking-believing-praying-planning-acting) in and for a particular society" (Kritzinger et al., 2019:4). How would one then see the contestation and questions about the Faculty and the choices to be made?

Pointers for the future

In terms of pointers for the future, I would, firstly, in line with the Keet-Naudé tradition, hold that the role and significance of the Faculty lie in its ability to raise public leaders, i.e. leaders who will impact personal and social transformation, where, at least in the current context of South Africa, the widening gulfs between rich and poor, genders and generations, among others, are bridged. This public call includes, but also goes beyond, narrow ecclesial and religious concerns. These are leaders who do this within an ethos of sustainable living – it is personal, but they are agents of change within the broader public. At our current juncture, I would argue that this emphasis on a public call challenges the Faculty and also the University, and also accentuates the need to read its history from the perspective of those who have been silenced and therefore excluded from this history. This question can be answered by how we start to re-read history from the perspective of the subaltern, from the bottom up, from the perspective of the *"noodlydende, die arme en die verontregte"* (the needy, the poor and the wronged) (NGSK, 1986:724).

Secondly, this public call has implications in terms of partnerships with various denominational and religious communities and it has implications for the Faculty. I would suggest that the following must be the character of these communities, namely a body that stands with people in any form of suffering, which includes, among others, to *"getuig en sal stry teen elke vorm van ongeregtigheid sodat die reg aanrol soos watergolwe, en geregtigheid soos 'n standhoudende stroom"* (witness and struggle against any form of injustice so that justice rolls down like streams of water and righteousness like a never-failing stream) (NGSK, 1986:724). A body that stands against injustice with the wronged – this means that this institution must also witness against those powerful and privileged, who, out of selfishness, seek their own interests and control over others and disadvantage them. These implications are inspired by a decolonising perspective that emphasises the centrality of the voices of the indigenous, the poor and those who were stripped unjustly of their humanity, as per the Belhar Confession.

This is, lastly, the perspective from which I suggest we must read the history of the Faculty of Theology at SU. Concretely, it means that we read it from Idas

Valley, Cloetesville and Khayamandi, and the call from Khoi communities for redress in terms of the future spatial planning of Stellenbosch. While this call relates – at least for my dialogue partners – directly to the sense of marginalisation and underdevelopment in communities who are descendants of the Khoi, there are also the needs and hopes (dreams) of faith communities excluded, vilified and ridiculed in the past by the white DRC. Today, this relates to the cries from the communities here in Stellenbosch and the broader Western Cape that still struggle to come to terms with the implications of forced removals. These implications today are glaring: a lack of housing; rising unemployment, which leads to the sprawling illegal underworld of drugs; human trafficking; violence; and subsequently the industrial-criminal complex, where black people in particular are criminalised and incarcerated for fighting (and dying) to eke out a livelihood – where seemingly black lives do not matter yet.

This understanding of redress – visual redress – is uncomfortable; it is not an easy term, but is must be faced head-on if we wish to engender systemic transformation, not merely *for* the University, but also *through* the University.

References

Agang, S.A. 2020. *African public theology*. Bukuru: Hippobooks.

Biscombe, H. 2006. *In ons bloed*. Stellenbosch: African Sun Media.

Bosman, H. 2018. Teologie. In: A. Grundlingh (ed). *Universiteit Stellenbosch 100: 1918-2018*. Stellenbosch: Universiteit Stellenbosch, 339-359.

Brown, E. 1994. Kweekskool teenoor teologiese fakulteit: Die ervaring van die Nederduitse Gereformeerde Kerk. *HTS Teologiese Studies / Theological Studies*, 50(1/2): a2544. https://doi.org/10.4102/hts.v50i1/2.2544

Chikane, R. 2018. *Breaking a rainbow, building a nation: The politics behind #MustFall movements*. Johannesburg: Picador Africa.

Cloete, D. 2018. *Vrede vloei soos 'n rivier: Oor die strome van my lewe*. Wellington: Bybel Media.

Coertzen, P. 2009. Die terrein en geboue aan die bopunt van Dorpstraat. In: P. Coertzen (ed). *Teologie Stellenbosch 150+: Die verhaal van teologiese opleiding op Stellenbosch - die mense en die geboue.* Wellington: Bybel Media, 73-96.

Combrink, H.J.B., Muller, B.A. & Hartney, J.M.N. 2009. Van Seminarium na Fakulteit Teologie: Besinning en ingrypende veranderings. In: P. Coertzen (ed). *Teologie Stellenbosch 150+: Die verhaal van teologiese opleiding op Stellenbosch - die mense en die geboue.* Wellington: Bybel Media, 35-52.

Costandius, E. & Brand, E. 2020. Redress at a higher education institution: Art processes and image theatre as embodied and rhizomatic learning. CriSTaL. 8(SI):92-110. https://doi.org/10.14426/cristal.v8iSI.277

Faculty of Theology. 2016a. Minutes of the Faculty Board, 18 February, Stellenbosch University.

Faculty of Theology. 2016b. Minutes of the Faculty Board, 12 May, Stellenbosch University.

Faculty of Theology. 2016c. Minutes of the Faculty Board, 4 August, Stellenbosch University.

Faculty of Theology. 2016d. Minutes of the Faculty Board, 3 November, Stellenbosch University.

Faculty of Theology. 2017a. *Annual report.* Stellenbosch: Stellenbosch University.

Faculty of Theology. 2017b. Minutes of the Faculty Board, 16 February, Stellenbosch University.

Faculty of Theology. 2017c. Minutes of the Faculty Board, 11 May, Stellenbosch University.

Faculty of Theology. 2017d. Minutes of the Faculty Board, 3 November, Stellenbosch University.

Faculty of Theology. 2018a. *Environment Plan* (2019-2023). Stellenbosch: Stellenbosch University.

Faculty of Theology. 2018b. Minutes of the Transformation Committee, 24 July, Stellenbosch University.

Faculty of Theology. 2018c. Report of the Transformation Committee, 10 May, Stellenbosch University.

Gericke, J.S. 1959. Die kweekskool en die Universiteit. *Die Kerkbode*, 84(17):671-673.

Gilliomee, H. 2007. *Nog altyd hier gewees: Storie van 'n Stellenbosse gemeenskap.* Cape Town: Tafelberg.

Habib, A. 2019. *Rebels and rage: Reflecting on #FeesMustFall.* Cape Town: Jonathan Ball.

Heese, H., 2018. Die ontstaan van die Universiteit Stellenbosch (US). In: A. Grundlingh (ed), . *Universiteit Stellenbosch 100: 1918-2018.* Stellenbosch, 3-26

Keet, B.B. 1959a. Die professore van die Kweekskool. In *Eeufeesuitgawe van die Kweekskool, Stellenbosch (1859-1959).* Cape Town: NG Kerk-Uitgewers, 27-31.

Keet, B.B. 1959b. Ná 100 jaar. *Die Kerkbode*, 84(17):659-660.

Kritzinger, J.N.J. 1988. Black Theology: Challenge to mission. Unpublished DTh dissertation. Pretoria: University of South Africa.

Kritzinger, J.N.J. 1990. Teologie vir wit bevryding. In M. Hofmeyer, J.N.J. Kritzinger & W. Saayman (eds.). *Wit Afrikane? 'n esprek met Nico Smith.* Bramley: Taurus.

Kritzinger, J.N.J., Mokoena, K.K. & Maponya, M.S. 2019. 25 years of ministerial formation praxis in the Uniting Reformed Church in Southern Africa: How Belharic have we become? *Studiea Historiae Ecclesiasticae,* 45(3):1-15. http://dx.doi.org/10.25159/2412-4265/6238

NGSK (Nederduitse Gereformeerde Sendingkerk). 1986. Handelinge van die twee-en-twintigste vergadering van die hoogeerwaarde Sinode.

Op sy mylpaal lees ons 100! 1959. *Die Kerkbode*, 134(17):658.

Plaatjies-Van Huffel, M.A. & Taljaard, A. 2017. Sy didaktiek. In: A. Grundlingh, R. Landman & N. Koopman (eds). *Russel Botman: 'n Huldeblyk.* Stellenbosch: African Sun Media.

Smit, D.J. 2017. Sy lewe as teoloog. In: A. Grundlingh, R. Landman & N. Koopman (eds). *Russel Botman: 'n Huldeblyk.* Stellenbosch: African Sun Media, 75-101.

SU (Stellenbosch University). 2017. *Stellenbosch University Transformation Plan.* Retrieved from https://www.sun.ac.za/english/learning-teaching/student-affairs/cscd/Documents/Career%20Services/Transformation%20Plan.pdf [Accessed 6 December 2020].

SU (Stellenbosch University). 2019. *Stellenbosch University Visual Redress Policy (draft).* Retrieved from http://www.sun.ac.za/english/transformation/Documents/Visual%20Redress%20Policy%20draft_eng.pdf [Accessed 6 December 2020].

Van der Merwe, W.J. 1959. Opleiding van sendelinge. *Die Kerkbode,* 84(17):674-675

Section C

Voice and agency enunciations amid visual redress experiences at Stellenbosch University

Chapter 10

Visual redress as restitution: Conversation

Renee Hector-Kannemeyer and Otto van Noie

Redress: To set things right (to remedy), to make up for something (to compensate), to remove the cause of grievance or complaint and to exact reparation for something (to avenge) – Merriman-Webster Dictionary

Figure 10.1: 80-year old Whaleed February, Lückhoff High School alumnus from Die Vlakte (photo by S. Els, November 2019)

INTRODUCTION

This conversation between Stellenbosch University (SU) through the Division for Social Impact and a voice from the Stellenbosch community was informed by the statement of the late Prof. Russel Botman, who encouraged the University to move from success to significance, to redefine success as being relevant to the oppressed and the marginalised, and to produce knowledge in the interest of society to the benefit of all.

The HOPE Project, inspired by Brazilian philosopher Paulo Freire, was launched at SU by the late rector and vice-chancellor, Prof. Russel Botman, in July 2010. The HOPE Project envisioned a long-term strategic plan, which the University committed to, with the application of its knowledge and expertise in a strategic and intentional approach to benefit society.

POSITIONALITY

Based on the pragmatic definition of the HOPE Project of the role of the University, the two authors of this chapter, Mr Van Noie and Ms Hector-Kannemeyer, started their three-year conversation on restorative justice as a basis for restoring community and healing the broken relationships that existed between the University and the local community. These conversations led to the establishment of a co-management forum between SU and various community leaders in and around Stellenbosch in 2018. The restorative justice framework that informs their collective work is a relational framework that aims to restore social imbalances within relationships and therefore outlines that the wrongs that were perpetrated against a person or community need to be addressed. In order to address the wrongs of the past, we need to have a deeper understanding of the current trauma of people of colour who were impacted by those wrongs. We have to explore, in equal partnership with the surrounding communities, what the appropriate redress and development initiatives, especially with regard to the forced removals and loss of community, need to address.

Mr Van Noie represents a Stellenbosch community voice. He is a retired teacher, community activist and member of the co-management forum. He was a student at Lückhoff School in Banghoek Road during the 1950s and a teacher at the school during 1969, at the time of the forced removals. He continues to engage with the University regarding its processes of redress and restitution.

Ms Hector-Kannemeyer was born in Idas Valley and has a familial connection to Die Vlakte. The connection between the authors is that they are both alumni of Lückhoff High School from different time periods. Ms Hector-Kannemeyer is employed at SU as the deputy director of the Division for Social Impact. She hopes to present methodological approaches that could unravel processes of redress that will be respected by all parties, heal broken social relationships and lay a foundation of restitution on which to build a shared future.

THEMATIC FRAME

As a point of departure, the two authors developed a set of key questions that served as themes for the ensuing conversation on their respective approaches to visual and broader redress at the University and the Lückhoff precinct. The following four questions guided the conversation, which, in turn, formed the themes of the chapter:

1. How are the authors positioned relative to the original Lückhoff School and to SU's involvement in redress initiatives related to the Lückhoff precinct?

2. How does the physical location of Lückhoff School in Die Vlakte position the school with respect to visual redress?

3. What is the history of SU's utilisation of transformation space and visual redress space at the Lückhoff precinct?

4. How can SU reconceptualise visual redress as restitution at the Lückhoff precinct?

THEME 1: THE AUTHORS' POSITIONS RELATIVE TO THE ORIGINAL LÜCKHOFF SCHOOL AND TO SU'S INVOLVEMENT IN REDRESS INITIATIVES RELATED TO THE LÜCKHOFF PRECINCT[98]

Otto van Noie: Stellenbosch community member

Stellenbosch has a submerged history that refuses to be buried. It resurfaces at odd times, proverbially calling forth, as if the stones in the walls themselves are crying out for justice, as in the words of the prophet Habakkuk. The history of the previous site of Lückhoff High School in Banghoek Road[99] is one such instance. Over the years, this site has repeatedly been highlighted as being of significance by persons

---

98 The first theme is discussed in the first person, as it reflects the individual backgrounds and narratives of the two authors. The rest of the chapter was written in the third person, so as to reflect a separation of voice in positionality, approach, methodology, interest and experience.

99 Identified as the Lückhoff precinct in this chapter to distinguish it from the current Lückhoff School property.

identifying with it: alumni of the school, descendants of those who lived in close proximity to the school in the area known as Die Vlakte and those who have other meaningful relationships with Die Vlakte, its people or institutions.-

I was born in the town and had been exposed to its segregationist and apartheid culture. My maternal grandfather was a market gardener in central Stellenbosch. This is where I first learnt that historical Stellenbosch consisted of at least two disparate parts: one was where 'coloured' and black people lived, and the other was where they could only work, and perhaps be allowed to walk along its streets.

I also attended the 'coloured' high school, engaging with young people not just from all over Stellenbosch, but also with Afrikaans-speaking fellow learners from the Boland, the Southern Cape and as far as present-day Namibia. This was a formative experience, as the school was a public institution where learners from across the economic spectrum were accommodated on an equal basis. Although subject tuition was exclusively in Afrikaans, it was attended by learners who were later classified as 'Native'/African. These learners were forced to attend schools established under the Bantu Education Act. Two of those learners were personal friends of mine who had lived in Idas Valley and had attended the Volkskool (later Volkskerk Primary School) with me.

Later, as a teacher at Lückhoff School, I endured the humiliation of forced removal of the school to Idas Valley. I was arrested by the security police in 1983 for activities related to the student unrests in the Western Cape and at Lückhoff. My family were also members of the independent Volkskerk van Afrika congregation, whose church building, primary school and manse were located a stone's throw from the high school building. That heritage was lost partly through statutory demolition and partly through forced alienation of property.

These were some of the early experiences that radicalised me in my becoming a political and educational activist. Lückhoff School that, for some reason, had been left standing amid the ruin and the rubble of forced removals, is a constant, taunting reminder not just of what has been lost and alienated in material terms, but also the continuing relationship of power and hegemonic dominance from the past that continue to shape the future of the town and its development.

I position myself as one of the many community voices – past and present – that have advocated for a consensus-based solution to the moral dilemma that faces the community. Currently, I serve as a member of the Lückhoff Advisory Board, established by the University, and as a board member of Matie Community Service, a University body functioning under the auspices of the Division for Social Impact.

Renee Hector-Kannemeyer: Stellenbosch University

For the research process of the Lückhoff visual redress initiative, I have taken the position of both an insider and an outsider. As cautioned by Tuhiwai Smith (2012), the role of insider in the research methodology needs to be reflective. In many ways it was easy to position myself as insider, as I was born in Stellenbosch and grew up in Idas Valley, with familial roots in Die Vlakte. My father was a teacher of English at the 'old' and 'new' Lückhoff School, and taught most of the school community of 1969. I matriculated from Lückhoff School in the early 1990s and am a proud alumnus.

Although my family moved from Stellenbosch, my late father is still held in esteem by the Idas Valley community, and especially by the Lückhoff alumni. My father passed away in the early 1980s, but when I mention that I am Pat Hector's daughter, I am always immediately received with warm trust and greeted with nostalgic stories of my father as teacher. I grew up in Kahler Street in Idas Valley, in the same street as Mr Van Noie. My paternal great-grandfather, Jan Hector, was one of the earliest members of the Volkskerk in Die Vlakte and the family is still recognised for their contribution to the church. The Volkskerk has been a prophetic voice in the community since its establishment in 1922 and particularly during the apartheid struggle. I attended the Volkskerk until my teenage years, when our family relocated to Cape Town.

I have been living in Cape Town for more than 25 years and although I have stayed in touch with many community members, I have not stayed connected with the ongoing conversations, hopes and challenges of the local community for more than 20 years. I am currently employed by SU's Division for Social Impact. My office is located in the former school building from where my father and my community were forcibly removed. Working in this building has challenged me ethically. It has also positioned me as somewhat of an outsider with regard to the Lückhoff visual redress initiative.

I am deeply grateful to be able to work so closely with Mr Van Noie, who is a dedicated community leader and intellectual. He has been playing a central role in the current Lückhoff initiative. The focus is on restitution for the local community. I have done research on the manifestations of trauma of the forced removals based on interviews with a past resident of Die Vlakte. My research focused on a community that had been forcibly removed from the centre of Stellenbosch, called 'Die Vlakte', during apartheid. Living and working with and among people who have experienced this removal, I was keen to research whether, and how, the impact of the trauma is currently manifesting in this specific community. For an insider researcher the parameters of any initiative have to be clearly defined and for that reason it was pivotal that any interventions, research process and methodology were co-defined by the local community, as recommended by Tuhiwai Smith (2012).

Within participatory action research it is vital to hold the space for contradiction and conflict, traditionally called choques, and invite all researchers with opposing understanding to explore difference and not fall back on the need for consensus before an idea can be advanced. It is on this basis that the lived experience of an intellectual such as Mr Van Noie in relation to the forced removals, Lückhoff School and ongoing conversations with the University is positioned as central to this chapter. This positioning assists SU to navigate from the individual to the social and ultimately to systemic analysis, which enables sustainable social impact.

Participatory action research is founded on the multiplicity of identities and varying worldviews and positions the work as deeply personal, political and emancipatory and an opportunity for knowledge creation in order to facilitate social justice. However, the emancipatory ability of any initiative depends on the concept of 'coming to voice', where space of agency and power to act are facilitated.

This agency of voice can only be achieved when the colonial power structures are reorganised and the afflicted community is intentionally positioned as the experts in the initiative or research conducted.

THEME 2: THE POSITIONING OF THE PHYSICAL LOCATION OF LÜCKHOFF SCHOOL IN DIE VLAKTE WITH RESPECT TO VISUAL REDRESS

SU admits to its 'strained relationship' with a section of the local community over its presence in that part of the town colloquially known as Die Vlakte (SU, 2019). The history of the town looms large in any genuine attempt to achieve reconciliation between the University and the people of Die Vlakte. The handling of the historic Lückhoff building will be an acid test of the ethical principles of transformation underlying redress initiatives impacting on this space. Two books derived from the oral testimony of people who had lived there deal with destroyed community life in this area. Both resonate with sentiments of regretful loss, nostalgia, indignation and anger. *In ons bloed* (Biscombe, 2006) is a narrative of events, stories and memories, while *Nog altyd hier gewees* (Giliomee, 2007) is a more academic account. Clark and Costandius (2020), in dealing with the iconography of apartheid, raise the relevance of socially produced space. They reference Lefebvre (1991), who points to the production of space, of how social relations are embedded in space and how such space may be commanded by hegemonic social formations as a means of establishing dominance and control.

For Mr Van Noie, dealing with the aesthetics of redress from the perspective of a community member who lived in the proximity of SU for eight decades, it is reasonable to distinguish between SU as a (South) African university *per se* and as an institution embedded in the town of Stellenbosch. As an African university its concerns are continental and global, but as a locally embedded institution it has had far different roles to play before and after the democratisation of the country.

Mr Van Noie reflects the reiterative voice from the community on the possible repurposing of the Lückhoff precinct. He is a proponent of a deeper form of restitution as opposed to the proposed visual redress initiatives currently being advanced by the University, which he believes do not go far enough in conferring dignity on the broader Stellenbosch community. He, too, supports a participative approach as a cornerstone of any restitution efforts. He believes that we need to consider how the local community responds to Stellenbosch University's many utterances regarding transformation, and how the community holds the University accountable for such redress and restitution. The University's embeddedness acknowledges the community's presence and its own role in the unfolding of the historic narrative of Stellenbosch, its culture, its socio-economic impact and the social relations stemming from the positioning of both the University and the community. SU's history is inextricably woven into the history of the town.

Die Vlakte as community

Figure 10.2: Lückhoff School, 1959 (source: Biscombe, 2006)

Lückhoff High School, although a state institution, shared Calvinist roots of origin with most of its feeder schools and the resident university. The school was established towards the end of the era of Cape liberalism, in 1937. The school, the only Afrikaans-medium secondary school for 'coloured' youths from the Boland area and beyond, had pride of place in the community and was its beacon of hope, inspiration and leadership. This was the school that had provided community leadership at the time of the Battle of Andringa Street in the person of one of its teachers, Mr Sean, who had been elected as secretary of the Vigilance Committee, which represented the community in negotiations with the University.

From 1960 onwards, as the threat of forced removals became a daily reality and the primary schools were faced with closure under legislation designed to undermine the independence and resistance of communities, the high school became a central focal and rallying centre. Eviction notices had begun to be served on tenants, some families were cautiously relocating elsewhere, while others vowed to fight to the bitter end. The community was being torn apart, and it was vital that a centre should hold for as long as possible. Lückhoff High School began to take on an added symbolism of community pride and achievement.

Forced removals and relocation: 1964-1971/1972

Mr Van Noie's view is that the recollection of these events is important; they were successive and almost continuous blows over two decades to the esteem and sense of security of the majority of Stellenbosch residents, and to the community that claimed Die Vlakte as their cultural home in particular. They radically changed social relations. In the end, it did not really matter whether 'the other side' was white and liberal or white and racist. The aesthetics of power and privilege were stark: white for dominance and black for subservience. He remembers that through all this turmoil of strife, imprisonment, killing and brutality, SU was firmly embedded in the town as a 'whites-only' university. There was a growing awareness and alarm at what the community regarded as the implication of the University in both the formulation of apartheid doctrine and its implementation. As an institution, it neither repudiated apartheid, nor did it resist its implementation as an institution, although, to its credit, there were many academics and others in some way connected to the University who became anti-apartheid critics, and some even activists against apartheid's injustices.

> It is therefore puzzling that the University, which took ownership of the empty shell of the school building after the illegitimate expropriation by the National Party regime, still holds the title deeds to a community asset. Is it this plea for the 'transfer' of ownership of this building that has led to the "nearly 40 years' division between the University and the coloured community of Stellenbosch" (SU, 2019:n.p.). Mr Van Noie reflects that there is perhaps more to the distant community attitude towards the University than the 'loss' of a building.

Lückhoff School has come to represent a space with possibilities for concrete transformation. Transforming the school is not merely constituted by the opportunity to rectify; it implies the obligation to do what is necessary to re-establish a moral-ethical environment that was unilaterally betrayed by fellow townspeople and, institutionally, by the University. The Lückhoff building, left standing among the ruins, echoes the collective voice of generations uttering the same cries for justice, which no other voice or message can ever supersede.

> Ms Hector-Kannemeyer shares that the role of the University is fundamentally to produce new knowledge, therefore the core of its business should be focused on research, teaching and learning, and social impact. The University should aim to address one of the core questions posed by Prof. Russel Botman when he reminds us that our focus should be centred around developing a pedagogy where the issues and concerns of the most marginalised are prioritised (Botman, 2007). Ms Hector-Kannemeyer states that although the sincerity of the relationship with the local community is not in question, the methodology and praxis of engagement after the incomplete HOPE Project need to be explored and even critically evaluated. Such reflection needs to be done by the very community who suffered this injustice.
> We need to ask how we as a university are advancing the project of redress and development and whether the current parameters of the Visual Redress Policy fall short of giving expression to our commitment to the local community. SU also has to consider whether its commitment to redress and development initiatives enabled the healing, restoration and reconciliation of a wounded community and moved us all closer to mending the broken trust between SU and Die Vlakte/the Lückhoff community. The University has to pay attention to the cries of the community and review its current praxis of engagement.

The importance of understanding place identity

For Ms Hector-Kannemeyer, a deepened understanding of place identity is a critical consideration in responding to the ongoing cries from the Lückhoff community. Such a view is expressed by Erasmus (2001:98):

> The places where people worked and lived, the spaces where children played, are fundamental to the development of both a community and an individual identity.

> It is the sense of belonging, togetherness and collectively participating and sharing activities which is a crucial element in the formation of identity.

When searching for an understanding of the connection between people and place, Hart (1988, cited in Jeppie & Soudien, 1990:137) states as follows:

> It has long been recognized that people are place and place is people. Interpersonal relationships play a central role in the making and meaning of place. In the history of South Africa however this intricate relationship has been persistently and wilfully damaged. People other than whites are either denied the freedom to define their own places, or those places which they have come to know and love are wrestled from them.

When seeking to understand place identity, it is critical to explore how a place is intrinsically connected to a sense of self and how a specific place is incorporated into who we are and our understanding of ourselves. The trauma of grieving the loss of home or community through forced removals is not only about the assault on property, but more deeply and more importantly also about an assault on the self (Krupat, 1983).

Manzo (2003) argues that place is political, especially in instances of racial discrimination. People are forced to carve out a safe space of belonging for themselves, and as researchers we need to understand how these directly contribute to people's sense of self and meaning making in the world. These emotional connections to place transcend time, which was so evident in community members' responses to/at the Lückhoff School renaming ceremony in 2007. Members of the school community who attended the ceremony, many of whom were learners at the school, remembered the school's removal in 1969 with deep emotions, accompanied by expressions of pain and tears. They remembered the humiliating act of carrying their benches away from their beloved school to a newly appointed school outside the town. The invitation to bring the very same benches back as 70-year-olds evoked memories of forced removal and the pain associated by uprooted lives. It is evident that for them, trauma is ongoing and recurring even 50 years after their forced removal from their beloved school (Hector-Kannemeyer, 2010).

It has become evident from the years of conversation, dedications and symbolic gestures that the Lückhoff community still feels alienated from their school. In the absence of healing and with the ongoing trauma, Ms Hector-Kannemeyer believes that a more participatory methodology and pedagogy are needed. Such pedagogy should not merely include the voices of the marginalised, but the University also needs to persuade the local community that their collective voice matters. As a University, we should facilitate the community's agency and participation in processes of restitution. For any meaningful and authentic change to occur, especially regarding issues that are critical to their own environment, the needs of those most impacted by the trauma or injustice will have to be prioritised.

It has also been clearly articulated in the draft Visual Redress Policy of SU that the University cannot implement the policy outside of the larger Stellenbosch community of which it forms part. Visual redress initiatives need to represent not only the history, but also the current involvement of a variety of stakeholders, both in and outside of the University community. This representation of the community voice requires an intentional process of collaboration and community agency, especially pertaining to a lost community asset, which is owned by the University. The policy instructs that collaboration should reflect in its procedures and therefore a deeply participatory method of engagement prioritising community needs is critical to honour the principles outlined in the Visual Redress Policy (SU, 2020). The Visual Redress Policy is also committed to the SU Transformation Plan, which invites SU to be the vehicle driving transformation in and of society and states that such societal impact needs to be evident in the very town of Stellenbosch, where SU is located.

THEME 3: THE HISTORY OF SU'S UTILISATION OF TRANSFORMATION SPACE AND VISUAL REDRESS SPACE AT THE LÜCKHOFF PRECINCT

The Lückhoff building in Banghoek Road is one of the few remaining vestiges of the buried history of a once vibrant community. An iconic aura has grown around it over the passing decades.

The early history through the eyes of Mr Van Noie

Lückhoff School is located in the centre of Die Vlakte, at the intersection of two historically important arterial roads. It has rightly been described as 'the heart' of the area. Lückhoff School could not escape the racialised political fall-out of apartheid, but in its cultural isolation, amid its sanitised surroundings, it has remained standing as a witness of what was perpetrated against a community.

This institutional background to the transformation initiatives at Lückhoff School is important in understanding the trajectory of transformation at the University in general. The only visually significant change from a transformational perspective that has been made to the school has been the photographic exhibitions along two of its corridors and in one of its larger rooms. These photos depict snatches of community life in Die Vlakte, some of the buildings that used to be part of the visual landscape and a collection of photos of alumni and teachers, school activities, newspaper cuttings and other memorabilia from the era before forced removals. This represents a fraction of the rich history of this area, its people and its vibrant culture. However well-meant this initiative was, it is a memorial – the dead hand of the past.

An observer of the memorabilia would see glimpses of Die Vlakte firstly as a stable, developing community, portraying a community's sense of permanence, entitlement and even complacency that characterised that earlier period in the area. Then there are a few photos depicting the devastating impact of forced removals.

Die Vlakte, once assumed by the community to constitute a part of an inclusive Stellenbosch, became a contested space as forced removals became a reality. It increasingly came to signify the betrayal of promises and assurances by white Stellenbosch in general, and SU in particular, because of the role of apartheid ideologues in its ranks. Lückhoff High School and the space it occupied within Die Vlakte became part of this contested space.

It stands to reason that any unilateral actions, however well intended, will be viewed with suspicion and mistrust because of the continued exclusion of community voice and the stifling of community agency. This may also help to explain why ownership of Lückhoff School through legal title by SU is regarded by the estranged community as morally reprehensible. The community, however, continues to extend an invitation to the University to rectify this situation, in other words, for the University to re-establish the school as an ethically infused environment. Such rectification cannot, once again, be decided on by the perpetrators or bystanders who acquiesced in the face of the forced removals.

One of the reasons for the paucity of material depicting life in Die Vlakte displayed at Lückhoff School is that many people who had been closely linked to the school and Die Vlakte refused to take part in any such initiative because of the untransformed character of SU. For them, supporting such an initiative would have been to legitimise the acquisition of the property by the University. Those who did contribute did so because of loyalty to, and love for, Lückhoff School as their alma mater. The school had been alienated from its original owners in a particularly hurtful and wrongful manner without any other cause except that of an unacceptable skin colour to fellow townspeople, including 'learned persons' at SU.

A key reason for the community's estrangement is the severe property loss suffered by the inhabitants of Die Vlakte. Examples of property loss are as follows:

- The Volkskerk School that was demolished and replaced by a local white-owned property
- The Dutch Reformed Mission School (Latsky School) that was destroyed to make way for a white-owned business complex
- The James Higgo School that was acquired by the Department of Correctional Services
- The Methodist school that was used as a white pre-primary school, named De Kleine Bosch; this property was later also acquired by SU
- The St Mary's Anglican school that was appropriated by the Stellenbosch traffic department.

The following religious denominations lost the use of their buildings:

- The Volkskerk became St Paul's church, with a majority of white members.

- The congregation of the Dutch Reformed Mission Church had to relocate to Idas Valley.
- The Methodist Church in Plein Street was demolished and its new church building had to be erected in Idas Valley. (Giliomee, 2007:205)

The Lückhoff School building was left intact and later became the property of SU. This is beside the loss of private and rental property and homes in Die Vlakte and across the broader Stellenbosch town, including properties in Dorp, Krige and Du Toit streets, and in Die Boord residential area.

The Botman legacy

In 2003, Russel Botman (2003) then a professor in Missiology at SU, addressing the issue of the importance of collective human dignity of social formations in a globalised world, voiced his concern about the elevation of monetary value above human value. He insisted that the restoration and fulfilment of human rights are fundamental to the restitution of human dignity. He reminded us that restorative justice "invites people into a certain memory of the past that also frees them from it. Simultaneously it frees people *for* the future, for each other …" Restorative justice, he said, "does not fly in the face of a victim's pain and continued suffering ignoring the dehumanization caused by conflicts" (Botman, 2003:33).

On assuming the rectorship at SU in 2007, Prof. Botman engaged extensively and with a wide variety of community groupings and stakeholders in the broad transformation project. He brought his pedagogy of hope to the religious community through a sermon and discussion session at the Volkskerk van Afrika, Stellenbosch.

A seminal occasion relates to the rededication of the Lückhoff High School building. The original Lückhoff School building in Banghoek Road in Stellenbosch was rededicated to its original community owners, the people of Die Vlakte, in 2007. In his declaration, Prof. Botman referred to his message delivered at his installation as vice-chancellor of SU, in which he explained his commitment to pursuing a pedagogy of hope and also his wish to live it out. He stated that the handing over of the building to its original owners is the materialisation of a pedagogy of hope. Prof. Botman explained that ownership would "serve as a balm of deep-rooted wounds and pain, which we believe, will heal with time" (Botman, 2007:n.p.).

In response, Pastor Godfrey Martin replied on behalf of the Lückhoff Gespreksforum as follows: "We have always been adamant that our property and heritage should be returned to us" (Martin, 2007:n.p.). Pastor Martin referred to the gesture by SU to return the old Lückhoff building as "a beacon of hope … for the transformation of Stellenbosch" (Martin, 2007:n.p.). Pastor Martin's words echoed those of Prof. Botman, who declared:

> We are here to say that the gruesome legislation that caused people to become uprooted will not have the last say, but that the hope for a non-racial and multicultural society is alive, and that the spirit of Lückhoff and of the Vlakte will live on. In this way, Lückhoff is a beacon of hope for today and for tomorrow. (Botman, 2007:n.p.)

This has always been the call of a community forcibly robbed of its heritage and deprived of a space that they could morally claim as their own to shape into a place of memorialisation and of hope and as a pedagogical instrument that would continue to proclaim the messages of hope, justice and restitution.

The HOPE Project initiated or strengthened a range of community empowerment initiatives under the directorship of Dr Jerome Slamat, located in the original Lückhoff School building. Dr Slamat had previously also overseen the restoration of the original name of the school building that had been chiselled off. These were interpreted by the community as a deliberate signal regarding the future destiny of the building, the beginning of a process of meaningful redress. Here, at last, the community could sense the tangible, visible embodiment of the advent of a pedagogy that offered the hope of redress that would be commensurate to the wounds inflicted.

Two other instances are worth mentioning to illustrate how Prof. Botman's pedagogy of hope opened up transformation space: In the late autumn of 2013, Pieter Nel, head student of Dagbreek men's residence, apologised to the country for the involvement of Dagbreek students in the Battle of Andringa Street of 1940, for the damage done to human relations between the University and the residents of Die Vlakte who were attacked in their homes, and for the culture of intolerance based on racial classification it helped to create.

In a similar vein, Prof. Nico Koopman (2018), current Vice-Rector: Social Impact, Transformation and Personnel, speaking about *ubuntu* and communality, mentions restorative justice as an example of an act that goes beyond the call of duty. He agrees that it is "the restoration of dignity" and "collective justice that seeks to deliver to all" (Koopman, 2018:2).

At the "Bring back the Benches" ceremony on 19 November 2019, the current rector, Prof. Wim de Villiers, committed the University to continue the work of Prof. Russel Botman. The return of the benches has become a renewed symbol of hope for the Lückhoff and Die Vlakte communities. One of the learners of the class of 1969 explained that the event evoked great emotion for him, as that day was the first time that he had returned to the Lückhoff building since the forced removals 50 years before.

Mr Van Noie further states that the visual redress approach in its current form does not offer an explanation for why the community voice has not been given greater prominence and space in the determination of what restitution should strive to achieve. He further states that any form of redress that would not continue the praxis of the HOPE Project or undermines or refutes the Botman legacy would be problematic in the eyes of the community.

THEME 4: HOW SU CAN RECONCEPTUALISE VISUAL REDRESS AS RESTITUTION AT THE LÜCKHOFF PRECINCT

Figure 10.3: "Bringing back the Benches" ceremony, 19 November 2019 (photo by H. Oets)

From her social impact perspective, Ms Hector-Kannemeyer maintains that a methodology that addresses the concerns highlighted by Mr Van Noie above is found through the process of engagement with the afflicted community. Processes of engagement are crucial in the healing process. Critical participatory action research (CPAR) is informed by the view that those who are most directly impacted by a challenge should take a central position in the research process. CPAR is a participative methodology based on the conviction that those most affected by a problem, those who hold significant knowledge, wisdom and unique expertise, should be at the centre of the restitution process. CPAR by its very nature questions what is deemed as accepted knowledge and challenges neutrality and objectivity. Inspired by Paulo Freire's critical pedagogy (Freire, 1970), CPAR positions community knowledge as central and affirms the role of community as essential in responding to the pursuit of justice.

CPAR is designed to inform, educate and organise all participants, from local community members to academics, to be able to recognise and respond to challenges in their lives and in their communities. The process of conceptualising the problem is critical to this approach, as well as how research is conducted, how it is analysed, the meaning of the data for the local community and how this research translates into action. This pedagogical process informs how researchers learn through inquiry, the production of knowledge, how knowledge is applied to people's lives and, most importantly, how it leads to the betterment of the lives of local communities. With a strong liberatory focus, CPAR directly confronts systems of oppression that prohibit local communities from confronting their own challenges, such as issues related to classism, racism, sexism, ableism and cultural bias. CPAR positions political education as a critical component of the research methodology. CPAR draws on Freire (1970), who believes that critical reflection is a precursor for social change combined with a dialectical fusion of theory and practice and the challenge of hegemonic approaches of knowledge creation.

A core principle of CPAR is informed by the true commitment to a collaborative methodology and pedagogy that encourage and validate the lived experienced, ideas, skills and contributions and incorporates local community knowledge into the research methodology in an intentional dialogical process (Fine & Torre, 2019).

The workshop that introduced the Lückhoff visual redress initiative involved the school community of 1969 as part of this dialogical process to participate in conversations on remembering Lückhoff School in Banghoek Road. Participants shared their memories about school discipline and the strong sense of community that they had experienced as they participated in the walk-through activity reflecting on the pictures in the corridors of the lives lived in Die Vlakte, to which they were deeply connected. The session also focused on the concept of the Lückhoff Living Museum and the symbolic return of the school community of 1969 in the "Bring back the Benches" event.

The creation of the Lückhoff documentary was also shared with the participants in exploring the concept of a Living Museum. The Living Museum is intended to present Lückhoff School as a multi-purpose venue for reconciliation, ethical pedagogy and cultural inclusivity. Perhaps even more important than any eventual outcome must be the process of arriving at restitutive outcomes. According to Mr Van Noie, critical for the realisation of a worthy outcome will be the centring of the community's voices that had been most affected by the loss of what had become the iconic presence of a survivor from a past of devastation. This would ensure the meaningful repurposing of Lückhoff School, as intended by the local community in 2007. It would also signify the process of memorialisation brought to life in cathartic and redemptive ways, creating new understandings and bringing buried history into perspective as pedagogical insight. Such a process would give effect to exactly what Lückhoff School always promoted, embodied in its motto, "Education is Light".

Ms Hector-Kannemeyer remarks that it was noteworthy that although community leaders shared their Lückhoff memories, they also spoke of the future and the educational needs and youth challenges of the community. The plans and ideas shared in this deeply emotional and engaging dialogue indicated that community members wanted action. They believed that these platforms initiated by SU provide real spaces for agency and they liberally shared their ideas and dreams and the needs of their community. CPAR is committed to a methodology that is both pedagogical and collaborative in what has been articulated as a problem-posing approach. SU, through its Division for Social Impact, has pledged ongoing commitment to not only hearing and acknowledging the voice of the community, but also to restoring community. The continued engagement with the community will follow the praxis of CPAR with the emphasis on understanding of how participation in research is influenced by politics and power (Fine & Torre, 2019).

CPAR can be described as a theory of knowledge that intentionally challenges what counts as knowledge, how it is constructed and who holds that knowledge. The primary role of the methodology is to question power and who has power in the conversation on engagement to determine how that power needs to be shifted in order to create knowledge together. Knowledge and perspectives from a diverse group of people and collaboration are encouraged, centred on those who have been the most directly impacted by the injustice. It is also critical to explore the connection between feminist psychologies and liberatory psychologies and how they are integrated into global structures of injustice. As with CPAR, there is a deep conviction that those who are oppressed, in partnership with and in support with others, need to facilitate their own liberation. It is, however, essential that researchers engage with a full critical analysis and a variety of practical approaches to effect social change guided by the needs of the oppressed (Lykes & Moane, 2009).

Mr Van Noie shared that in the University's attempts at redress, SU acknowledges past wrongs and its determination to rectify and make good for suffering, hurt and loss. Provided that it is authentic, such redress becomes the living embodiment of restitution. From this historical account it follows that visual redress is political: it is influenced by political-philosophical and theoretical aesthetic cross currents prevalent at the time and embedded in the warp and woof of the community. It is, therefore, a terrain of struggle regarding what is appropriate and apposite, given the broad scope of what 'redress' can be deemed to constitute. Its acceptance of an agenda of 'redress' implies the acceptance of a political imperative to transform, based on the moral principles enshrined in the Constitution of the Republic of South Africa.

According to Ms Hector-Kannemeyer, the Division for Social Impact's commitment to restitution is further imbibed by the Vice-Rector: Social Impact, Transformation and Personnel, who provides some insight into and explains the scope of acts purporting to redress, restitute or transform, by describing them as healing, inclusive, reconciling and, importantly, righteous and just so as to give effect to social justice (Koopman, 2020).

Mr Van Noie, however, cautions that the University needs to be mindful of the method of community engagement when issues of redress (in whatever form) are contemplated. He references an article in the February 2020 issue of the campus newspaper, *Die Matie*, which stated: "According to the Visual Redress Policy draft … '[the visual changes] will assist SU in its drive for transformation in and through visual redress'" (Visagie, 2020:n.p.). He further emphasises that the article pointed out that such initiatives had already been included in a budget for, among others, a history lane to connect "the histories of the town on the one hand … with the university on the other hand" and a "remembrance garden at the Ryneveld/Merriman intersection [to] highlight the history of Die Vlakte" (Visagie, 2020:n.p.).

Mr Van Noie voiced his concern and said that while not doubting the intentions of the University, it still fails to grasp the enormity of the past wrong in which the University is implicated. This information regarding proposed projects is of material interest to the descendants of Die Vlakte residents, Lückhoff alumni and interested and affected parties even outside the municipal boundaries of the town, yet they were never consulted.

Mr Van Noie quotes Voloshinov (1929:23) on signifiers and acts of signification as "having two faces, like Janus"; that innate quality or ability to reflect an object's dual or multiple realities as perceived by a recipient. For example, what may be presented as a garden of remembrance could be conceived as just another burial site to commemorate previous spaces that have been bulldozed. A history walk could be interpreted as a transformational cul-de-sac; the end of a history, redress without any form of restitution. Although the intent of the University might be honourable, the impact of any initiative when the community voice is not included might have a completely different, and even detrimental, impact.

Ms Hector-Kannemeyer responds to this distressing, yet legitimate, concern of Mr Van Noie and re-emphasises the point that SU should pause any initiatives relating to Die Vlakte and Lückhoff School, especially when it comes to redress, development and healing initiatives, if the very people whom it aims to support are not part of the conversation. She states that as a University, we need to consider as a matter of urgency who is not part of the conversation and who should be in the room when decisions regarding the afflicted community are made. We need to look at who is not present to contribute to the conceptualisation and implementation of an initiative that aims to honour and restore the afflicted community. We need to ponder on the reflection that ideas, creations, initiatives and narratives are as much shaped by who is not there as by who is present (see Fine, 2002).

This reflection compels us to honestly review the various methodologies being implemented and initiatives and solutions being provided for the afflicted or marginalised communities without considering who is absent in these conversations. Why do we as researchers believe that those who are at the centre of the trauma or injustice could not offer any meaningful contribution to how this challenge needs to be addressed? In response to the concerns raised by Mr Van Noie, Ms Hector-Kannemeyer states that the proposed visual redress initiative has not centred the voices, experience, ideas or reflection from the local community in the conceptualisation of the proposed memory walk and garden as part of these initiatives. She emphasises that it is critical that when we implement these initiatives, we move away from mere inclusion of all voices, but that we move deeper into the power that the local voice holds; that we enable a space of agency and that the marginalised voices are repositioned to hold power in determining the most suitable initiative that will facilitate healing, remembrance and restoration of their own loss and trauma. We need to hear the critique from a community voice to inform a methodology that will address these concerns. Fine (2002) argues that a lack of inclusion and participation stands the risk of compromising, misrepresenting and even falsifying collaborative work and begs academics to consider an alternative methodology found on CPAR principles.

The 'Bring back the Benches" memorialisation initiative, involving SU Lückhoff School, alumni and Die Vlakte community representatives – harking back to 2007 and the Botman legacy – already has had a significant impact across the Boland in particular. It awakened new interest in and excitement about similar projects elsewhere, but not just as heritage initiatives. The Living Museum concept has drawn attention to the possibilities of how divided pasts can be cemented into common, joint and shared futures.

We need a methodology that is deeply aware of the cultural hegemony that exists within the University/community intersection and accepts that the values held by our communities are not always aligned to the values of our institutions. Our work therefore has to be emancipatory, focused on social justice and consistently drawing on and prioritising the knowledge of the community; work that it is participatory, centring the community's experience.

CONCLUSION

SU's visual redress project presents the University and the local community with an opportunity to implement an initiative that could institute visual redress that is community-centred, jointly implemented and deeply transformational. The healing is in the process and in order for the process to be truly participatory, we need to have all role players presented from the project's conceptualisation stage to the implementation of the initiative. This is an incredible opportunity to explore a praxis that is guided by those who have been the most impacted and traumatised by the forced removals. This process would enable healing, restoration and emancipation for Die Vlakte community.

As an institution we are invited to reflect on and respond to Mr Van Noie's view that visual redress is not only found in a memory garden or walkway, but in the restoration of a community's sense of belonging in, and ownership of, the town of Stellenbosch.

We conclude with the insights of Clark and Costandius (2020), who caution that although the aim of visual redress is an attempt to right the wrongs of the past through the removal of hurtful symbols and the addition of more inclusive symbols, this is not enough. Healing the wounds of the past has to accompany visual redress activity. In the case of the previous Lückhoff High School building, the call for the handing over of the building to its rightful owners must be given concrete expression.

The question of who the current rightful owners are remains complex 50 years after the removal, as Die Vlakte community is only found in its dispersed, fragmented form. What is called for is to redefine what community is with respect to Lückhoff School. For both the community and the University voice, the engagement through this process has illuminated a 'new community', easily defined, consisting of residents from the dispersed Die Vlakte community that hold diverse religious and cultural views.

This defined community of the Lückhoff alumni has the power to not only guide visual redress as a restitution project, but also to unite the alumni of the pre-1969 Lückhoff School in Banghoek Road with the new Lückhoff School in Idas Valley. Clark and Costandius (2020:3) argue that "the relations between people and context should be taken into consideration to enable redress as cultural, social, economic and environmental or political events and discourses are always embedded in physical, emotional and lived experiences".

Clark and Costandius (2020) further state that the violence held in these institutional spaces cannot simply be replaced and that it is critical to understand

and respond to the traumatic histories, especially when those proposed initiatives to address the violence are challenged at grassroots or community level. A process that does not permit alternative voices perpetuates the continuation of oppressive hegemonic structures. Clark and Costandius (2020:17) suggest that "to be silenced is to be rendered invisible. But for [higher education] institutions to attempt to speak on others' behalf or to 'invite' others to speak is to risk paternalism or even practise condescension". They caution higher education institutions to be aware that this form of engagement still holds to a colonial praxis and does not enable agency of voice or encourage equality of power in the conversation.

This chapter further invites a deeper reflection on the current nature of University/community relationships to carefully examine how colonial thinking frames engagement, interaction and conduct when formulating these hierarchical partnerships. The relationship that predominately exists with the 'community' as partners in research or collaboration is based largely upon the premise that the indigenous are not active role players in the research, outside of being the subject of the research. This understanding is based in the conception that the 'community' possesses neither the capacity for research, nor the interest (Tuhiwai Smith, 2012). It becomes imperative to critically review the nature of the relationship between the researcher and the researched, especially as the researched seems to be assigned a passive role in the relationship: that of need, loss of power and lack of autonomy. The issues to explore in 'relationships' of deep inequality are questions of where power is located and how power has been ascribed to the initiator of the relationship, especially when community members are invited to 'participate' on already-agreed initiatives by the University, which Clark and Costandius (2020) expose as condescending and paternalistic.

The chapter invites us to interrogate and explore through a process of CPAR an alternative to these hierarchical 'partnerships' of unequal power, to create authentic partnerships based on equality and agency of voice between higher education institutions and the communities with whom they have an opportunity to collaborate within a truly reciprocal relationship.

References

Biscombe, H. 2006. *In ons bloed*. Stellenbosch: African Sun Media.

Botman, H.R. 2003. *Human dignity and economic globalisation*. In: K. Sporre & H.R. Botman (eds). *Building a human rights culture: South African and Swedish perspectives*. Retrieved from https://www.diva-portal.org/smash/get/diva2:152505/FULLTEXT01.pdf [Accessed 12 November 2020].

Botman, H.R. 2007. Speech made at the symbolic hand-over ceremony of the previous Lückhoff School building to the local community, 15 October (unpublished).

Clark, M. & Costandius, E. 2020. Redress at higher education institutions in South Africa: Mapping a way forward. *de arte*, 55(3):26-48. https://doi.org/10.1080/00043389.2020.1728874

Erasmus, Z. 2001. *Coloured by history, shaped by place: New perspectives on coloured identities in Cape Town*. Cape Town: Kwela Books.

Fine, M. 2002. Carolyn Sherif Award address: The presence of an absence. *Psychology of Women Quarterly*, 26:9-24. https://doi.org/10.1111/1471-6402.00039

Fine, M. & Torre, M. 2019. Critical participatory action research: A feminist project for validity and solidarity. *Psychology of Women Quarterly*, 43(4):433-444. https://doi.org/10.1177/0361684319865255

Freire, P. 1970. *Pedagogy of the oppressed* (Trans. M.B. Ramos). New York, NY: Continuum.

Giliomee, H. 2007. *Nog altyd hier gewees: Die storie van 'n Stellenbosse gemeenskap*. Cape Town: Tafelberg.

Hector-Kannemeyer, R. 2010. Current manifestations of trauma: Interviews with a former Vlakte inhabitant. Unpublished MA thesis. Bellville: University of the Western Cape.

Jeppie, S. & Soudien, C. 1990. *The struggle for District Six: Past and present*. Cape Town: Buchu Books.

Koopman, N. 2018. We still need ubuntu - but we need to understand it. *Cape Argus*, 8 October 2018. Retrieved from https://www.iol.co.za/capeargus/opinion/we-still-need-ubuntu-but-we-need-to-understand-it-17178885 [Accessed 24 August 2020].

Koopman, N. 2020. *Om teenstand teen sosiale geregtigheid te oorkom [Overcoming resistance to social justice]*. Stellenbosch University. Retrieved from https://www.sun.ac.za/english/Documents/newsclips/2020%20Overcoming%20resistance%20to%20social%20justice.pdf [Accessed 20 February 2020].

Krupat, E. 1983. A place for place identity. *Journal of Environmental Psychology*, 3:343-344. https://doi.org/10.1016/S0272-4944(83)80037-1o

Lefebvre, H. 1991. *The production of space*. Oxford: Blackwell.

Lykes, B. & Moane, G. 2009. Editors' introduction: Whither feminist liberation psychology? Critical explorations of feminist and liberation psychologies for a globalizing world. *Feminism & Psychology,* 19(3):283-297. https://doi.org/10.1177/0959353509105620

Manzo, L. 2003. Beyond house and have: Toward revisioning of emotional relationships with places. *Journal of Environmental Psychology,* 23(1):47-61. https://doi.org/10.1016/S0272-4944(02)00074-9

Martin, G. 2007. Speech made at the symbolic hand-over ceremony of the previous Lückhoff School building to the local community, 15 October (unpublished).

SU (Stellenbosch University). 2019. Historical background. Retrieved from http://www.sun.ac.za/english/Pages/Historical-Background.aspx [Accessed 12 November 2019].

SU (Stellenbosch University). 2020. *Visual Redress Policy (draft)*. Retrieved from http://www.sun.ac.za/english/Documents/Visual%20Redress%20Policy%20draft_eng.pdf [Accessed 1 August 2020].

Tuhiwai Smith, L. 2012. *Decolonizing methodologies: Research and indigenous peoples*. Second edition. London: Zed Books.

Visagie, C. 2020. Say yes to the SU redress. *Die Matie*, February. Retrieved from https://diematie.com/2020/02/say-yes-to-the-su-redress/ [Accessed 13 May 2020].

Voloshinov, V.N. 1929. *Marxism and the philosophy of language* (Trans. L. Matejka & I.R. Tutunik). New York, NY: Seminar Press.

Chapter 11

Work IN Conversation: Discussing one artist's creative interventions on Stellenbosch University campus

Gera de Villiers and Charles Palm

Introduction

The red-bricked Rooiplein (Red Square) is an important, highly trafficked pedestrian throughway and communal gathering area at the heart of the main campus of Stellenbosch University (SU). It is a semiotically charged space, where multitudes of people from different social and cultural backgrounds converge. The Rooiplein pays homage to the University's origin with a prominent statue of diamond magnate Jan Marais, whose philanthropy helped to establish the institution in the early 1900s. It was against this backdrop that the Rooiplein became a meeting place during the student protests of 2015 and 2016, which addressed a myriad of issues such as decolonisation of university space and curriculum, university fees, outsourcing and student housing.[100]

In 2018, a shipping container-turned-exhibition space was installed on a grassy expanse just off the Rooiplein. This container gallery was initially proposed and managed by Charles Palm, a visual artist and SU student, and funded by the visual redress project of the University. Palm also became the first exhibitor in this space with his *Obscure Stellenbosch* (2018) installation, which was made possible with support from the Andrew Mellon Foundation. This chapter presents a discussion with Palm about this and two other works that he enacted on the Rooiplein – *Work IN Progress* (2018) and *Die Voo'kamer* (2019) – by Dr Gera de Villiers, postdoctoral fellow for the visual redress project.

Both the Rooiplein and these three works of Palm's are immersed in social semiotics and it is therefore important to provide the reader with a brief understanding of this concept. Semiotics, a linguistically based theory, was developed independently – but at roughly the same time – by both Swiss linguist Ferdinand de Saussure and American philosopher Charles Peirce as the study of signs and how people use them to create meaning (De Villiers, 2018). Social semiotics is a branch of the theory that broadened the study into areas other than linguistics, as it understood that "meaning

---

[100] These protests took place on university campuses throughout the country during this time.

resides so strongly and pervasively in other systems of meaning, in a multiplicity of visual, aural, behavioural and other codes, that a concentration on words alone is not enough" (Hodge & Kress, 1988:vii). This means that a person reads a sign with the help of these decoding devices (visual, aural, behavioural, etc.) along with their own historical, cultural and social codes (Hooper-Greenhill, 2000). These codes, which are shared between the same or similar socio-cultural groups, allow us "to read the world in terms of the codes and conventions which are dominant within the specific sociocultural contexts and roles within which we are socialized" (Chandler, 2002:156). For instance, as was discussed in the interview, Palm often wears a bright neon high-visibility vest. This vest is something that traditionally signals a labourer – a construction or road worker – or, in a uniquely South African context, a car guard or parking lot attendant. However, Palm is none of these things and, instead, he uses it to question people's reading of this sign; to play with their perceptions.

An understanding of semiotics – and social semiotics – allows one to see that meaning making is not static, that we are active participants in the construction of our realities. We do not have to accept things at face value, but can – and should – question the signs with which we are confronted. Being aware of social semiotics is an acknowledgement of one's role in the constant and active process of making meaning, of creating social realities (Chandler, 2002).

Social semiotics as artistic process

De Villiers: Social semiotics seems to be integral in your creative process. What does this mean to you in your practice?

Palm: I see art as a language; it's just a means of communicating with people in a non-verbal manner. As an artist you're constantly dealing with social semiotics in this way – whether you are aware of it or not. I believe most of the decisions that we make are generally emotionally motivated and not entirely rational. And most of those decisions are grounded in knee-jerk reactions we have based on visual cues. So, having a firm grasp on the concept of social semiotics helps as a visual artist.

De Villiers: Yes, exactly. It's about how people make meaning – about their space, others, themselves, etc. – through all sorts of different signs that we are confronted by daily. How have you explored and played with this perspective in your works – and life?

Palm: I enjoy that sort of thing. Before I started studying, I started playing with social semiotics; playing with perceptions. I think we all do to some extent – in the way that we dress and project ourselves socially. In my own experience, having a particular skin colour in a particular environment here in South Africa already gives off certain perceptual cues to South Africans, which were learned over generations. I like to challenge and explore such perceptions. Often people's responses would reveal much more about them than what it might reveal about me. You know? If I walk around in a chicken costume all day long, you might not know why I'm wearing that chicken costume, but the way that you respond to that chicken costume will tell me a lot more about you than you about me. So, to me it's a way of gaining information and manipulating perceptions around these interactions in social and public spaces.

De Villiers: You mentioned to me that you often wear a hi-vis [high-visibility] vest in social situations to play with people's perceptions.

Palm: I love the fact that it's kind of steeped into our consciousness. I remember when hi-vis became a thing in people's visual language – through cheap consumer goods and sports apparel in the 90s – and then suddenly it was everywhere in a more official manner: police and security, emergency vehicles – it's just a background phenomenon now. It's kind of strange to me that high-visibility colours can sometimes make people invisible. If I wear it in an urban environment, I'm practically invisible. I'm like a cog in the wheel of this big machine. I might as well be like a robot or a traffic cone. The human element is almost completely removed from the person. It's like I'm seen as just a tool. To me it can be fun to play with these perceptions. I have to be very resourceful with my methods because I don't always have the money to buy what I need for my work, so I find things – I scavenge around. If you look like a worker or a technician, people often just open the door for you! I like digging into this background stuff that we are immersed in but not really paying attention to. You need to interrogate it and ask, "What does this mean to me and how does it function in my reality?"

Work IN Progress (2018)

Figure 11.1: Work IN Progress, S.E. Williams, 2018, digital photograph

Work IN Progress (Figure 11.1) was a collaborative experimental public performance piece during which Palm and Babalwa Tom projected images onto the pedestal of the JH Marais statue on the Rooiplein. The performance was a creative attempt at putting the pedestal into context; it was "a visual meditation on the work and workers who historically provide a pedestal for progress" (Palm, 2018) but are often excluded from the historical narrative. Various digital and live video projections were mapped onto the pedestal, such as an animated high-visibility chevron, the keyhole from the front door of the Ou Hoofgebou (Old Main Building),[101] diamonds and live animations by Tom using water and pigments. Marais was a

---

101 "The Ou Hoofgebou was inaugurated in November 1886. The Faculty of Law, that will celebrate its centenary in 2021, has been housed in the Ou Hoofgebou since its inception in 1921" (SU Corporate Communication and Marketing, 2020:n.p.).

diamond-mining magnate and politician whose substantial financial contribution helped to establish SU. This piece, which also included a fire performance by Tom, served as a commentary on "human and natural resources, as well as the social and circumstantial factors involved in individual successes, historically celebrated through monuments of this nature" (Palm, 2018).

De Villiers: This is perhaps a good point to talk about *Work IN Progress*, a piece in which you utilised both a hi-vis vest and these hi-vis colours. How did you go about accessing the space? And what was the content of the performance?

Palm: It was executed in a very hushed manner to avoid bureaucratic delays – this whole thing was done a bit guerrilla style! I didn't ask anybody's permission to plug a projector into the Rooiplein's electrical grid. I went out beforehand to check which electrical plugs around the Rooiplein worked but I wore a yellow vest, so it may have helped me to go about my business unnoticed. On the night of the performance, I was wearing my hi-vis vest and Babalwa was wearing a uniform that's typically worn by the cleaning staff of Stellenbosch University. We were both in character in that way. So, this was part of the semiotic language that we were using throughout this performance.

That [red-orange and lime-yellow] chevron was actually a painting that I did in my second year as a student. I don't think that my lecturer was amused with the initial painting because I found the exact colours that I needed and painted the chevron stripes directly as it came out of the tube. At the time I knew that I was going to use this in an extended way later on – I just didn't know how or when or where – but I was creating content for some future project. So, [for this project] I processed the painting digitally to become a continuous video loop. I layered this with other content like an animated spinning diamond, photographs of the Law Faculty's front door keyhole, and Babalwa's live water projections.

De Villiers: What would you say the message of this work was?

Palm: Most of my ancestry comes from slaves and the town that I grew up in – and where both of my parents and grandparents were raised – was established because of the abolition of slavery in the mid-1800s. The early British government in the Cape had a policy of establishing mission stations specifically for freed slaves. So, they created these little labour pools under the control of Christian missionary societies. To some extent I would assume that this was also a measure to undermine the free burgher establishment in the Cape during this time. The earliest 'Palms' that I could trace in my family were working in Kimberly during the diamond-mining boom in the early 1900s. So, there is this direct link in this particular case [with Marais].

Drawing upon these histories that are tied to my ancestry got me interested in the phenomenon of labour. I have found that labour seems to be an abject phenomenon in South Africa. For example, many South Africans may feel like they are entitled to have access to a domestic worker, but there's also this historical reluctance to deal with the politics of domestic workers or the socio-economic issues within that relationship – this is perhaps more true for most of the local industries that carry the South African economy. And in South Africa, there seems to be little acknowledgement about how these relationships are still fundamentally based on a very colonial construct. I think it's very tightly intertwined with early globalised capitalism and the idea of creating an 'other'. So, the work is trying to bring attention to the historical 'other'. It was a creative attempt to put the pedestal in context to some extent – the thing that's raising Marais above everybody else. It's an attempt at redressing some of the symbols and monuments on Stellenbosch University's campus.

Camera obscura experiments

De Villiers: A great mediation on daily campus life was your *Obscure Stellenbosch* installation. However, I think that we should first talk about how you became interested in camera obscura as a technique.

Palm: When I started my studies, I was very intensely engaged with my subject matter and struggling to work within the constraints of the course structure. This was also a time when campus was a really tense and hostile space for me because, since my first year, there were constant mass protest movements on this campus for reasons that I could completely identify with. So, after a few years of this I wanted to give myself a break from all the stress and just meeting my deadlines. I decided to have some fun and delve into something interesting that I had wanted to try for a long time: camera obscura. There's a drawing room in the Arts Department with screens that you can close over the windows on the inside to darken the space completely. So, I thought the easiest way for me to experiment with camera obscura was to use one of these rooms with these screens. I just opened one of the screens a little bit, built a cardboard insert that blocked out the rest of the opening, and I put a lens in there to play around with the projected image. The first iteration was magical, but then I got frustrated that I could only point it towards the scenes outside of this particular room. [At the time] I was at the Thupelo artist residency in Nyanga[102] with one of my classmates. We were driving into Nyanga every morning and she mentioned, "Why don't you just put it [the camera obscura] in the back of your bakkie?" I thought this was a great idea and started in the residency to move towards experimenting with that. I cut all the cardboard in the residency space, but the first experiment in the back of the bakkie was actually in Stellenbosch – the first image that I got going was of the Kruithuis[103] [see Figures 11.2 and 11.3]. I didn't know much about the armoury building at this time.

Figure 11.2: Bakkie camera obscura experiment, Kruithuis, C. Palm, 2017, digital photograph

Figure 11.3: The Kruithuis projection, C. Palm, 2017, digital photograph

---

102   Nyanga is a township in the Western Cape approximately 35 km from Stellenbosch and 20 km from Cape Town.

103   A VOC (Vereenigde Oost-Indische Compagnie – Dutch East India Company) era armoury building erected in 1777 in Stellenbosch central. However, "Stellenbosch has always been a peaceful town and not once during its 300 years of existence has it heard the sound of guns fired in war" (Stellenbosch Museum, 2005:n.p.).

De Villiers: How did you become interested in this building? Or was it just a random choice?

Palm: No, I was drawn to it for a while. Purely because I thought that it was a bit odd, that it had some sort of dark vibe about it. There was a secret there that attracted me. I thought that it may be some kind of masonic building because there were no significant windows and it faced east. But I also knew that it was an armoury and if this building was a first line of defence, what was the defence for? Why would it face inland and not towards the sea, towards the coast? I really thought this was weird. Maybe this was because of some inland threat?

I took that picture of the Kruithuis in May. The building was closed at that time and only opened again in September. When September came around, I went in there during that first week at about 12 noon. This time I had questions, but the guy there didn't really have any satisfying answers and there was no information inside about why exactly it was built. But I walked around and then – by accident – I discovered this seemingly naturally occurring camera obscura on the first floor of the building [see Figure 11.4]. I didn't know that I would find a camera obscura and none of the people that I spoke to who work in or manage the building knew about this. Currently, we don't even know if it occurs in this building by design or if it was a weird coincidence.

*Figure 11.4: Kruithuis camera obscura, C. Palm, 2017, digital photograph
(the two curved projections are buses from across the road)*

De Villiers: You went on to expand this project from a static experiment in the back of your parked bakkie into a mobile immersive experience accessible to the public. You transformed it into a moving camera obscura and took people on "Obscure Detours" through Nyanga, Stellenbosch, Pniël, Cape Town and other areas.

Palm: Yes, during the period between May and September – after that first image [of the Kruithuis in the back of the bakkie] – I started working towards making it a mobile installation [see Figure 11.5]. I wanted to take people on little journeys. In Nyanga, I did this with a planned route into the town centre. I drove from the artist residency space to a derelict old cement factory. It looked like a post-apocalyptic site and there was controlled access at the entrance. But, because I was wearing a hi-vis vest, security may have assumed I was the contractor coming in and out with this bakkie.

I would later also take many other people through a route around Stellenbosch. I would always stop at the Kruithuis, open up [the back of the bakkie], and then we would chat there for a bit. Not necessarily about the Kruithuis, because this was before I'd had an opportunity to go inside, but that would just be the last image people saw before I opened the canopy. We would chat about the whole idea and technology within the camera obscura phenomenon and so forth and then I would go back and drop them off. Then there were also some journeys in Cape Town and surrounding areas with friends.

I tried to keep the camera obscura up in the bakkie as much as possible so that at any time if somebody wanted to check it out, I could just say, "Ja, get in the back!" I tried to make it somewhat comfortable back there. I always had a mattress in the back and friends later donated pillows and the backrests of a couch. So, towards the end it was quite finely tuned. I got some black stretchy fabric and had some fixing points on the inside of the canopy so that it had this cocoon-like feeling to it; a womblike environment. It was cosy and soft, there were no sharp edges or hard surfaces anywhere, so you could just sit and relax in the back. But what was funny was the level of trust that people had! They just climbed into the back, no one asked where we were going or if I had a driver's license.

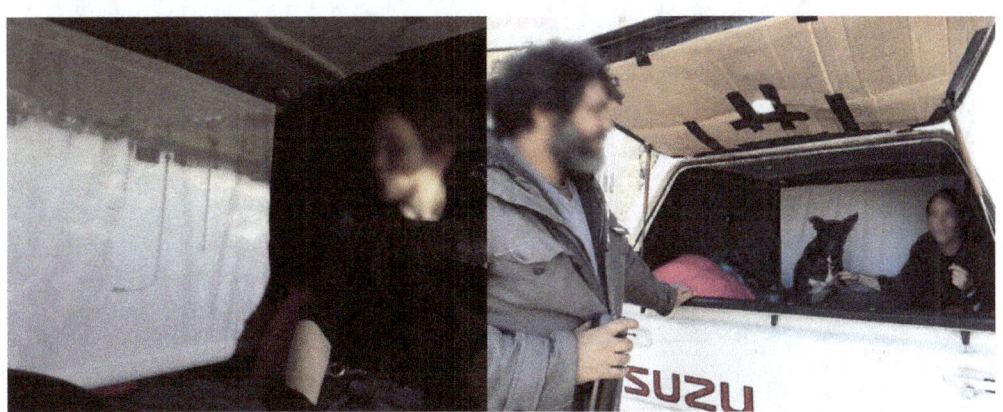

Photo 11.5: Obscure Detour, Nyanga, C. Palm, 2017, digital photographs

I also had some humorous experiences in Stellenbosch. For instance, one day I was driving around in town and was waved down by a female classmate with a group of friends. They seemed very excited, waving me down in the middle of the road, screaming at me to pull over, and asked if they could all jump in the back! Because most of the time I was wearing a dirty hi-vis vest, I easily looked like a building contractor or perhaps a technician. As this group of students climbed in the back I saw three old ladies standing on the other side of the road with open mouths looking at us like, "What is going on? What's happening here?"

It started off as me trying to have some fun with my work. Because, as a student you can be consumed by the deadlines and the subject matter of your work and it definitely gets stressful and all that. So, by the end of my second year I really felt like freeing myself from this construct, and that's how this project was initiated.

Obscure Stellenbosch (2018)

Figure 11.6: Obscure Stellenbosch interior, S. Louw, 2019, digital photograph

Obscure Stellenbosch was the first work to be featured in the gallery space within a modified shipping container that was placed on the edge of a grassy area adjacent to the Rooiplein. A small aperture and lens on the front of the structure facilitated a camera obscura projection of the outside campus scene (see Figure 11.6). Through this aperture, an upside-down mirror image of daily campus life was projected onto a large curved screen inside of the container; the inside of which had been covered in black fabric to facilitate the clarity of the image. Visitors were encouraged to enter the space and stay for at least 15 minutes to fully experience the installation (seating was provided). In pointing the lens at the University's buildings and one of its most populated communal areas (a space that was also used as a gathering place for students during the protests of 2015 and 2016), this piece asked viewers to consider the historical, ideological and institutional constructs of the University as it celebrated its 100th year.

De Villiers: So, Charles, you then took what you learned in these experiments and you put that experience into your *Obscure Stellenbosch* installation on the Rooiplein in 2018. Let's talk a little about the background for this project. How did you get the container? Was that always going to be its location – and why?

Palm: In early 2018, I was invited to an early brainstorming session in our department for the visual redress project organised by Professor Elmarie Costandius. One of the items discussed was a movable creative space on campus. I put forth the suggestion of using only the frame of a shipping container and building something more sculptural onto this frame. But, after some drawings were done, we settled on something that was closer to a typical container [see Figure 11.7]. Costandius managed to secure funding for a curator of this space through the Andrew Mellon Foundation in the United States and this enabled me to be formally employed to work on the container project until the end of 2018.

Figure 11.7: Container gallery space exterior, C. Palm, 2019, digital photograph

[The container] was always going to be on the Rooiplein somewhere. It's the biggest common space on Stellenbosch campus and Elmarie presented the idea for it to be positioned here from the start. In many ways [the Rooiplein] also projects the ideologies of the institution through the surrounding architecture and spatial planning, especially the Jan Marais statue and all that it represents. He was an early diamond-mining magnate and a major stakeholder in the De Beers Corporation along with Cecil Rhodes at the turn of the century. He was also an early pioneer of Afrikaner nationalism through his philanthropy towards Afrikaans print media outlets, cultural institutions, and as a local politician. At his passing, Marais bequeathed a substantial amount of funding towards the building of Stellenbosch University as we know it today. As far as we know, he didn't have any children and most of his inheritance was left towards the development of Afrikaner nationalist culture. I originally wanted to place the structure next to – or close to – Jan Marais, or include him in the frame somehow. At this point I knew that I would try to build a camera obscura installation inside the container at some point. Structural concerns about the library roof below prevented a placement close to Jan and I settled on the best frame I could get within these types of constraints.

De Villiers: The Rooiplein, as a central communal space on campus, was also a gathering space during the 2015 and 2016 student protests. Were you involved in these protests?

Palm: I wasn't directly involved in any of the protests. I'm not at all comfortable with emotionally charged crowds, especially when there is a high chance of fire arms in the vicinity. I did, however, contribute creatively towards events and talks in support of the protest movements. It was inspiring when students and staff were gathering peacefully, addressing each other en masse on the library steps, especially here on Stellenbosch campus, because you don't see that kind of thing happening often. It's generally a very divided space – at least in my experience. There are definitely many factors and constructs here that have been historically keeping us from finding common connections in this space. When we stand together around subjects and things that are retarding our growth in this way, then changes – big changes – may be possible.

De Villiers: It sounds like there was an amazing sense of camaraderie and togetherness, which brought to light issues that had previously been left in the dark. But the container – and your installation – came about after these protests. The Rooiplein's history became a backdrop for your work.

Palm: This was after the protests; there was a heavy environment around campus for the next year – or two years. It really felt tense. When things quieted down after the protests, it felt to me like a bomb could go off on campus any day. That was the environment where this installation came into being. For me, it was a way of providing some kind of a release valve in the form of a space for quiet reflection. That's all that I had in mind from the get go. That was all I wanted to do – to use this container to facilitate mindful reflection on the space.

De Villiers: Your background is in interior design and architecture. Do you feel like that was helpful to you in this project? Do these still influence your work?

Palm: Yes! Very much. If you want to get people's attention, it helps to make big gestures and to make the experience immersive. Architecture and any spatial design is immersive in nature. I kind of cringe at traditional art display constructs, where you put something on a wall or a sculpture in a white space with bright lights on it, surrounded by other works. To me, if you want to draw attention to a subject, or you want to communicate something to somebody that you feel is important or urgent, you need to immerse the 'viewer' in that subject. Just in terms of scale and the immersive qualities of architecture, it's definitely a tool that can be applied effectively in this sense.

It's also important for me to mention that there was no allowance made for a designer or architect in the budget of this container's construction process. I don't think anyone on the committee thought this was needed, but the contractors definitely expected this element on the project – because they only build according to the specifics of a particular design. I had some understanding of these processes and, so, I took on this role to a large extent. However, the project ended up taking much longer than expected but, because I was already being paid to facilitate the space, I could justify this added service on my behalf. But it was far from ideal because I was a full-time student at the time and I feel that the contractors took advantage of this at times, as many things didn't turn out the way that I had instructed and there wasn't time to have them redo parts of the build as needed. As a result of all this, I suffered some personal losses, as the project had a negative effect on my academic career – to the extent that I had to repeat some of the subjects from that year, which cost me time and money. But, overall, I think the project was largely a success. I definitely saw the value and potential in this project from an early stage and towards the end of the build I felt that it was important that I have an opportunity to use the space for my own work. I already had an idea for an immersive installation and the container offered me the scale and platform suitable for this work. So, soon after the container was delivered, I got straight to work.

De Villiers: Well, this installation was very much an immersive experience. You invited people into a dark container and introduced them to camera obscura. You showed them their world upside down and allowed them to quietly contemplate this moving image that you had facilitated. What did the container look like inside – what would a visitor encounter?

Palm: So, visitors would typically approach from the grass, walking over a short path lined with square concrete slabs towards the open doorway. A thick black felt-like curtain hung over the entrance to help block out sunlight from the interior and most of the interior was lined with more black fabric. On entering, visitors would find a second layer of black curtains that formed a small foyer. They would typically be asked to wait in this foyer space for a minute to let their eyes adjust to the darkness and when they pulled this second curtain aside, it revealed two brown faux leather bean bags placed close to the large glazed panels. This seating arrangement was later replaced with a couch and an armchair along with a side table and a vinyl chequered floor for better visibility in the dark. As visitors stepped into this space they would see a large projected moving image on their left – the camera obscura lens was located in the centre above the seats, and behind the large glass panel in the centre of the structure.

De Villiers: For how long was *Obscure Stellenbosch* open? Did you advertise it or did you wait for people to figure it out and approach you?

Palm: Throughout most of the autumn and spring months the container's door stood open between 13:00 and 14:00 on weekdays. Student facilitators from the Visual Arts Department and myself guided curious students, staff and the public into the space to experience the installation. There were some discussions around signage and visibility of the installation, but we observed that people were naturally inquisitive and during a typical lunch hour we would be approached by at least five people. Over a total of four months, I think the installation had about 400 visitors. I liked the idea of having people's curiosity rewarded by inviting them to experience or access the installation inside, so no signage was put up anywhere on the exterior for the time that the installation was open.

De Villiers: Were you able to get any feedback from visitors – what do you think people thought about this work? Is there a particularly memorable interaction that you had with a visitor?

Palm: There were many memorable moments. The camera obscura experience is very difficult to record or document, though. It will just look like an upside-down image on a screen or a page. It's really about the immediate experience, the magic of viewing the here and now as a visual spectacle. You get to see the moment when a visitor realises that there are no electronics involved in this moving picture; that everything is created just with sunlight and a Pyrex lens. You can't capture this type of realisation with a photograph.

I have learned that it takes a while to understand camera obscura. People say, "Ok cool, so where's the projector? Is it behind here?" And I'm like, "No, no, there's no projector. It's really just that hole and the sunlight." [One day I showed the installation to one of the oldest staff members at Stellenbosch University] and about 10 to 15 minutes afterwards, when he understood how this whole thing worked, he said to me, "This is really something special. But, is there no way you can turn this image the right way up?" When he said this it kind of clicked with me: His discomfort with the image is exactly part of what I'm trying to articulate here – and he appreciated this aspect of the work immediately. For many people, it feels like life on Stellenbosch University campus is a bit upside down most of the time – and this can be very traumatising to live through; it's a very slow and consistent trauma. So, in some respect the work also speaks to that, or it embodies a kind of discomfort inherent in a lot of people's experience on campus as expressed during the protests.

De Villiers: That's a really great example. I'm sure that people had a whole range of emotions when interacting with this work – from amazement and awe to discomfort – and that's a good representation of how people react to the same space in different ways because of the social semiotics surrounding it, because of how they have been taught to read and react to a space. Stellenbosch and the Rooiplein mean different things to everyone because of a person's own personal history and the histories of the ways that each space was and is used. It's great that you use social semiotics as a 'fun' tool because that also makes it possible to address these bigger, heavier issues.

Die Voo'kamer (2019)

Figure 11.8: Die Voo'kamer, visual redress launch, H. Oets, 2019, digital photograph

The piece shown in Figure 11.8 – an ephemeral installation lasting for only one evening – was created for the formal launch of the visual redress project in 2019. *Die Voo'kamer* transformed the shipping container space from the *Obscure Stellenbosch* installation into a cosy living room with furniture and décor from the 50s and 60s. The installation also included video projection mapping onto two picture frames. To the right of the couch, projected onto a small frame, was a little animated gif and above the couch hung a large elaborately framed piece of white board with digitally projected video footage from SU student and staff gatherings during the protests in 2016. The footage consisted mostly of students gathering on the steps leading down to the University library – which forms an informal amphitheatre – where students and staff took turns addressing one another during this time.

De Villiers: The last of your projects that we're discussing also utilises social semiotics and historical issues – *Die Voo'kamer*.[104] How did you conceptualise this work?

Palm: The concept for this work was to create a space for coming together and sitting down in a cosy Stellenbosch lounge. So, I decided to use a reference to Die Vlakte, which was the last multiracial community in Stellenbosch before the Group Areas Act[105] came into effect. It also has connections to Stellenbosch University because HF Verwoerd (who initiated the Group Areas Act along with many National Party cabinet members of the time) was an alumni of the University. Also, some of Stellenbosch University's buildings were later built on areas that were once part of the Die Vlakte neighbourhood.[106] That community is historically, geographically and spatially tied to Stellenbosch University. Since 2015, there has been a resurgence in debates on campus around the history of Die Vlakte in relation to Stellenbosch University. This was the conceptual starting point for the installation.

De Villiers: How did you decorate the space so that it referenced this community?

Palm: It had a bit of a grandma's lounge vibe. I had a black and white vinyl chequered floor and an armchair and a couch that I found amongst the props in the University's Drama Department. On the couch I laid a knitted blanket, a patchwork with various colours that belonged to my late aunt. I put a copy of *A history of inequality in South Africa 1652–2002* **(2002) by** Sampie Terreblanche on the coffee table along with a candle that was burning. I got an old large frame from a framer in Stellenbosch to hang on the back wall. That frame was used to put a projection into and I also had a small frame that I got from my mother. I put a white piece

---

104   In Afrikaans, a 'voorkamer' means 'front room'. In South Africa, a 'voorkamer' denotes a large front entrance room typically found in an old Cape Dutch homestead.

105   The Group Areas Act, which aimed to regulate and separate residential areas along racial lines, was one of many apartheid era legislations that denied rights and upheld segregation in favour of the white minority.

106   "During apartheid, Stellenbosch forcibly removed coloured residents from the centre of the town – an area called Die Vlakte ('The Flats') – and relocated them to an area farther away. The university received some of this land and established part of its campus here; this caused a deep rift between the university and the previous residents of Die Vlakte that the university is still in the process of addressing" (De Villiers, 2018:74).

of hardboard inside both of these frames so that I could project onto them. All of the little side tables had doilies on them that I had borrowed from family members. There were also a few kitsch ceramic ornaments in the space that I borrowed from [SU printmaking lecturer] Stephané Conradie and from the University's Drama Department.

Inside the small frame was this little gif by Conradie of her young niece wearing one of her [bricolage assemblages] as a headdress. And I was looking for footage of the 2015 and 2016 gatherings or protests and I found the work of Dean Tucker – he studied Visual Design Communication at Stellenbosch – he had some really good footage on his YouTube channel. I contacted him and asked if I could use some of it and he gave me permission. So, I downloaded some from YouTube and then I cut sections of that video footage that I could use and cropped it according to the big frame in the centre over the couch. That's how the whole thing [*Die Voo'kamer*] came together. And it was just for this one evening [for the launch of the visual redress project].

Influences

De Villiers: You've mentioned to me that history is something that you are particularly interested in. How does that influence your work?

Palm: [My work is] mostly based in history. I have a love for South African history and I kind of eat it up like chocolates. Especially Cape history and especially histories from this area – Stellenbosch history – because during the apartheid years history was tightly curated. It was not as accessible as it is today. Now we are living in a time where there is a lot that we have to relearn about our own histories. Especially people in the Cape – everybody who has ancestry in the Cape has access to a rich history that probably was often not promoted during the apartheid years. So, it is a great environment for people like me to come into and make work about because most of us just don't know much about it. And I'm surprised most South African artists – or young artists – well, no, I'm actually not surprised that more people aren't delving into this. It seems to rather be exclusively historians and people studying history that are. Generally, there seems to be a lot of frustration with this, I suppose, for 'people of colour' because [our history] was not part of the dominant historical narrative in South Africa for a very long time. To be clear, I don't think these histories were ever a secret, but they were certainly not promoted by the dominant institutions or the media. And I can't really get too frustrated because it gives me a lot of material to work with today. It's a whole area of research that's left largely untapped and I suppose it may secure a lot of work for me – and others like me – in the near future.

I feel it's my responsibility as somebody who's not in the 'historically dominant grouping' of Stellenbosch University to contribute academic work or creative work from my own vantage point. I must admit that when I came to study here I was worried I may be presented with an exclusively Eurocentric art education. But the time that I came to study was well aligned with a new wave of post-colonial studies that was being delved into in our department and faculty. And for the most part, it wasn't at all like I imagined it to be. In many cases it was confirming a lot of the ideas that I was already grappling with on my own – like global corporate discourse or colonial and capitalist discourse.

One of the factors for me coming to study was that I started delving into my own heritage and trying to look up my own genealogy in the years leading up to my application here. I was hoping to develop some research skills as a student in this regard, because I ran into some challenges early on. You often hit a dead end at some point with slave ancestry. There's a point where you can't go any further because they didn't have surnames and didn't belong to any institutions by choice, so their names weren't consistently registered anywhere – at least not by name and surname. I could only go as far [back] as 1843 – when slavery was abolished – and then a lot of these people started to be baptised in churches; only here can one start to find a thread of records tied to these individuals. So, I was already immersed in this process. I've often felt like I should bring my perspective and the perspectives of my ancestry into my work in some respect.

De Villiers: What did you learn from your experiences creating these three works – and seeing the pieces in action, being interacted with? What future works are you considering?

Palm: What I learned about most throughout this project is synchronicity as a result of trust, which can be a sublime phenomenon to experience. The circumstances and environment around my work seemed to fall into place in unexpected ways as I let go of my own preplanned ideas and started trusting the paths presented to me. The questions that these works were built around were all attempts at observing and understanding the environment that I was immersed in at the time. Many of these questions I carried with me for years before I became a student at Stellenbosch University. The process of working through these questions illuminated much about trust and letting go – trusting and following your nose, in an immediate sense, when something peaks my attention.

I wasn't intending to produce reactionary artworks as a student; I actually had hopes of making and working with compost. I started experimenting with gardening about 10 years ago in Pniël and I became fascinated with soil ecology – nurturing micro-organisms and fungi that promote plant growth. I was, in fact, moving towards building a greenhouse in the Arts Department for my fourth-year final project at the same time that I started to get involved with the projects mentioned here. That process was disrupted by my own curiosity and my personal circumstances, and I had to let go and trust the disruption as it were. In a strange way, I think I may have made [metaphorical] compost in these works and I hope it will contribute towards a fertile substrate for positive growth. In terms of future work, I'm planning to revisit and develop shelved projects as opportunities arise. I've recently moved back to my home town in Pniël, where I'm planning to rebuild the greenhouse I started in the Arts Department and continue the compost-making process in one way or another.

Conclusion

Palm's works discussed in this chapter situate themselves at the intersection of history and social semiotics, simultaneously finding fun and meaning through playing with perceptions. He uses his art to invite people into seemingly comfortable spaces, while also confronting them with immediate discomforts – as demonstrated in his retelling of being asked to flip the upside-down *Obscure Stellenbosch* image the right way around. The positioning of his works on and around the Rooiplein provides them with a richly semiotic environment full of many competing narratives. Through the performance and installations discussed, Palm provides a space for previously marginalised histories – such as his own – to be considered and contemplated.

References

Chandler, D. 2002. *Semiotics: The basics*. London: Routledge. https://doi.org/10.4324/9780203166277

De Villiers, G. 2018. *Investigating the semiotic landscape of the house museum in Stellenbosch, South Africa*. Doctoral dissertation. Stellenbosch University. Retrieved from http://hdl.handle.net/10019.1/103441 [Accessed 23 August 2020].

Hodge, R. & Kress, G. 1988. *Social semiotics*. Cambridge: Polity.

Hooper-Greenhill, E. 2000. *Museums and the interpretation of visual culture.* New York, NY: Routledge.

Palm, C. 2018. *Work IN Progress*. Vimeo. Retrieved from https://vimeo.com/308587925 [Accessed 22 June 2020].

Stellenbosch Museum. 2005. *The VOC Kruithuis in Stellenbosch*. Retrieved from https://stelmus.co.za/voc-kruit-huis/ [Accessed 28 August 2020].

SU Corporate Communication and Marketing. 2020. *'Ou Hoofgebou' artwork to celebrate Constitution*. Retrieved from https://www.sun.ac.za/english/Lists/news/DispForm.aspx?ID=7626 [Accessed 27 August 2020].

Terreblanche, S. 2020. *A history of inequality in South Africa, 1652-2002*. Pietermaritzburg: UKZN Press.

Chapter 12

Indexing visual redress at Stellenbosch University: Ways of viewing and reading while walking through the Arts and Social Sciences Building

Faaiz Gierdien

Introduction

The visual images (visuals hereafter) in the hallways of the Arts and Social Sciences Building at Stellenbosch University (SU) allude to several issues. They depict various aspects of the violent removal of the Die Vlakte residents, some of whom lived on the very site of this building. From 2018 to 2020, while walking through this building on my way to teach my Postgraduate Certificate in Education Mathematical Literacy Teaching class, I began to notice these visuals. This period afforded me an opportunity to view and read the range of visuals and their related captions. Moreover, I started reading De Certeau's (1984) 'walking in the city' as a way to help me to think about this walking exercise and what it afforded me. Over time, 'walking' and 'city' acquired deeper meanings for De Certeau. The Arts and Social Sciences Building forms an integral space of SU, situated in peri-urban Stellenbosch, which becomes, in my view, De Certeau's proverbial 'city'. Like an index finger, my acts of walking, viewing and reading these visuals 'point to' a synchronic system (see De Certeau, 1984:94) of a present/past set of historical, geographical, political and social issues. As for the visuals, I discovered that they originate from a visual arts[107] project of Prof. Elmarie Costandius and her students. In addition, I started reading the text of a document titled "Visual Redress Policy" at Stellenbosch University",[108] which alerted me to the thinking behind the visuals and similar redress efforts at other SU spaces. This chapter is based on, and framed by, two data sources, namely words or expressions such as the name 'Arts and Social Sciences Building' and selected visuals related to Prof Costandius' visual arts project. Also, in the case of the visuals there are accompanying texts, namely expressions or words.

This chapter speaks to more than a local, SU redress set of issues. Today we read of analyses of "troubling images" (Freschi, Schmahmann & Van Robbroeck, 2019:1)

---

107 http://www.sun.ac.za/english/management/wim-de-villiers/Documents/Vlakte%20Student%20project%20panels_AAF.pdf

108 SU (Stellenbosch University). 2020. *Visual Redress Policy. Draft*. Retrieved from http://www.sun.ac.za/english/transformation/Documents/Visual%20Redress%20Policy%20draft_eng.pdf [Accessed 29 September 2020].

and "exchanging symbols" (Nettleton & Fubah, 2020:1) referring to the pre-1994 apartheid South Africa. Notions of images and symbols relate to the visuals' data source. Moreover, in the case of the South African higher education landscape, there is a growing body of literature on redress at historically white universities. Currently, these universities are coming to terms with their legacies and are forging ways to address and redress historical issues (Bentley & Habib, 2008). The titles "Redress at higher education institutions in South Africa: Mapping a way forward" (Clark & Costandius, 2020), "Decolonising university in South Africa: Rigged spaces?" (Hendricks, 2018) and "Picturing change: Curating visual culture at post-apartheid universities" (Schmahmann, 2013) reveal the extent of this redress debate in the current South African higher education landscape. Keywords in these titles speak to both data sources. Given this unfolding visual redress scenario, I pursue the organising question: what are the indexical issues related to my walking, viewing and reading the visuals in the Arts and Social Sciences Building? The question speaks intimately to my history, something I point out below. Responding to the question requires unpacking meanings and relations between index, indexicality, visuals, visuality and illusions. In addition, I came to know of a "haunting presence" (Tayob, 2019:11) of issues I had never thought of before. First, I review relevant analytic tools, followed by a note on selecting the visuals' data. Second, I examine the name 'Arts and Social Sciences Building' in addition to a visual depiction of its location. This is followed by an analysis of selected visuals in the Arts and Social Sciences Building.

Index and indexicality

An index refers to words or expressions that serve a "directive function" (Hanks, 1999:124). The names 'Arts and Social Sciences Building', 'GG Cillié Building' and 'Old Main Building' on the SU campus come to mind. These different names point to, as in an 'index finger', details about their histories, for example. Although the first one informs the reader about different University departments that fall under the broad category of arts and social sciences, there is a history behind this name, as I point out below. The same can be said about the second name, a person's name, which houses the Faculty of Education. The last name reveals some details about the historical significance of the building. Evidently, these names reflect a mix of personal, historical and generic names, such as arts and social sciences. In other words, building names, which form words or expressions, have an indexicality (Hanks, 1999); that is, they are context-dependent and point the reader in particular directions. What these directions are depend on the history of the viewer or reader. In brief, indexing a building name or any set of words, for that matter, implies going back and forth in time to discover its meaning and related history.

Visuals, visuality and/as illusions

The visuals I viewed inside the Arts and Social Sciences Building index or point to an illusion and have the goal of meeting myself as the viewer 'halfway', as Gombrich argues in his book *Art and illusion* (1961) (see also Krieger, 1984). Clearly, the visuals inside said building depicting the violent removal of Die Vlakte residents do not equate to the actual violent happenings associated with the implementation of the Group Areas Act of 1950. The designers of these visuals created an illusion with the past. In a temporal sense, they wanted to take me as a viewer back in time. These visuals as images possess a 'visuality', meaning they point the viewer in different directions, dependent on the history of the viewer. All viewers have historicised selves that can frame their feelings when viewing visuals. Feelings are therefore ways in which the visuals meet the viewers halfway. In their project related to Die Vlakte titled "Memorialising forced removals in the Arts and Social Sciences Building", Costandius and Alexander (2019) report on what I see as ways these visuals, as illusions, meet viewers halfway. In particular, Costandius and Alexander mention feelings of ignorance, disinterest, affective responses and shame. For example, 'ignorance' tells me that certain viewers had no knowledge of the Die Vlakte residents and their erasure and banishment from Stellenbosch, the town. Likewise, 'disinterest' informs me that some viewers were not concerned about the forced removals represented in the visuals. Therefore, there exists the possibility of Gombrich's 'art and illusion' orientating the viewer towards a 'decolonial' reading of visuals. One reason has to do with my realisation that designers of visuals insert their particular presence in a dominant, hegemonic or colonial ethos, a point I elaborate on later. In brief, visuals and/as illusions are far from being an all-or-nothing affair; illusion in these contexts is always a matter of degree, contingently dependent on the history of the viewer and how he/she interprets the 'visuals as illusion' over time. In my case, based on the coloured 'group' classification according to the Group Areas Act, my family and I may have been victims of forced removals, like the Die Vlakte residents. Therefore, for me, over time, viewing these visuals evoked and continue to evoke feelings of possible victimhood. Put differently, visuals have a different appeal to different viewers/readers.

A note on the data and method of analysis

My historicised self influenced the data I selected to answer my organising question. Based on my walking and reading noted in the introduction, data included the name 'Arts and Social Sciences Building' and selected visuals from the "Memorialising forced removals in the Arts and Social Sciences Building" project. In my method of analysis I adapted and used index, indexicality, visuals and illusion. This task hinges on the notion of an index as having a directive function that 'points to' something that points to something else. These concepts are also threaded throughout the chapter and used in appropriately justified ways to answer the chapter's organising question. The selected data excerpts, made up of words, expressions, quotes and screenshots of visuals, therefore become analysable, examinable and 'intelligible', all dependent on my historical frame of reference.

Indexing the name 'Arts and Social Sciences Building'

The first name of the Arts and Social Sciences Building was the BJ Vorster Building, which signals several indexical issues. Being a building name, it points to a close and comfortable relation between SU and apartheid South Africa. In fact, BJ Vorster was a prime minister of the apartheid regime as well as a chancellor of SU. This personal name, coupled with 'Building', became integral to a system of building names associated with physical spaces on the SU campus and, in turn, with apartheid, globally considered as a crime against humanity (see Chapter 2 in this book for more details on apartheid-era politician names of buildings). Moreover, it is not far-fetched to imagine how this person's name reminded and grated the Die Vlakte residents, some of whose homes occupied the very same space as this building. In addition, this name affirmed an image of SU and its power space to the Die Vlakte residents, the South African higher education landscape at the time and the apartheid-divided South African communities as a whole. The unambiguous message that the name signalled to the Die Vlakte residents was that the University endorsed their banishment and marginalisation from Stellenbosch, the town, as well as SU.

The BJ Vorster Building underwent two more name changes. In 2002 it became the Arts Building and eventually the Arts and Social Sciences Building in 2007. Here the pressure and political ethos of a democratic, post-apartheid South Africa on the SU administration become evident. These two name changes index a kind of curatorial move, one where the SU bureaucracy responded to its role as a university and a place of higher learning in a new just political order. Liberal factions within the SU administration and its academic community rallied for these name changes as a way to distance SU from the brutal implementation of the Group Areas Act of 1950 by the apartheid state, and the accompanying trauma experienced by the Die Vlakte residents. The current name, 'Arts and Social Sciences Building', signals a more neutral and generic name, one that can be associated with disciplines that fall in the broad category of arts and social sciences. As an index, this name fits in with a name reference system common to a university campus that could be anywhere in the world, for that matter.

Indexing the physical location of the Arts and Social Sciences Building

The screenshot (see Figure 12.1) as a visual points to several indexical issues not only confined to a geographical level. For example, the design or layout of Figure 12.1 takes the viewer back in time by projecting a 'past/present simultaneity' in terms of a geometric overlay indicating where the Die Vlakte residents once lived in relation to the Arts and Social Sciences Building (see letter L). To orient the reader in this respect, I superimposed a dotted line oval to point out that this building actually stands on "properties occupied by coloured people 1951/52" and an "area of Die Vlakte affected by the removals" on the current space of the SU campus (see the legend on the bottom right side of Figure 12.1). At a scalar level, the graphic formatting of 'properties' and 'areas' as colour traces meets the viewer halfway. It rests on the viewer to imagine that these shadings correspond to the actual, current geographical locations, as in the case of all flat maps of geographical spaces. In other words, Figure 12.1 portrays a two-dimensional flatness that approximates to actual physical spaces. On paper, therefore, there emerges a reconstitution between a grid layout of the current SU campus space and the past, namely the Die Vlakte 'properties' and 'area'. What I look at in Figure 12.1 is a degree of an illusion, because this figure meets me more than halfway, something unbeknown to me until I studied the geometrical and geographical outlines represented on it. I have walked around the depicted SU areas many times, but could never imagine the Die Vlakte homes until I studied what Figure 12.1 brings to the fore, namely the haunting presence of the geographical location of the homes of the Die Vlakte residents.

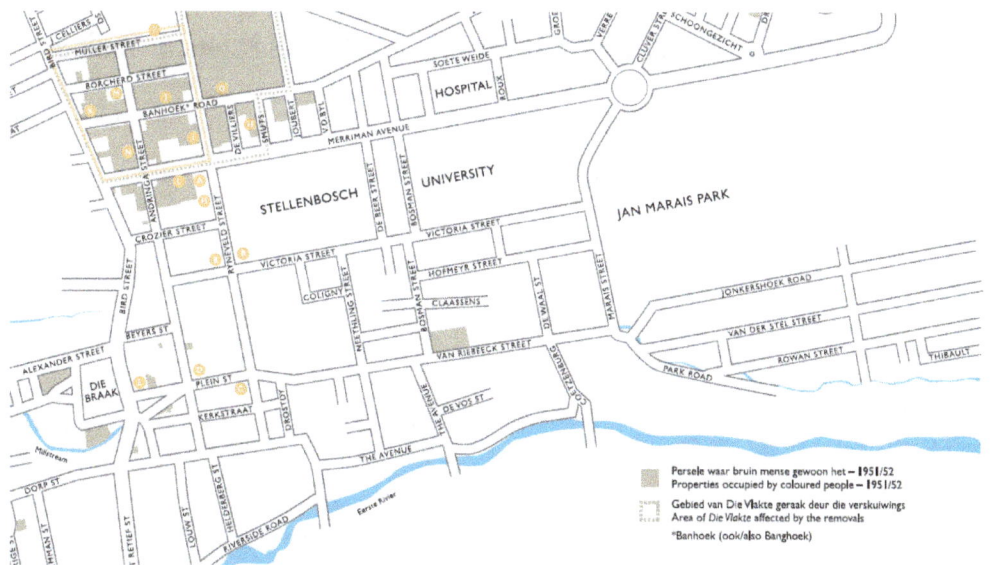

Figure 12.1: Screenshot indicating the location of the Arts and Social Sciences Building (Source: "Forced removals in Stellenbosch – Die Vlakte"[109], page 1)

---

109   https://dievlaktehistoryproject.wordpress.com/2015/08/

In fact, the indexed two-dimensional 'properties' have the goal of informing me that real homes once stood on these shaded areas. In addition, the geometricity of Figure 12.1 has been cropped, reduced and self-evidently flattened to render it as part of 'the data' for purposes of analysis. For me, Figure 12.1 represents a haunting presence of properties that were once occupied by the Die Vlakte residents. In other words, there exists the haunting presence 'on paper', as in Figure 12.1, of the homes and areas where these residents once lived. By decree of the Group Areas Act, these 'properties' were bulldozed and flattened. Nevertheless, as the reader I am directed to a past/present reference system which the designers of this visual had in mind. What comes to the fore in Figure 12.1 is a convergence of geography, history and affect, captured poignantly in a 2017 article (Hauser, 2017) about Wilfred Damon, a Die Vlakte resident, who pointed to a parking lot in the vicinity of the Arts and Social Sciences Building, where his family once lived. I can only imagine the political and psychological violence and related trauma that Wilfred Damon and his family must have experienced, and still are experiencing.

Indexing visuals at the entrance of the Arts and Social Sciences Building

The two plaques as visuals draw the reader's attention to the Arts and Social Sciences Building as a geographic site in particular ways (see Figure 12.2).

Figure 12.2: Screenshot showing two plaques from "Mapping Emotions" (Source: see footnote[110])

The wording on each of the two plaques directs me to two facts regarding Die Vlakte. These plaques emanate from a project called "Mapping Emotions", which indicates how affect issues relate to geography, the location of Die Vlakte in this case. The upper left plaque depicted in the picture above directs me to the date when the apartheid-sanctioned Group Areas Act was implemented in Die Vlakte. The wording also spells out why the Die Vlakte residents were "forcefully removed from their own homes". In this instance, the underlying referencing is apartheid legislation on 'groups' and 'race classification', which certainly included me. The lower right plaque, appropriately placed at the entrance of the Arts and Social Sciences Building, points me to a geographic location of Die Vlakte, using street names. One of the students suggested the entrance position for this plaque.

---

110 See https://dievlaktehistoryproject.wordpress.com/2015/10/ or https://www.slideshare.net/jakobp78/exploring-the-potential-of-visual-art-in-negotiating-social-transformation-at-stellenbosch-university

These details on both plaques meet me halfway. For example, further orientation would mean that I as the viewer would want to get a kind of a topographical view of these streets in relation to the Arts and Social Sciences Building. In this regard, Figure 12.1 becomes helpful. In addition, a deep or 'decolonial' reading of "Mapping Emotions" potentially becomes more grating to me, because I know the apartheid-era name of this building, namely the BJ Vorster Building. The SU administration has proverbially 'forcefully removed' this apartheid-associated name in favour of the generic 'Arts and Social Sciences Building'. The wording on the two plaques meet me more than halfway because they jolt my attention to the Die Vlakte homes that were once there. In summary, the details on the plaques strike my emotions and in turn, they point to me a haunting presence of Die Vlakte and its residents.

Indexing selected visuals inside the Arts and Social Sciences Building

Based on spatial consideration, I chose to analyse a mural that uses feet on tiles on the floor and another mural using hands on the wall inside the Arts and Social Sciences Building (see footnote 106), because they index to several interrelated issues. First, through information from the visual arts project I found out that the first mural is from learners at Lückhoff Primary School, while the second stems from learners at Rietenbosch Primary School. I interpret the choice of the two primary schools to be a way to connect them, albeit through visuals, to the Arts and Social Sciences Building. The building of these two schools on the periphery of Stellenbosch is a result of the political role played by Stellenbosch the town and SU in the banishment of the Die Vlakte community together with its schools from peri-urban Stellenbosch. Second, there is no doubt that many of these learners have filial connections to the Die Vlakte residents who were violently removed from Stellenbosch, the town, from 25 September 1964 – the implementation date of the Group Areas Act – onwards. Third, the choice of the two schools located in Ida's Valley and Cloetesville, respectively, is significant. These are two coloured townships outside the 'whites-only' proclaimed areas in Stellenbosch, built by the apartheid regime soon after the violent erasure of the Die Vlakte residents. In fact, these forced removals left many residents destitute. Evidently, this fact points to criminal acts of basic human rights violations, enforced by a regime headed by BJ Vorster, which was also the first name of the Arts and Social Sciences Building What comes to light for me is how SU acted to remove the name BJ Vorster Building 'in time' and replaced it with a more neutral name of 'Arts and Social Sciences Building'. The feet and hands visuals therefore take me back 'in time,' thereby reminding me, through my walking and reading, of ways SU works on reinventing itself in a post-1994 democratic South Africa.

A complicated picture of my reading and viewing of the feet and hand murals or visuals, emerges. On the one hand I can argue that these visuals amount to an outright illusion; for example, the hands and feet are not real. They index and therefore point to the actual hands and feet of real learners at the two primary schools. On the other hand, these visuals instantiate the haunting presence of the hands and feet of the descendants of the Die Vlakte residents on a section of the historical site of Die Vlakte. Over time and through discussion with colleagues, I realised that these murals, in a visual sense, entangle the Arts and Social Science Building as an SU space and the two primary schools in particular ways. The former, through its triumphalist architecture and previous name especially – BJ Vorster Building – conjures up feelings of injury in the memory of the Die Vlakte residents. The latter, indexing primary school learners, contain seeds for healing and redressing the complicity of SU in the destruction of the homes of their parents and even grandparents. In summary, looking back at these murals and starting from Figure 12.1, I am more aware now of how the visuals I have analysed aim at meeting me halfway.

Concluding remarks

The idea for this chapter started during my walks on my way to present lectures in the Arts and Social Sciences Building. I became intrigued by this building name, the visuals inside it and Die Vlakte and its residents. I started reading about the generative meanings of 'indexing' and visuals and related notions as a way to understand my reading of selected visuals inside the said building while walking. As a mathematics education lecturer I could easily have glossed over the visuals by focusing solely on their surface and artistic features and still commented on ways they aim at engaging me as the viewer. However, it is the other half, namely the politically entangled legal violence and accompanying social upheaval that traumatised the Die Vlakte residents, indexed in the data sources, that I came to discover (see Behar, 2014). By deploying the notions of index, indexicality and visuality, I became aware, albeit in a contingent way, of the name changes of this building and what some of the visuals in it depict in relation to entangled historical, geographical, political and social issues. Central to my argument is that a 'deep' reading of the visuals of the visual arts project related to this building implies going back and forth in time, being and becoming aware of how any viewing of the visuals will be contingent, because there will always be more to know and to discover in terms of the visuals and the haunting presence of the Die Vlakte residents and their homes. Taking the cue of apartheid – now globally classified as a crime against humanity – the Arts and Social Sciences Building geographically stands on the site of a crime scene. The casual reader and viewer of the visuals will not easily be able to discern this fact because of the physical erasure of homes and residents. It requires a 'decolonial viewing' of the visuals viewed as 'troubling images' to arrive at such a sobering position regarding SU's visual redress as a whole.

Visual redress at SU as an indexical expression is at once vague and particular. It is vague because for me visual redress can have different meanings. It was only after I read about the rationale for the murals, for instance, and the involvement of the two primary schools located in the coloured 'group' area that I saw how particular the visual redress issue really can become. In particular and as a start, those learners, and all learners, for that matter, from the Ida's Valley and Cloetesville schools have a right to a free education at SU. Visual redress at SU works to reduce conflict and maintain the pursuit of incompatible but desirable goals within the spaces of Stellenbosch and its surrounds and the University. For me, desirable goals need to include a move from redress to reparations; that is, financial compensation, for example. The injury inflicted on the Die Vlakte residents is deep and long-lasting, but has to be addressed. As I read it, a main goal of visual redress at SU is to handle references of redress issues in the South African higher education landscape in productive ways, as Fataar, in his chapter in this book, succinctly points out. Currently it implicates Stellenbosch, the town, and SU with their roles in the destruction of the homes of the Die Vlakte residents and associated social, political and economic upheavals.

References

Behar, R. 2014. *The vulnerable observer: Anthropology that breaks your heart.* Boston, MA: Beacon Press.

Bentley, K. & Habib, A. 2008. Conceptualising an alternative framework for redress and citizenship. In: K. Bentley & A. Habib (eds). *Racial redress and citizenship in South Africa.* Cape Town: HSRC Press.

Clark, M. & Costandius, E. 2020. Redress at higher education institutions in South Africa: Mapping a way forward. *de arte,* 55(3):1-23. https://doi.org/10.1080/00043389.2020.1728874

Costandius, E. & Alexander, N. 2019. Exploring shame and pedagogies of discomfort in critical citizenship education. *Transformation in Higher Education,* 4(a73):1-8. https://doi.org/10.4102/the.v4i0.73

De Certeau, M. 1984. *The practice of everyday life* (Trans. S. Rendall). Berkeley, CA: The University of California Press.

Freschi, F., Schmahmann, B. & Van Robbroeck, L. 2019. *Troubling images: Visual culture and the politics of Afrikaner nationalism.* Johannesburg: Wits University Press. https://doi.org/10.18772/22020024716

Gombrich, E.H. 1961. *Art and illusion.* New York, NY: Pantheon Books.

Hanks, W.F. 1999. Indexicality. *Journal of Linguistic Anthropology,* 9(1/2):124-126. https://doi.org/10.1525/jlin.1999.9.1-2.124

Hauser, A. 2017. 'That parking lot was my home' - Stellenbosch man revives interest in area demolished under apartheid. *Times Live,* 15 November. Retrieved from https://www.timeslive.co.za/news/south-africa/2017-11-15-that-parking-lot-was-my-home-stellenbosch-man-revives-interest-in-area-demolished-under-apartheid/ [Accessed 23 October 2020].

Hendricks, C. 2018. Decolonising universities in South Africa: Rigged spaces? *International Journal of African Renaissance Studies - Multi-, Inter- and Transdisciplinarity,* 13(1):16-38. https://doi.org/10.1080/18186874.2018.1474990

Krieger, M. 1984. The ambiguities of representation and illusion: An EH Gombrich retrospective. *Critical Inquiry,* 11(2):181-194. https://doi.org/10.1086/448283

Nettleton, A. & Fubah, M.A. 2020. *Exchanging symbols: Monuments and memorials in post-apartheid South Africa.* Stellenbosch: African Sun Media. https://doi.org/10.18820/9781928480594

Schmahmann, B. 2013. *Picturing change: Curating visual culture at post-apartheid universities.* Johannesburg: Wits University Press. https://doi.org/10.18772/12013045805

Tayob, H. 2019. The unconfessed architectures of Cape Town. In: L. Ameel, J. Finch, S. Laine & R. Dennis (eds). *The materiality of literary narratives in urban history.* New York, NY: Routledge. https://doi.org/10.4324/9780429325052-11

Section D

Reflexive considerations on the transformative potential of visual redress

Chapter 13

Functions and uses of visual redress initiatives

Nico Koopman

Introduction

In this chapter, five functions and uses of visual redress are discussed. In drawing upon various earlier publications of mine[111] on the public role of religion in society, I distilled five possible functions and uses of visual redress in public life. In my development of five modes of public engagement, I drew especially on the work of ecumenical theologian James Gustafson. Visual redress might aim to firstly, envision and imagine a new reality of dignity, healing, justice, freedom and equality, and secondly remember and reject an old and still prevailing reality of dehumanisation, injury, injustice, oppression and inequality. Visual redress might, thirdly, involve the telling of stories of hurt and of healing. The visionary and imaginative, as well as criticising and subversive potential of visual redress, might nurture and inform, fourthly, our scientific and technical analyses, which might, fifthly, serve our quests for policies and practices in service of dignity, healing, justice, freedom and equality for all.

Visual redress is given expression in names of buildings, statues, plaques, pictures, portraits, creative works of art, expressions of culture, music and architecture, among other things. Various forms and items of visual redress can become vehicles of envisioning and imagination, criticism and rejection, storytelling, technical analysis and policymaking.

Visual redress, envisioning and imagination

The vision of a new, democratic South Africa is clearly articulated in the 1996 Constitution of the Republic of South Africa. This vision entails that we want to be a South Africa where there is human dignity in the context of the integrity of creation, where there is healing of the wounds of our people, and where there is

---

111   I reappropriated work that had focused on the public functions and uses of religion, and applied it afresh to the quest to develop functions and uses of visual redress initiatives on university campuses and other institutions in democratic societies. See, among other sources, Koopman (2014:625–639; 2019:94–108).

justice for all, freedom for all and equality for all. These visionary principles are also articulated in the Transformation Plan of Stellenbosch University (SU).

Visual redress might fulfil an envisioning and imagining function. According to ecumenical theologian James Gustafson (1988:13–14), visionaries portray an alluring vision of the future. They see a new world in which the strife and suffering that we currently experience are overcome. This vision may indict the contemporary broken reality, but its main function is to allure and attract people to act concretely and to attempt to approximate the vision. Visionaries use utopian language, symbols, analogies, similes and metaphors that move us. Their speeches are not technical moral arguments or policy statements. Hearers are moved by aspects such as the passion of the speaker's voice, the cadences and the figures of speech, many drawn from classical texts, and also the moral authenticity of the speaker. Such visionary language moves us from indignation with the present to aspiration for the future.

Brazilian social scientist Rubem Alves (1972) offers a strong plea for envisioning and imagination. He calls for the task of envisioning and imagining, specifically in so-called post-liberation societies. Alves (1972:183) talks about societies that have struggled against oppression, but that do not fulfil the vision of an alternative society years after victory from oppression has been achieved. Alves (1972:183) speaks, in fact, about societies that had become democracies, but that had forgotten the vision of a liberated society, the vision that had strengthened them during their struggle for liberation.

He writes remarkably about the disappointments that followed various liberation experiences. After World War II, the expectation was that the two handmaids of reason, science and technology, could bring about peace, harmony and prosperity in the world. What followed, however, was an era of various wars, especially the Cold War, the international arms race, the growing gap between rich and poor among and within nations, hunger, exploitation, oppression, and political and economic imperialism.

The revolutionary movements of the 1960s were also not succeeded by good ages of harmony and prosperity (Alves, 1972:183–184). The frustration about the absence of the new in post-liberation contexts indeed reminds one of the post-liberation context in the young democracy in South Africa, which came into being in April 1994 when our first inclusive democratic elections took place. Although we made good progress towards building a country where all South Africans enjoy a life of prosperity and dignity, for millions of poor South Africans, this new life remains an illusion.

Alves (1972:188–189) identifies three ways in which people deal with the frustration of the non-fulfilment of the vision of a new society of dignity and justice for all. Some people give up on the ideal and vision of a new society and argue that the attempt to fly should be abandoned. They start to live as fat, domestic ducks that cannot flap their wings. They view the current world of suffering and injustice as the best possible world. In the case of Christian believers, they live with a type of realised eschatology as if Jesus Christ's second coming had already taken place.

A second response is that people start pretending that victory had been achieved and that we should start enjoying life (Alves, 1972:180–191). We should view life as a party. He compares this life to sexual intercourse and joy without the exciting prospect of pregnancy and the birth of the new. There is no dimension of creation present in this response to unfulfilled visions and ideals.

A third response is the so-called Christian realism of Reinhold Niebuhr (Alves, 1972:189). According to Niebuhr, the best that Christians can achieve in this situation of frustration is a tolerable life in a kind of confusion of purposes. The realism of Niebuhr, according to Alves (1972:194), gives up on notions such as vision, imagination and hope.

What is hope? It is the presentiment that imagination is more real and reality less real than it looks. It is the hunch that the overwhelming brutality of facts that oppress and repress is not the last word. It is the suspicion that reality is much more complex than realism wants us to believe; that the frontiers of the possible are not determined by the limits of the actual, and that in a miraculous and unexpected way life is preparing the creative event that will open the way to freedom and resurrection.

According to Alves (1972:189),[112] Niebuhr's frustration about the broken realities makes room for pessimism and resignation:

> Social creativity is dismissed as either a utopian dream or an ideological demon, with its ultimate roots in man's selfishness and self-deception. The hope of the past are identified with illusions. And if one's hope are illusions, so are one's frustrations – ultimately 'healthy' experiences which bring us back to reality. And frustration is displaced by resignation.

Over against these three responses, Alves (1972:200–201) pleads for the restoration and revival of creative imagination and renewing hope. This vision of hope is born among people who suffer, and not among people who enjoy prosperity and well-being and who are more easily tempted to view this one as the best possible world. Hope and suffering function in tandem. Alves (1972:200) explains as follows:

> Those who live in the pain-delivering sectors of our society, however, even before they can articulate in speech the evil of this world, are already doing it by means of their inarticulate groans (Rom. 8:26). And this is the raw material the spirit takes unto Himself. In other words: this is the emotional matrix which is the beginning of the creative event. Suffering prepares the soul for vision. Personality refuses to take things as they are. It spreads its wings and the heart emigrates to the horizons of the future.

Alves (1972:203) explains in a striking manner that suffering reminds us of the political work of liberation that is still unfinished:

> For creation to take place, suffering and hope cannot be separated. Suffering is the thorn that makes it impossible for us to forget that there is a political task still unfinished – still to be accomplished. And hope is the star that tells the direction to follow. The two, suffering and hope, live from each other. Suffering without hope produces resentment and despair. Hope without suffering creates illusions, naiveté, and drunkenness.

---

112 Elsewhere, I (Koopman, 2010:41–56) had argued that this criticism of Alves of Niebuhr's realism does not take away the important contribution of Christian realism in public policy discourses in pluralistic contexts where morally acceptable compromises should be sought.

This hope and creative imagination bring forth a new, surprising creative event, which cannot be scientifically analysed, cognitively dissected and eventually duplicated (Alves, 1972:197–198).

With an appeal to Nikolai Berdyaev and Martin Buber, Alves (1972:185–186) argues that revolutionary movements have led to frustrating outcomes because they focused too much on the wrong that they had to break down, and not on the good that they had to bring into being. Their euphoria about victory over evil soon disappeared, because during their struggle against evil they did not adequately envision and embody the new reality. Through this grave negligence and omission, they actually had paved the way for a society where the old would be repeated.

Alves offers a thorough analysis of this neglect and its consequences that is of disturbing relevance for South Africa. Alves's analysis challenges South Africans to remember the vision of a new, post-apartheid society that we had once adhered to. This vision is articulated in a document such as the Freedom Carter and it was voiced at the launch of the United Democratic Front in 1983. It was expressed in the South African Constitution of 1996 as the vision that is shared by South Africans from all political, ethnic, religious and cultural communities. In the Bill of Rights, i.e. Article 2 of our Constitution, this vision entails a society of dignity, equality, freedom, justice and equity. Various religious documents resonate with this vision of the type of society for which South Africans want to work.

Without vision we shall perish. Faithful prophetic work entails, in these days of amnesia and forgetfulness, the public proclamation of the vision of a new society of justice and joy! This is now our joint political task, in the words of Alves (1972:197):

> If ours is not the harvest season, it may well be a time for sowing ... In spite – and because – our tall trees have been cut down, our air polluted with fear, and our soil turned into a heap of refuse, a new seed must be planted: the seed of our highest hope.

People with vision and imagination remember the dream of a new society. They remember the future – the future of dignity, healing, justice, freedom and equality for all.

Visual redress at our institutions can help to keep the dream of a new society alive. Visual redress as visual envisioning and imagination can mobilise us to work for the realisation of the long-cherished dream of new campuses and new societies. Names of buildings, plaques, statues, portraits, pictures, other works of arts and architecture as vehicles of visual redress can in this manner become vehicles that mobilise us to make visions become realities.

Visual redress, criticism and rejection

Gustafson's (1988:7–11) reflections on criticism help us to develop contours for the function of visual redress as that of criticism and rejection of what is dehumanising, injuring, unjust, oppressive and discriminating. Besides annunciation, criticism involves the task of denunciation. Besides the task of announcing the vision of a new society, critics perform the task of denouncing the reality that is in conflict with the vision of a new society. The critic, according to Gustafson, addresses what is perceived as the root of the problem. The problem is not merely viewed as a matter of policies that are inadequate and wrong, but a matter of moral and social waywardness. The critic names the devil that presumably underlies the various wrongs in society. Critics get to the roots of problems that pervade institutions and cultures, or that pervade the actions and behaviour of individual persons. On the basis of statistical indicators and social analysis they expose the causes and roots of social and personal wrongs. They do not engage in detailed policy recommendations and matters of strategy and tactics. The indictments of the critic construes the human condition in deep and broad proportions. And these indictments lead to conviction of guilt and constitute a call to a fundamental repentance and a radical turn from unfaithfulness to faithfulness.

During apartheid, the notion of apartheid as a heresy was employed to expose the deepest religious and moral causes and roots of what went wrong in our society. The notion of colonialist empire is currently employed to express what is going wrong in contemporary societies in local, regional and global contexts. US scholar Joerg Rieger (2007:1–3) identified various features of the contemporary understanding of empire. 'Empire' neither only refers to historical empires such as the Hellenistic,

Roman, Japanese, Spanish, Portuguese, English and many others, nor does it only refer to the United States of America (USA), which is described in terms of notions such as power, superpower and hyperpower in a so-called mono-polar world, which came into being after the fall of the Soviet Union. Empire also does not only refer to the hyperpower of multinational corporations and the interests of the powerful nations of the G8 in today's globalising world. For Rieger (2007:2–3), empire …

> … has to do with massive concentrations of power that permeate all aspects of life and that cannot be controlled by any one actor alone … Empire seeks to extend its control as far as possible; not only geographically, politically and economically – these factors are commonly recognized – but also intellectually, emotionally, psychologically, spiritually, culturally, and religiously.

Rieger (2007:3) describes empire in terms of notions such as control, as a dispersed reality that is embodied in various dependencies maintained through less visible ties, as primarily an economic reality that is tied to the growth of global capitalism, as a political power, as something that exerts power through cultural and intellectual webs that work in hidden ways. With an appeal to Michael Hardt and Antonio Negri he describes power as biopower, i.e. a form of power that regulates social life from its interior and that welds together economic, political and cultural forces.

The globalisation research initiative of the Evangelisch Reformierte Kirche in Germany and the Uniting Reformed Church in Southern Africa offers a helpful definition of empire. This research collaboration, which was hosted by the Beyers Naudé Centre for Public Theology at SU, is one attempt among many to advance the reception of the Accra Declaration on global justice by so-called Northern and Southern churches. Boesak, Weusmann and Amajad-Ali (2010:3) explain as follows:

> We speak of *empire*, because we discern a coming together of economic, cultural, political and military power in our world today, that constitutes a reality and a spirit of lordless domination, created by human kind yet enslaving simultaneously; an all-encompassing global reality serving, protecting and defending the interests of powerful corporations, nations, elites and privileged people, while imperiously excluding, even sacrificing humanity and exploiting creation; a pervasive spirit of

destructive self-interest, even greed – the worship of money, goods and possessions; the gospel of consumerism, proclaimed through powerful propaganda and religiously justified, believed and followed; the colonization of consciousness, values and notions of human life by the imperial logic; a spirit lacking compassionate justice and showing contemptuous disregard for the gifts of creation and the household of life.

The definition of these two churches focuses on empire not only as specific nations, corporations or institutions. This definition is deeper, wider and more inclusive than attempts to attribute the notion of empire only to such clearly definable institutions. It implies these institutions, but also unmasks the spirit, gospel and ethos that constitute and nurture them, and that they in turn reinforce. This definition concurs to some extent with Rieger's perspectives on empire.

This definition of empire helps to unmask the spirit of empire in the practices, policies and institutions in all walks of life, on local, regional and global level. Moreover, it helps to unmask the spirit of empire in the hearts of humans and in the life of churches as well. Notions such as empire enable us to pay attention and to become conscientised about what is going on around us and in us. These concepts shock in order to restore. And critics are called upon to, among others things, shock in order to restore.

Criticism also entails self-criticism. We should, however, guard against a form of self-criticism that has pacifying effects, a self-criticism that serves as excuse to terminate public involvement, because we are ourselves so very imperfect. What is required is a self-criticism that shows that we are aware of our sinfulness and fallibility as human beings. Because we are imperfect beings, even our best efforts might be contaminated. Without constructive self-criticism we cannot speak legitimately in the world. Without self-criticism we can easily absolutise our own position, and tolerate no other opinion. Where there is no healthy self-criticism we open the door for the stereotyping, stigmatisation, demonisation and annihilation of all views that differ from ours.

Besides the self-criticism with regard to justice in racial and class matters, we need to practise prophetic self-criticism with regard to various other justice matters, among others sexism, misogyny, heterosexism, patriarchalism, homophobia, nationalism, ableism, ageism, ecocide, exclusion and exploitation. In our own ranks these evils are still tolerated too often.

Envisioning and criticism are also prompted by protests on South African campuses for accelerated and radical transformation towards justice; for the decolonisation of universities and an end to rape culture and discrimination against LGBTIQA+ persons; for respect for black bodies. Envisioning and criticism is required amid accusations that South African struggle heroes such as Nelson Mandela and Desmond Tutu have made immoral compromises during the negotiations for a new South Africa. Student leader Rekgotsofetse Chikane (2018), son of struggle hero Frank Chikane, argues that people such as Mandela and Tutu have made wrong compromises during the negotiations for a new South Africa.

Criticism should be informed by technical analysis and policy discourses. On the other hand, clear and courageous criticism should inform our technical discussions and our formulation of policies that seek to serve justice. In the same vein, our vision should inform and guide our technical analyses and policy discussions. Engagement in such analyses and discussions enrich vision discourses, because they challenge us to be continuously in search of ways in which to concretely embody the vision. And in all of these, narrative discourse plays an indispensable, illuminating and energising role. The narrative mode of discourse continuously reminds us of the plight of the poor and wronged, the vulnerable and suffering ones in this world. Narratives also bring to our attention humble and hopeful materialisations of the vision of dignity, healing, justice, freedom and equality.

Visual redress initiatives can sharpen our critical edge, and help us to diagnose, identify, acknowledge, expose and reject betrayals of the vision of a new society of dignity and justice.

Visual redress and storytelling

Gustafson (1988:19–20, 22–24) identifies three functions of stories in communities. Stories form the ethos and identity of a community and its members. Furthermore, stories inform and guide the moral choices of people. Stories form moral identity by rehearsing the community's history and traditional meanings as they are portrayed in classical texts and other sources. The living tradition and truth transmitted through narratives, liturgies, rites and other concrete terms and symbols shape the ethos, vision, virtue and character, the values and outlooks as well as the moral interests and determine the moral convictions of the moral and religious community. The ethical methods of Jesus and the rabbis demonstrate that narratives can illuminate casuistic moral argumentation. They do not provide single, clear and argued answers to specific moral cases, but they do provide nuanced and subtle illumination of the challenges that are faced and of possible outcomes. They show us features of life that are somehow excluded from technical abstract casuistry. Narratives do not offer distinctions and arguments, but they evoke imagination and stimulate our moral sensibilities and affections. And although they do not give clear and decisive conclusions, they do enlarge one's vision of what is going on. Where casuistic moral arguments call us to act in conformity with them, narratives invite us to act in the light of the vision they convey.

Gustafson (1988:20) argues that stories do not offer theories of justice or injustice. But they do have a moving effect. African theologian John Mbiti (1975) uses African prayers, poems, idioms and sayings to narrate how African people deal prophetically, hopefully and with resilience with the various plights that they face, especially the plight of poverty.

Stories especially reveal the plight of people living at the margins of our societies. The level of civility and dignity of a society is measured by how we care for the poor, the vulnerable and the marginalised. The narratives of vulnerable people are determinative for the type of society we strive to be. Their stories provide the epistemologies and knowledge without which civilizing democracies cannot flourish.

Visual redress initiatives offer the possibility to tell stories of injury and hurt, and also stories of healing and hope, in a remarkable and transformative manner.

Visual redress and technical analysis

Gustafson (1988:42) states that visual redress also has the function of ethical, technical and scientific analysis. Ethical discourse provides the concepts, the modes of appropriate argumentation and important distinctions that lead to greater precision and stronger backing for what religious and secular moral communities think is the right thing to do, the good thing to do.

Gustafson (1988:31–32, 37–40) admires the constant attention to the ethical mode of moral discourse in the Roman Catholic tradition. He argues that in the second part of the 20th century, Protestant ethicists started to give attention to the ethical, or philosophical, moral discourse. He notes that the ethical writings of his teachers and of his pupils differ significantly in this regard. Ethical discourse, under the influence of especially Anglo-American moral philosophy, encourages a more precise use of concepts such as justice, virtue, rights and duties. It offers more careful distinctions between concepts and classes of moral issues. It requires stronger logical arguments in support of moral prescriptions or moral condemnations. Gustafson states that ethical or philosophical analysts are challenged to employ different ethical theories in a complementary manner in their analyses – as is done in the Bible – e.g. teleological (Aristotle, Augustine, Thomas Aquinas), deontological (Kant, Barth, Bultmann), utilitarian or consequentialist (Jeremy Bentham, John Stuart Mill) theories. In addition to the teleological (human as maker) and deontological (human as citizen) theories, H. Richard Niebuhr calls attention to the cathecontic (human as answerer) theory.

Drawing upon the work of Gustafson, American theologian B.V. Brady (1998:146–147) states that the ethical discourse is drier and less exciting Wording must be painstakingly accurate. Concepts need to be defined in a clear, comprehensive and concise manner. Clear thinking, precise use of words and compelling reasoning facilitate engagements. The ethical discourse helps to make narratives public and to translate the passionate pleas of the visionary and critic into rationally defensible public positions. And by assisting these discourses to be more vocal and public in credible and constructive ways, an impact is made on the formation of public opinion, public ethos, public Zeitgeist/thinking and eventually public policy.

Accompanied by such thorough technical analysis of various public challenges, the task of envisioning, criticism and storytelling can be accomplished with intellectual sophistication, authority and credibility.

Especially in academic contexts, visual redress initiatives can serve the purpose of stimulating and enriching technical and scientific analyses that do not paralyse and oppress, but that are active and liberating.

Visual redress and policymaking

In order to have an impact on public life on campuses and broader society, we need to participate in policy discourse. According to Gustafson (1988:43, 46, 52), the policy mode distinguishes itself from the other discourses in two ways. The first is that people who have the responsibility to make choices and to carry out the actions that are required by those choices conduct this discourse. Visionaries, critics, storytellers and technical analysts can all function with the external perspective of observers, but policymakers function with the internal perspective of persons and agents who are responsible for making choices in quite complex and specific circumstances that constrain their possible actions. The second is that policy is developed in particular conditions that both limit and enable the possibilities of action.

The first question of the policymaker is likely to be "What is going on?" and not "What ought we to do?" Or, at least, both of these questions have to be kept in mind in a tandem and finally integrated way. The policymaker has to know what is possible, as well as what is the right thing to do, or what the most desirable outcomes are. What is desirable is always related to what is possible; it is always under the constraints of the possible. And a critical factor of judgement is precisely what is possible.

The ethical should give direction to policy, but according to Gustafson (1988:49–51), more is required for final decisions and policies: estimates and assessments of what is possible with the help of sociological, economic and other concepts; information on how to move the institution with efficiency from where it currently is to where it could be and ought to be within a specific timeframe. For the policymaker the ethical is not the only consideration, it is just a dimension of the economic, social, personal and historical.[113]

Within the framework of limited space, time, information and possibilities, policymakers are challenged to make compromises and even decisions that might seem morally wrong or morally inadequate to the storytellers, critics and visionaries (Gustafson, 1988:51). Brady's (1998:48–153) elaboration on and application of the work of Gustafson is helpful. He argues that in policymaking the variety of vulnerable people need to be given priority, among others children, women, oppressed racial groups, poor people and exploited workers. This notion of the priority of the most vulnerable will help ensure that the unavoidable compromises do not have a negative impact on them. This notion of the option of the most vulnerable serves as benchmark with regard to policymaking and especially the adoption of compromises. Gustafson (1988:51) emphasises that the enabling dimension of policy discourse resides in the fact that policymakers have sufficient power to implement decisions and policies.

Visual redress initiatives can illuminate and inform policymaking and policy implementation processes. Visual redress as envisioning, criticising, storytelling, and technical and ethical analysis advances sound policymaking and policy implementation.

Conclusion

This chapter attempted to identify and briefly discuss five functions and uses of visual redress initiatives on campuses and at other institutions of democratic societies. These functions might assist our serious quest to develop visual redress policies and practices and to launch visual redress initiatives that serve dignity, healing, justice, freedom and equality for all. This chapter seeks to prompt questioning such as the following: what type of visual redress initiatives help us to keep the vision of dignity and justice alive; to expose betrayals of the vision; to tell the stories of hurt and the stories of healing, especially from the margins of society; to facilitate

---

113   For a discussion of the potential of Christian realism and middle axioms for policy discourses, see my essay "Churches and public policy discourses in South Africa" (Koopman, 2010:41–56).

liberating analyses; and to develop humanising and just policies and practices of policy implementation?

References

Alves, R. 1972. *Tomorrow's child: Imagination, creativity, and the rebirth of culture.* New York, NY: Harper & Row.

Boesak, A., Weusmann, J. & Amajad-Ali, C. 2010. *Dreaming a different world: Globalisation and justice for humanity and the Earth; The challenge of the Accra Confession for the churches.* Stellenbosch: The Globalisation Project.

Brady, B.V. 1998. *The moral bond of community: Justice and discourse in Christian morality.* Washington, DC: Georgetown University Press.

Chikane, R. 2018. *Breaking a rainbow, building a nation: The politics behind MustFall movements.* Johannesburg: Picador Africa.

Gustafson, J. 1988. *Varieties of moral discourse: Prophetic, narrative, ethical, and policy.* Stob lectures of Calvin College and Seminary. Grand Rapids, MI: Eerdmans.

Koopman, N. 2010. Churches and public policy discourses in South Africa. *Journal of Theology for Southern Africa,* 136:94-108.

Koopman, N. 2014. Theology and the building of civilising democracy in South Africa. *Nederduitse Gereformeerde Teologiese Tydskrif,* 55:625-639. https://doi.org/10.5952/55-3-4-657

Koopman, N. 2019. Envision and criticize: Doing public theology when democracy seems to fail. *International Journal of Public Theology,* 13(1):94-108. https://doi.org/10.1163/15697320-12341564

Mbiti, J. 1975. *The prayers of African religion.* New York, NY: Orbis Books.

Rieger, J. 2007. *Christ and empire: From Rome to postcolonial times.* Minneapolis, MN: Fortress Press.

Chapter 14

Bibliography on visual representational culture at Stellenbosch University

Mimi Seyffert-Wirth

The Special Collections division of the Stellenbosch University Library is home to several resources, from manuscript collections to published works and digital collections, covering a wide range of disciplines. Some of these pertain to the history of Stellenbosch University as well as the town of Stellenbosch – histories inevitably intertwined.

The purpose of this bibliography, compiled from Special Collections and other library resources, is to present to the reader a selection of resources that may put the visual representational culture of Stellenbosch University into historical, cultural and social context. Most of the resources cover a time period preceding the chronology of this publication and offer a reader consulting these resources a holistic historical view leading up to where we are in terms of visual redress today. Some resources cover spatial design, art, artefacts and architecture of the University and may shed some light on decisions made or directions followed at certain points in the history of the University and the town, influenced by the thinking and philosophy and other factors of that time.

Manuscript collections

Manuscript collections of previous Stellenbosch University rectors

These collections typically contain information related to the development of Stellenbosch University and its infrastructure.

Cillié, G.G. 1900-1958. Manuscript collection. MS 205. Manuscripts section, Stellenbosch University Library and Information Service.

De Villiers, J.N. 1970-1979. Manuscript collection. MS 393. Manuscripts section, Stellenbosch University Library and Information Service.

De Vries, M.J. 1979-1993. Manuscript collection. MS 254. Manuscripts section, Stellenbosch University Library and Information Service.

Smith, J.J. 1883-1949. Manuscript collection. MS 333. Manuscripts section, Stellenbosch University Library and Information Service.

Thom, H.B. 1663-1985. Manuscript collection. MS 191. Manuscripts section, Stellenbosch University Library and Information Service.

Van Wyk, A.H. 1966-2001. Manuscript collection. MS 320. Manuscripts section, Stellenbosch University Library and Information Service.

Stellenbosch University and Victoria College collections

These collections typically contain information related to Victoria College and Stellenbosch University from a cultural perspective.

Gericke, J.S. 1911-1991. Manuscript collection. MS 203. Manuscripts section, Stellenbosch University Library and Information Service.

Neethling, J.H. 1903-1959. Manuscript collection. MS 268. Manuscripts section, Stellenbosch University Library and Information Service.

Ons Spreekuur (student society). 1895-1913. Manuscript collection. MS 97. Manuscripts section, Stellenbosch University Library and Information Service.

University of Stellenbosch Memorabilia Collection. 1913-1987. Manuscript collection. MS 216. Manuscripts section, Stellenbosch University Library and Information Service.

Van der Merwe, F. 1881-1985. Manuscript collection. MS 283. Manuscripts section, Stellenbosch University Library and Information Service.

Van Niekerk, J.A. 1906-1948. Manuscript collection. MS 117. Manuscripts section, Stellenbosch University Library and Information Service.

Victoria House (men's residence). 1918-1931. Manuscript collection. MS 235. Manuscripts section, Stellenbosch University Library and Information Service.

Wilgenhof Residence Collection. 1952-1989. Manuscript collection. MS 213. Manuscripts section, Stellenbosch University Library and Information Service.

Architecture collections

These collections contain information related to historical Stellenbosch architecture.

Pretorius, A. 1970-2004. Manuscript collection. MS 408. Manuscripts section, Stellenbosch University Library and Information Service.

Smuts, F. 1673-1987. Manuscript collection. MS 229. Manuscripts section, Stellenbosch University Library and Information Service.

Van der Merwe, H. 1924-2005. Manuscript collection. MS 195. Manuscripts section, Stellenbosch University Library and Information Service.

Walton, J. 1911-1999. Manuscript collection. MS 247. Manuscripts section, Stellenbosch University Library and Information Service.

Collections on art and artists

These collections typically contain information about donations of artwork to Stellenbosch University as well as artists affiliated with the University.

Bouman, A.C. 1926-1946. Manuscript collection. MS 8. Manuscripts section, Stellenbosch University Library and Information Service.

Cussons, S. 1942-2004. Manuscript collection. MS 244. Manuscripts section, Stellenbosch University Library and Information Service.

Laubser, M. 1907-1975. Manuscript collection. MS 79. Manuscripts section, Stellenbosch University Library and Information Service.

Scholtz, J. du P. 1875-1990. Manuscript collection. MS 165. Manuscripts section, Stellenbosch University Library and Information Service.

Scully, L. 1945-2002. Manuscript collection. MS 330. Manuscripts section, Stellenbosch University Library and Information Service.

Vroue-Vereniging Universiteit van Stellenbosch Collection. 1925-1992. Manuscript collection. MS 287. Manuscripts section, Stellenbosch University Library and Information Service.

Digital collections

Botman, R. 2007-2014. Available at: http://digital.lib.sun.ac.za/handle/10019.2/4433

Die grondeienaars van Stellenbosch. 1693-1860. Available at: http://digital.lib.sun.ac.za/handle/10019.2/5911

IMS (Information in connection with Stellenbosch Municipality). 1946-1966. Available at: http://digital.lib.sun.ac.za/handle/10019.2/222

Pretorius, A. 1850-2006. Available at: http://digital.lib.sun.ac.za/handle/10019.2/870

Solomon, H. 1570-1860. Maps. Available at: http://digital.lib.sun.ac.za/handle/10019.2/653

Solomon, H. 1729-1901. Pictorial Africana. Available at: http://digital.lib.sun.ac.za/handle/10019.2/4277

Stellenbosch Discussion Forum. 1993-1994. Available at: http://digital.lib.sun.ac.za/handle/10019.2/869

Stellenbosch University and Victoria College Historical Photographs. 1880-2001. Available at: http://digital.lib.sun.ac.za/handle/10019.2/14837

Thom, H.B. 1937-1983. Available at: http://digital.lib.sun.ac.za/handle/10019.2/3433

Visual Arts student project. 2018. Available at: http://digital.lib.sun.ac.za/handle/10019.2/15462

Walton, J. 1911-1999. Available at: http://digital.lib.sun.ac.za/handle/10019.2/312

Books

Books on Stellenbosch University

Ballot, M., Nel, Z. & Van der Merwe, H. 2001. *Huldigingsbundel vir Andreas H. van Wyk: Rektor en visekansielier, Universiteit van Stellenbosch.* Stellenbosch: Corporate Affairs, Stellenbosch University.

Booyens, B. 1995. *Die Universiteit van Stellenbosch Biblioteekdiens, 1895-1995.* Stellenbosch: Stellenbosch University.

Botha, A. 2007. *Chris Brink: Anatomy of a transformer.* Stellenbosch: African Sun Media.

Brouckaert, R. 2015. A history of the Endler hall as cultural space. Unpublished master's thesis. Stellenbosch: Stellenbosch University.

Cloete, T.E. & Breedt, K. 2018. *Stellenbosch University buildings.* Stellenbosch: Stellenbosch University.

Dreyer, L. 2018. *A particular frame of mind: Faculty of Science, Stellenbosch University 1918-2018.* Stellenbosch: Faculty of Science, Stellenbosch University.

Fensham, F.C. 1986. *Ou Hoofgebou, 'n eeu oud.* Cape Town: Printpak.

Fourie, H. & Crouse, P. 1998. *Stellenbosch: University town on the banks of the Eerste River.* Cape Town: Human & Rousseau.

Grové, I.J. 2005. *Konservatorium 1905-2005: Die Departement Musiek en die Konservatorium aan die Universiteit van Stellenbosch by geleentheid van die eeufees 1905-2005.* Stellenbosch: African Sun Media.

Grundlingh, A.M. 2018. *Stellenbosch University 100: 1918-2018.* Stellenbosch: Stellenbosch University.

Grundlingh, A.M., Landman, R. & Koopman, N. 2017. *Russel Botman: A tribute, 1953-2014.* Stellenbosch: African Sun Media.

Kapp, P.H. 2015. *Nalatenskappe sonder einde: Die verhaal van Jannie Marais en die Marais-broers.* Cape Town: Tip Africa.

Kotze, D.J. 1969. *Professor H.B. Thom.* Stellenbosch: Stellenbosch University.

Lombard, P.J. 1993. *Prof M.J. de Vries.* Stellenbosch: Stellenbosch University.

Marais, W.T. 1949. *Vooruitgang: Uitgawe ter herdenking van die 25-jarige bestaan van die Fakulteit van Handelswetenskappe van die Universiteit van Stellenbosch en by die geleentheid van die inwyding van die nuwe gebou vir sosiale wetenskappe.* Stellenbosch: Stellenbosch University.

Pienaar, M. 2007. Die institusionele beeld en die impak daarvan op die kommunikasie binne die Universiteit van Stellenbosch. Unpublished study project. Stellenbosch: Stellenbosch University.

Stellenbosch University. 1984. J.S. *Gericke-Biblioteek*. Stellenbosch.

Thom, H.B. 1950. *Jannie Marais*. Stellenbosch: Stellenbosch University.

Thom, H.B. 1966. *Stellenbosch 1866-1966: Honderd jaar hoër onderwys*. Cape Town: Nasionale Boekhandel.

Universiteit van Stellenbosch Unie van Oudstudenten. 1918. *Gedenkboek van het Victoria-Kollege*. Cape Town: Nasionale Pers.

Van Rooyen, E.M. 1993. Prof. H.B. Thom se rol op kultuurgebied en die algemene volkslewe, onderwys uitgesluit, 1953-1969. Unpublished master's thesis. Stellenbosch: Stellenbosch University.

Van Wyk, A.H. 2000. *Professor Jannie de Villiers*. Stellenbosch: Stellenbosch University.

Books on Stellenbosch and surrounds

Barnard, W.S. 2004. *Introducing Stellenbosch: Natural, rural and urban landscapes*. Stellenbosch: Centre for Geographical Analysis, Stellenbosch University.

Biscombe, H. 2006. *In ons bloed*. Stellenbosch: African Sun Media.

Botha, C.S. & Fransen, H. 1979. *Ontdek historiese Stellenbosch*. Cape Town: Hollandsch-Afrikaansche Uitgevers-Maatschappij.

De Waal, L.M. 2015. *Jamestown, Webersvallei, Jamestown: "'n Stukkie van die paradys"*. Stellenbosch: African Sun Media.

Engelbrecht, H.S.J. 1972. Historiese skatte van Stellenbosch: 'n Bibliografie. Unpublished paper. Stellenbosch: Stellenbosch University.

Fourie, H. 2003. *Stellenbosch winelands*. Stellenbosch: Maxprod CC.

Fourie, M. 1990. 'n Oorsig van die bewaringsaksies t.o.v. bouwerke in die dorpskern van Stellenbosch. Unpublished master's thesis. Stellenbosch: Stellenbosch University.

Fransen, H. 1967. *The Stellenbosch Museum (Grosvenor House): A descriptive guide to the building and the collection, with short notes on the history of Stellenbosch and its other historic buildings.* Stellenbosch: Raad van Trustees.

Fransen, H. 2006. *Old towns and villages of the Cape: A survey of the origin and development of towns, villages and hamlets at the Cape of Good Hope, with particular reference to their physical planning and historical townscape.* Johannesburg: Jonathan Ball.

Fransen, H. & Cook, M.A. 1965. *The old houses of the Cape: A survey of the existing buildings in the traditional style of architecture of the Dutch-settled regions of the Cape of Good Hope.* Cape Town: Balkema.

Giliomee, H. 2018. *Always been here: The story of a Stellenbosch community.* Pinelands: Africana.

Gründlingh, M. & De Villiers, J. 2018. *Die Stellenbosse Heemkring: 50 jaar.* Stellenbosch: Stellenbosse Heemkring.

Hofmeyr, A. 1982. *Die Laan en sy mense.* Stellenbosch: Stellenbosse Heemkring.

Hofmeyr, S.M. 1993. *Carl Otto Hager van Stellenbosch.* Stellenbosch: Stellenbosch Museum.

Hoskyn, M. 1979. *Stellenbosch village, 1920-1950.* Cape Town: Tafelberg.

Hugo, A.M. & Van der Bijl, J. 1963. *Die kerk van Stellenbosch, 1686-1963: 'n Geskiedenis van die kerkgeboue van die Nederduits Gereformeerde gemeente te Stellenbosch, en van die mense wat hulle gebou het, vanaf die dae van Simon van der Stel tot op die huidige dag, in opdrag van die Kerkraad van Stellenbosch geskryf.* Cape Town: Tafelberg.

Johnson-Barker, B. & Balfour, D. 1992. *Stellenbosch: Place of gables, oaks and wine.* Cape Town: Struik.

Krige, O. 2015. *Carl Otto Hager: Argitek tot eer van God, 1813-1898.* Hermanus: Hemel en See Boeke.

Meiring, H. 2004. *My country in line and colour: An unconventional look at South African architecture.* Vlaeberg: Fernwood Press.

Neethling, M. 1995. Pikturale Stellenbossiana 1679-1950: Register van kunstenaars met 'n kultuurhistoriese ontleding van geselekteerde kunswerke. Unpublished master's thesis. Stellenbosch: Stellenbosch University.

Olden, P.L. 1990. Towards a morphological understanding of the Stellenbosch townscape: An analysis of the historical town plan. Unpublished study project. Stellenbosch: Stellenbosch University.

Proust, A. & Pennewaert, D.A. 2006. *Stellenbosch: A visual promenade*. Place: La Compagnie.

Rock, D. 2011. The location shall be called Kaya Mandi: A history of Kaya Mandi. Unpublished master's thesis. Stellenbosch: Stellenbosch University.

Smuts, F. 1974. *Stellenbosch, ons oudste dorp, our oldest village*. Stellenbosch: Stellenbosch 300 Aksie.

Smuts, F. 1979. *Stellenbosch three centuries: Official commemorative volume*. Stellenbosch: Stellenbosch Town Council.

Starke, A. 1979. The Braak and surrounding monuments. Unpublished study project.

Stellenbosch, 1679-1929. 1929. Stellenbosch: Hortors.

Stellenbosch argitektuur: Tentoonstelling in die kunsmusem van die Universiteit van Stellenbosch – Stellenbosch architecture: Exhibition in the art gallery of the University of Stellenbosch. 1979. Stellenbosch: Studiegroep van Stellenbosche Argitekte

Thom, Q. 1992. Kognitiewe kartering: Die vorming van 'n stedelike beeld. Unpublished master's thesis. Stellenbosch: Stellenbosch University.

Van Huyssteen, T. & Meiring, H. 1985. *Hart van die Boland*. Cape Town: Tafelberg.

Viljoen, V.A. 2015. Socio-spatialities of visual art in Stellenbosch. Unpublished master's thesis. Stellenbosch: Stellenbosch University.

Vorster, L.W. 1999. Die bydrae van Walther Blersch as stadsklerk tot die argitektoniese nalatenskap van Stellenbosch. Unpublished master's thesis. Stellenbosch: Stellenbosch University.

Vos, H.N. 1993. An historical and archaeological perspective of colonial Stellenbosch, 1688-1860. Unpublished master's thesis. Stellenbosch: Stellenbosch University.

Yang, Y.J. 2015. Producing post-apartheid space: An ethnography of race, place and subjectivity in Stellenbosch, South Africa. Unpublished master's thesis. Stellenbosch: Stellenbosch University.

Journals and newspapers

Die Matie. 1941. Stellenbosch: Stellenbosch University.

Matieland. 1957. Stellenbosch: Stellenbosch University.

Stellenbossiana. 1977-2008. Stellenbosch: Stellenbosch Museum.

NOTES ON CONTRIBUTORS

Stephané Conradie is a lecturer in Visual Arts at the Department of Visual Arts at Stellenbosch university where she is currently also a PhD candidate.

Elmarie Costandius is an associate professor in Visual Arts, coordinates the MA Visual Arts (Art Education) course and supervises PhD students in Art Education at Stellenbosch University.

Gera de Villiers is a Postdoctoral Research Fellow for Stellenbosch University's Visual Redress Project.

Faadiel Essop is currently the director of the Centre for Cardio-metabolic Research in Africa (CARMA) based in the Faculty of Medicine and Health Sciences and a full professor in the university's Department of Physiological Sciences (Faculty of Science).

Aslam Fataar is currently a research professor attached to the Transformation Office at Stellenbosch University and a professor in the university's Department of Education Policy Studies.

Khairoonisa Foflonker is a diversity and inclusivity facilitator, and is currently the Manager of Student Affairs at the Faculty of Medicine and Health Sciences at Stellenbosch University.

Faaiz Gierdien works as a mathematics education academic in the Department of Curriculum Studies, Faculty of Education at Stellenbosch University.

Renee Hector-Kannemeyer is the Deputy-Director: Division Social Impact at Stellenbosch University and the Head of Matie Community Service (Stellenbosch University NGO).

Nico Koopman is a professor of Public Theology and Ethics, and Deputy Vice-Chancellor for Social Impact, Transformation and Personnel at Stellenbosch University.

Reggie Nel is a professor in the Department of Practical Theology and Missiology, with a special interest in postcolonial theories and youth movements. He is currently the dean of the Faculty of Theology at Stellenbosch University.

Charles Palm is an honours Fine Arts student in the Visual Arts Department at Stellenbosch University.

Mimi Seyffert-Wirth is currently Deputy Director: Digital Scholarship at Stellenbosch University's Library and Information Service.

Bradley Slade is an associate professor in the Department of Public Law, Stellenbosch University, and currently the chairperson of the department.

Ellen Tise is Senior Director: Library and Information Services at Stellenbosch University.

Otto van Noie is a Board member of the Matie Community Service Governing Board and a member of the Lückhoff Advisory Committee. He is a community activist. He is a former pupil and teacher at Lückhoff High School based in Die Vlakte until the forced removals of inhabitants from the area in the late 1960s. He taught at various schools as well as the Lückhoff High School at its new location in Idas Valley.

Leslie van Rooi is the Senior Director: Social Impact and Transformation at Stellenbosch University.

www.ingramcontent.com/pod-product-compliance
Lightning Source LLC
Chambersburg PA
CBHW080728300426
44114CB00019B/2513